IN BED WITH ADAM AND EVE

IN BED WITH ADAM AND EVE

Your guide to a healthy marriage

Dr Emma Peacock

Sacred Psychology Publishing

Cambridge, United Kingdom

Contents

Contents

Introduction

Your guide to a healthy marriage

Emotional pain in marriage is tough. One day I was walking alongside a Christian friend of mine who was talking about her marital pain. She could see what the problems were in her marriage, but her husband just couldn't bear to hear her voice any of her pain or talk about what was wrong. As she talked it became clear that he couldn't tolerate the reality that he may have done something wrong or contributed to causing any pain in their marriage. Losing face and letting go of his image as a dependable, solid, husband was part of it, as well as the intense feelings of shame that he would have to come into contact with.

As we were making sense of what was going on for her in her marriage from a psychological point of view, it struck me that this echoed the story of Peter in the Bible, a disciple who Jesus had described as 'The rock'. Peter couldn't bear to face the prediction made by Jesus prior to his crucifixion that he would betray Jesus three times before the next day. Specifically, before the cock crowed to herald a new dawn. Whilst Peter was in a different position as a disciple of Jesus, he may have faced a similar dilemma to my friend's husband who probably thought: *'How can I be your rock and at the same time betray you and let you down?'* As Peter heard the cock crow the next morning, he had just denied knowing Jesus for the third time. Then poignantly we're told:

> *... Suddenly, the Lord's words flashed through Peter's mind: "Before the rooster crows tomorrow morning, you will deny three times that you even know me." And Peter left the courtyard, weeping bitterly.*
>
> — Luke 22:61–62

It is so unbelievably sad for Peter who seemed crushed by his betrayal of Jesus. Yet this was a very healthy moment. One it seemed like Jesus knew that Peter would experience as part of his journey and progression in his faith. Similarly, in marriage it's painful to have a full realisation of some of the mistakes we have made and actions that we're responsible for. But it's only from this point that healing, and growth can take place. The parallel story was interesting for my friend to think about and to share with her husband. Eventually she was able to encourage him to attend couples therapy with her and over time they experienced transformation in their marriage.

I'm a practising Christian and a clinical psychologist with a special interest and training in relational couples therapy. Over time, it became clear to me that I could help to provide a bridge for couples interested in exploring their relationship issues – helping them to connect valuable psychological insights with their existing Christian framework. There are plenty of fascinating relational patterns that we see in couples described in the Bible. So I've used the Bible stories, like historical case studies as a way to illustrate psychological concepts that would be useful for married couples to understand.

When I first started writing this book the term Christian marriage guidance was being typed into google search engine 18,000 times a month. This highlighted to me the need for more support for Christians in their marriages and how 'In Bed with Adam and Eve' could be a valuable resource.

This book may help couples who are looking for some accessible self-help resource to improve their relationship and resolve unhelpful patterns of interacting. It may also act as a stepping stone for some couples who after reading the book then choose to enter couples therapy. However, for some couples just reading the book on its own may be enough to set you off on the right path and help you move towards the direction you want to go in your marriage. Even if all you want to do is see your couple relationship grow and reach its full potential, this book will be a useful guide.

My aim in writing this book has been to provide the richest, most informative self-help material that I could. So it's not a lightweight read, and there is no promise of three easy ways to resolve your relationship problems. Overall, the written material in this book is relatively complex. But I believe this helpfully matches the complexities of the issues that couples encounter in their marriages. It is also worth pointing out that the themes in this book may bring a range of emotions to the surface. These emotions may take some time to process before healing can take place and for you to discover new, deeper levels of connection in your marriage.

Whilst this book is aimed at Christian couples, my hope is that it is accessible, of interest and can help couples from all backgrounds. I believe that you do not have to be a Christian to use or enjoy this book. There are some 'Spiritual Reflection Points' at the end of each chapter and suggestions for prayer. I have purposefully kept these separate from the main psychological 'Joint Reflection Points', so please feel free to skip these if they feel difficult to engage with.

Throughout the book I use a variety of terms interchangeably when referring to couples. These terms include: spouse; husband; wife; partner; couple relationship; and marriage. If you are reading this book and you are not married, feel free to substitute the term that you feel most comfortable with to describe the significant other in your life and your relationship.

The psychological 'Joint Reflection Points' are there at the end of the chapter for couples who wish to sit down and explore important issues from the chapter together. My hope is that these exercises will help you to digest some of the material, provide you with some valuable insights, and help you to grow together in your marriage.

However, whilst the psychological 'Joint Reflection Points' are there to stimulate helpful discussions, they may also generate strong emotions. You may want to decide whether you as an individual and as a couple feel ready to engage in such discussions. If you feel that your couple relationship is not ready for this, or is particularly fragile at this moment in time, you may just want to read the chapters and arrange to see a trained couples therapist. They can facilitate discussions and provide the support that you need as you share your thoughts and feelings with one another. Alternatively, you may end up enjoying the discussions that arise from the psychological 'Joint Reflection Points' but feel that you need more time and space to process important issues that have emerged. If this is the case, then making a decision to attend couples therapy together could be a good option for you.

There are some couples for whom this book would not be appropriate, and this includes relationships where there is domestic violence or individuals with significant addiction problems, such as alcohol and substance misuse. In these instances, it is best to seek professional help and to access individual/couples therapy to address these issues. Individuals with significant mental health issues may also benefit from face-to-face therapy if there are issues that need resolving in their couple relationship.

The combining of the psychological and spiritual

One of the unique features of this book is that I use quotations from the Bible, beautiful poetry from the *Song of Songs*, and examples of couples featured in the Bible to amplify the psychological points. The aim of this is to enrich the material by interweaving the psychological and spiritual concepts together. However, you do not have to have any prior knowledge of the Bible, as all of the Bible stories that I relay are explained in a way that is accessible and interesting for modern-day couples.

This is primarily a psychological guide to couple relationship issues, which carefully attempts to bring in the spiritual side, thus providing a way for Christian couples to enter and hopefully understand the psychological world of their marriage. I believe the spiritual points amplify the psychological points, adding an extra layer of meaning. This may help couples from all walks of life, regardless of whether they have an active spiritual faith.

A friend of mine who had just finished reading Chapter 4, entitled: 'The ideal couple and feelings of betrayal' - which features the infamous Biblical couple Samson and Delilah - told me: *'It has opened my mind up to lots of new ways of seeing what was going on between Samson and Delilah.'* I hope this experience is shared by others and the added psychological perspective will bring the Bible stories to life in new, meaningful ways.

In terms of the expertise behind the content of this book, it includes: my training as a clinical psychologist and additional training in couples therapy; lessons learned from my experiences of providing therapy for individuals, couples and families; and my personal experience and understanding of the Christian faith. My area of specialism is primarily psychological, although I do refer to ideas, books, and commentaries written by theologians. I believe the Christian concepts help to enrich the psychological material and vice-versa.

Throughout the book I have included some modern-day, fictional case studies of couples who are portrayed as Christians, each with their own particular marital problems. These have been inspired by my knowledge and understanding of couples therapy and the stories have been tailored to exemplify some of the core issues and recurring themes that emerge for couples during therapy. The three couples that I will introduce to you in this guide are: 1) Mike and Jenny, a teacher and lawyer; 2) Rose and Andy, a missionary couple; 3) and Tom and Lucy, an accountant and nurse. The themes that are presented in the case studies are true to life and closely reflect issues that arise time and time again in couples therapy, but they are not based on any specific 'real-life' couples. My hope is that the case studies will help to bring to life some of the psychological theory and make it easier to understand.

Your couple relationship journey: tips on using the guide

I am aware that as you look through the contents of this book you may be drawn to certain chapters that spark particular interest. Each chapter can be read separately as a stand-alone topic. You will be able to understand the premises in some of the later chapters even if you have not read the start of the book. However, at the same time, each chapter does build on the previous chapters and ideas are expanded throughout the book. In fact, your understanding of the concepts in the earlier chapters will enrich your understanding of later chapters. So, in order for you to get the most out of the guide, I would recommend reading the chapters sequentially if you can.

At the end of Chapter 1, one of the self-help exercises is to draw what psychologists refer to as a 'genogram' – more commonly known as a family tree. I provide detailed guidance on how to do this. It can be quite an involved process, so it is a good idea to allow enough time to complete this exercise in an unhurried, relaxed way. I am drawing your attention to this now because in subsequent chapters I ask couples to refer back to their genograms in order to use them as a starting point for a range of discussions. So, I would like to encourage you to draw your genograms together at the end of Chapter 1 and keep them for future reference. Hopefully you will get a lot out of doing this exercise.

It can take a lot of time and effort for us to see change in our relationships, and herein lies one of the key issues that married couples face. Namely, there is an idea in society that we shouldn't have to work on relationships, that if we're in love, our relationship should be good and there should be little conflict. Also, another unhelpful tenet is that good sex just happens, it's not something that should require effort. However, like all other areas of life we benefit when we dedicate sufficient time and energy. This is reminiscent of the Biblical principle that you reap what you sow.

> *Remember this—a farmer who plants only a few seeds will get a small crop. But the one who plants generously will get a generous crop.*
>
> — Corinthians 9.6

'You reap what you sow' is also a common phrase that is widely used in our society, and even in popular songs. Perhaps it is because the truth of this principle resonates so strongly with us all: you are likely to get the most out of something the more that you put in. Holding this in mind, you may benefit most from this self-help guide as a couple if you arrange a regular time to meet and discuss each chapter: allowing yourselves the space that you need to complete the self-help exercises. Having your own copies of the book and annotating points that stand out to you as you read the chapters may also help you to get the most out of this self-help guide. Marriage is one of the most precious things in which we could invest our effort, yet it is easy to get caught up in the day-to-day activities, routines and general demands of life. Being purposeful and using this guide to work on your couple relationship could be one way of prioritising your marriage.

This self-help guide is a resource for you, and there are multiple ways in which couples may be helped to pinpoint some of their key issues. However, it's possible that the relational issues depicted in the couples from the Bible, the psychological theory, and in the modern-day case studies may not resonate with you entirely. If this is the case, my advice to you – as the experts on your own marriage – would be to try to make connections with the overall themes that could be similar in some way. Even if it doesn't feel like an exact fit for your particular situation you may still be able to discover a useful link. My hope is that this self-help guide will engage you and inspire you to think about your relationship in new ways.

The decision to enter therapy

At certain points in this self-help guide couples may feel prompted to consider whether entering therapy may be beneficial for them. With this in mind, it may be helpful to briefly explore viewpoints connected with going to therapy. As a clinical psychologist I can disclose something that won't be a surprise. Namely that I'm an advocate for therapy and couples therapy. It's one of my passions, something I've spent years training to do and I have the privilege of supporting people in this way. For others, therapy is a new unknown. Some Christians may be more comfortable seeking support from church or through prayer rather than seeking out the support of a trained therapist as well.

There is perhaps still some stigma in our society about formally seeking out this type of support. I'd like to acknowledge that and challenge that. When Christians encounter physical health problems, although prayer for healing may be requested, the church would also typically advise individuals to seek medical help. Similarly, when we encounter psychological problems and issues within marriage, there are trained professionals equipped to help resolve emotional pain. I believe that entering therapy can fit in perfectly with God's desire to see that *'captives will be released'* Isaiah (61:1) and for positive change to take place.

Exploring our past, psychological theory and our unconscious

I do ask couples to reflect on and think about their past: patterns of interactions in the family that they grew up in, and what their parents' couple relationships were like. The reason to reflect on and make connections with our past is simply to understand ourselves better. My premise is that if we can truly examine ourselves and understand why we do things (particularly why we may act in certain ways in our couple relationship) then we have a better chance of changing unhelpful patterns of relating. So, it is not a question of looking into our past or at our family to apportion blame, but rather to bring greater understanding, opportunities for change and healing. Understanding, rather than blame, is the key here, and that is the path that I am trying to help people find.

I want to underline that the ideas I present here are only ideas and not facts. As a psychologist I recognise that psychological theory is not a 'truth' per se, but rather a helpful lens that we can use to look at our marriages. Therefore, I would like to suggest that the best approach to reading this book is to consider the ideas that I present as clouds, drifting by and to be curious as you watch them float past you. The points I outline are not hard facts that you can easily grasp, but psychological theories; and like the clouds you may be interested in the various shapes that you can make out and the personal meaning that you can draw from the chapters. I'm aware that for some people this will be easy, but for others, particularly those used to working with hard facts, just allowing yourself to be open and curious will present a new challenge.

For this book to be as useful as possible I have incorporated some in-depth psychological theory. The theory has been simplified, but without watering it down too much. However, if this way of thinking is new to you, you may benefit from reading a chapter more than once in order to try to digest it fully and make sense of the material. There is one particular psychoanalyst who I refer to throughout the book and who has influenced my way of thinking and this is Carl Jung. Jung was interested in the spiritual domain and his father was a minister in the Swiss Reformed Church. Jung's mother had also been heavily influenced by her Christian upbringing. Her father, Jung's maternal grandfather, had been a pastor and a celebrated academic who taught Hebrew and Old Testament at a theological seminary. Jung used Christian imagery within his theory; he recognised and valued the spiritual side of life. As one of the early, pioneering psychoanalysts Jung introduced some ground-breaking insights about the unconscious.

The unconscious is that aspect of the mind or 'psyche' that lies outside of conscious awareness. It can be thought of as an invisible backpack where unwanted aspects of ourselves may be placed or 'repressed'. There may also be some valuable treasures hidden in the unconscious that are waiting to be discovered and will help us realise more of who we are. Difficult life experiences that have not been processed fully may also be stored in the unconscious. The significance of the unconscious is that it can have a huge impact on our interactions with others and of course within couple relationships. The reasons why certain arguments and patterns of relating seem to crop up time and time again may relate to what is stored in the unconscious.

On a spiritual level, I believe that God as our healer can bring unhelpful unconscious patterns more into our consciousness. Sometimes this can happen through the prompting of the Holy Spirit during activities such as: meditation; dreams; prayer; reading the Bible; or worship. Engaging in therapy or other forms of self-reflection can also make unconscious patterns of behaviour more conscious. Once we are more aware of what the unhelpful patterns are, we are enabled to make active attempts to change, or at least the unhelpful patterns are harder to ignore. The couple relationship and making the unconscious more conscious will form the first chapter of this book.

I hope that you enjoy a deepening of your couple relationship as you read on and explore your guide to a healthy marriage.

Part One

Lifting the painted veil:
a journey of fear and hope

Chapter 1

Revelations: making what is unconscious, conscious

Lift not the painted veil which those who live
Call Life: though unreal shapes be pictured there,
And it but mimic all we would believe
With colours idly spread, — behind, lurk Fear
And Hope, twin Destinies ...

Sonnet by Percy Shelley, 1818

This chapter is all about 'lifting the painted veil' and exploring your relationship in order to understand what lies beneath the surface. This may help you to experience a new revelation. A revelation of something that acts as a catalyst for change and transformation. If you are a Christian, you may have experienced the Holy Spirit revealing things to you about yourself. You may well have listened to a sermon and felt as if the Holy Spirit has shown you something about yourself, of which you had not previously been aware: something that resonates strongly. This new knowledge can reorientate you and create a shift in attitude that supports you to implement change. Exploring our internal emotional world, our attitudes, and pattern of thoughts is also something that we can ask God to help us with:

Search me, O God, and know my heart; test me and know my anxious thoughts.
Point out anything in me that offends you, and lead me along the path of everlasting life.
— Psalm 139:23–24

Similarly, therapy, or engaging in other forms of self-reflection, may help to provide insights and make conscious what has previously lain dormant in the unconscious. Entering a couple relationship or marriage may stir up feelings that emanate from the unconscious. This may be related to the fact that the couple relationship is the most physically and emotionally intimate relationship that we can experience. The only comparable relationship is that between the infant and the mother, although the physical nature is all encompassing (the baby resides within the mother's womb and may feed from the mother's breast) it is not sexual, thus making the couple relationship unique.

However, entering such an intimate relationship can be filled with ideals and hopeful questions about whether all of your needs will be met by this important 'other' person. This can feel very similar to the mother–infant relationship; sometimes there is an unconscious desire for a blissful merging with the 'other'. Perhaps this is linked to our infant desire to be completely taken care of. Therefore, entering a couple relationship can raise very primitive unconscious fears about being completely merged and overwhelmed by the 'other' and of losing one's identity. On the other hand, it can raise an equally primitive fear of being abandoned by the 'other' and of our needs not being met.

We could therefore hypothesise that within couple relationships there tends to be an unconscious tension between being close, yet not merged, versus being separate, yet not feeling abandoned. This tension is like the image of a pair of porcupines who long to be together, edging themselves closer until they prick each other. This causes them to move apart, but as the desire to be close remains strong, they try again and again to make it work. There is an eternal hope of finding the right balance between togetherness and separateness; a balance that feels comfortable for both partners.

Marriage can provide the opportunity to develop both spiritually and personally, although this type of transformational experience can be painful. This process is referred to by the psychoanalyst Jung as 'Individuation', which he describes as a *coming to selfhood*, a process of *self-realisation* (Jung, 1977) and *achievement of a greater personality* (Jung, 1977). Jung has also described the process of individuation as taking on the *burden of completeness* (Jung, 1978), by becoming more in tune with feelings of pain, suffering, and conflict: this subsequently has the power to transform (Samuels, 1995).

Sometimes there is a wish to avoid this process, even Jesus asked God to *'Please take this cup of suffering away from me'* (Mark 14:36). However, Christ's suffering and death brought transformation and new life. His suffering also resulted in all followers being enabled to have a close, personal relationship with God. The individuation process involves integrating aspects of ourselves that we may not be conscious of, aspects that perhaps have been repressed in the unconscious, because they are too painful to look at. However, if we are willing to be curious and explore what may be hidden in the unconscious, we also can have the opportunity to experience transformation, new life, and a deepening of our personal relationships. The Bible tells us that God: '... *divided the light from the darkness. He called the light 'day time' and the darkness 'night time'. Together they formed the first day.'* (Genesis 1: 4–5).

It is possible for us to compare day time with consciousness and night time with the unconscious. During the night it is harder to see, objects may be hidden in the darkness: things may seem unclear and possibly scary. We cannot have day without night, both are valuable and together they make a whole. Yet how much do we value our unconscious? How much time or attention do we pay it?

At the start of this chapter there is a quotation from a sonnet by Shelley called 'The Painted Veil'. This speaks about our human caution and fear of lifting the veil that protects us from seeing life in its true form. Or, in modern language, removing the rose-tinted spectacles. It is a challenge we often do not want to face for fear of what we may come across. Yet, if we do not lift the veil, we prevent ourselves from entering life fully. There is a parallel here with being brave enough to allow issues to surface from the unconscious and examine what our couple relationship may be trying to reveal to us.

The unconscious 'couple fit'

Our unconscious is always trying to influence our conscious mind – or what Freud referred to as our 'ego' – to be more aware of its presence and the knowledge that it wants to impart. How does our unconscious get our ego to listen and pay attention? Entering a couple relationship presents the ideal opportunity. Each individual will have unconsciously formed an idea of what it means to be in a couple relationship. This is usually internalised from the dynamics of our parents' marriage, which will lay down unconscious ideals and challenges for us. Quite simply put, in order for these unconscious dynamics to be made conscious, they need to be acted out. Therefore, each individual requires a partner who can help them act out their personal, unconscious story. The unconscious is prompting our ego to choose a partner who will fit into this role: a person who unconsciously knows how to bring the previously hidden drama to life because their unconscious story dovetails perfectly. This is referred to as the 'couple fit'.

Case example 1 – Jenny and Mike

Let me describe a case example that will help us to apply some of the above ideas. Jenny and Mike both had very different upbringings and there was no awareness of any problematic dynamic until after they got married. Mike was the youngest child in his family but was close in age to his sister towards whom he felt particularly protective. His parents had a volatile relationship: his father was an alcoholic, very controlling and verbally aggressive towards his mother, often putting her down and blaming her for unforeseen problems. Mike's childhood role in the family was to help mediate the conflict within the family, try to keep the peace between his parents and look out for his sister. He would often take the blame for small incidents that had angered his father in order to protect his sister and mother.

Jenny's family could not have been more different. She was the eldest of three children and in her family anger and difficult emotions were not easily expressed. This was particularly apparent when her younger brother, who was being treated for leukaemia, died suddenly just when they thought he was getting better. The grieving process for the family was suppressed and difficult. Strong feelings such as anger were shut away in Jenny's family, although they inevitably seeped out through more indirect, passive aggressive means. Superficially there was a sense that everyone was happy and family life was 'perfect'. Her brother's death was not talked about. Underneath the surface there was a lot of anxiety in Jenny's family background and this was managed by staying close together as a family. There was an underlying fear of leaving the family unit and of separateness.

Each individual in a couple helps to create a structure that works together even if they seem as opposite as chalk and cheese. A useful illustration is to imagine that everyone is walking around with very heavy overcoats on, which make them feel uncomfortable and hot; in the couple relationship one person is looking for another person who has a hook on which they can hang up their coat. The couple system often functions so that both parties can hang their uncomfortable, hot overcoats on each other. Technically, this term is referred to in the world of psychology as 'projection'. One of the uncomfortable hot overcoats that Jenny needed to get rid of was her anger and Mike came from a family who knew how to express anger directly, which created the perfect hook for Jenny to hang her overcoat on (or perfect partner to project her anger onto).

Usually, if one person is expressing all of the emotion in the couple relationship, they are often holding a lot of the emotion for the other person. In couple psychotherapy terms one of the partners can be seen to have a 'double dose' of the emotion. This does not have to be anger, it could be that one partner is very ambitious and driven and the other is extremely passive. This is something to look out for: when one partner is holding a lot of one emotion and the other partner seemingly has none. Jenny would project her anger unconsciously onto Mike through passive aggressive means, for example: forgetting important conversations; not listening to Mike properly; forgetting to pick up Mike's dry cleaning after promising to do so, and these types of events would repeat until Mike would explode with annoyance and frustration. There was no conscious understanding on Mike's part that his decision to marry Jenny – who was from a seemingly happy, positive, quiet family – would result in him marrying the very same problematic family dynamic that he had grown up with: being embroiled in repetitive intense arguments with a loved one who was angry.

This defensive, punishing dynamic was of course very uncomfortable for Mike and Jenny. Mike was labelled by his wife as the angry one, like his father: a label he did not like. Jenny took no responsibility for making Mike annoyed. She said that she just simply forgot important things time and time again as her job as a lawyer was very demanding. Her excuse was that she did not mean to or that she was tired or stressed from work. It turned out later on in couples therapy that Jenny often 'disassociated' during interactions with

Mike by becoming focused on work plans, a strategy that she had unconsciously developed following the death of her brother as a way of shutting off feelings of grief. She blamed Mike for his 'overreaction' and withdrew from him, telling him that it was difficult for her to be close to him because he had been so angry.

For Jenny, being confronted with direct anger, which was expressed by Mike, was uncomfortable for her because this emotion had been fiercely repressed in her family of origin. Of course, the anger was more intense because Mike was expressing both his own sense of anger at not being listened to by his wife (which triggered painful feelings from his childhood of being overlooked) as well as Jenny's anger that she felt unable to express directly: Mike had been given a 'double dose' of anger.

The helpful thing about these types of projections happening in a couple relationship is that once they have been made conscious each partner has the opportunity to take their projection back and integrate their anger, sense of ambition or whatever the projection may be. What you see in your partner may actually be a reflection of yourself. Your partner provides you with a mirror and an opportunity to look at the unconscious aspect of yourself and hopefully take responsibility for it. The issue has been described perfectly in the Bible:

> *How can you say, 'Friend, let me help you get rid of that speck in your eye' when you can't see past the log in your own eye? ...*
>
> — Luke 6:42

Mike had his own speck of anger, yet Jenny came to realise that she had a whole log's worth of it.

With lots of work Jenny was able to become more conscious of the repressed and disowned anger that she had experienced whilst growing up: the anger she felt at the sudden death of her brother and the anger she felt towards her parents who became distracted and distant following her brother's death. She also realised that on some level she feared that Mike would leave her suddenly if she expressed feelings of anger. However, she learned to be more assertive and express her anger in a more direct, healthy manner.

Eventually Jenny came to see that conflict and expressing anger could be a good thing for her marriage and did not mean that Mike would reject or leave her. In fact, it often led to very deep conversations about how each of them was feeling and genuine negotiations about how to overcome issues in their relationship. Anger was no longer viewed as a negative feeling that needed to be fiercely repressed, but rather a 'real' emotion that was good to express in a loving direct way. Mike was forced to be more in touch with just how uncomfortable aspects of his childhood had been. He became more conscious of the pain involved in the interactions between his mother and father and of how having to mediate the anger in the family meant that his own needs had often been pushed to one side and overlooked.

The influence of the Christian culture

It is important to note here the influence of the Christian culture on Jenny and Mike's relationship, particularly in relation to the emotion of anger. Mike's family attended church sporadically and Mike went on to develop a deep and meaningful personal Christian faith. Jenny's family went to church regularly and they were well respected in the Christian community. Her father was an elder of the church and Jenny was brought up to uphold Christian ideals and values in a strict and somewhat dogmatic manner. One of the reasons why Jenny found it so difficult to express feelings of anger openly was because she was taught that these very real, genuine emotions were somehow wrong.

Verses from the Bible were used by Jenny's family to reinforce positive ways of Christian living, but they were also used to help suppress difficult emotions, like anger. Examples of the type of verse that Jenny used to hear whilst growing up included:

And now, dear brothers and sisters, one final thing. Fix your thoughts on what is true, and honourable, and right, and pure, and lovely, and admirable. Think about things that are excellent and worthy of praise.

— Philippians 4:8

and,

Always be joyful. Never stop praying. Be thankful in all circumstances, for this is God's will for you who belong to Christ Jesus.

— 1 Thessalonians 5:16–18

Whilst these are positive, encouraging verses, very applicable to day-to-day life, sometimes we need space to explore more difficult feelings. If we look to the example of Jesus, he was not always rejoicing. In the garden of Gethsemane when he was contemplating his upcoming suffering, he said to his disciples:

My soul is crushed with grief to the point of death. Stay here and keep watch with me.

— Matthew 26:38

There are times in life when we experience sorrow, pain and difficult emotions, including anger. These feelings need to be expressed and shared with others. Sometimes it can be tempting to switch off from our own or our partner's painful emotions and fall asleep to them, like Jesus' disciples in the garden of Gethsemane, but staying awake and exploring them is important:

Then he returned to the disciples and found them asleep. He said to Peter, 'Couldn't you watch with me even one hour?'

— Matthew 26:40

Symbolically, we could say that falling asleep may be the equivalent to allowing these emotions to remain in our unconscious, where – as we saw from Mike and Jenny's example – they have the potential to create havoc. Eventually Mike and Jenny had a more complete sense of themselves and which emotion belonged to whom. When the circular loop of relating to each other through anger was broken, they were freed up to relate on a deeper and more intimate level.

Case example 2 – Andy and Rose

The case example of Mike and Jenny has helped us think about how anger may be projected in a couple relationship and some of the reasons for this. But what about other emotions, like sadness or depression? Let us take a look at another couple relationship where depression, feelings of loneliness and disconnection seemed to linger.

Andy and Rose were a missionary couple who for eight years had been working overseas until they returned to the UK for a year's furlough. Rose had given birth to their three children over that time and as a result she had been a full-time mother. Andy on the other hand had been extremely busy as a full-time Christian worker. He had been involved in a variety of projects to help the local population: his goal was to improve health and living conditions in the local area. Rose had periodically been very depressed during the eight years overseas, whereas Andy seemed to be a very calm, hard-working Christian man. In fact, Andy did not appear to be very emotional at all, he seemed pragmatic and logical.

Once again, Andy and Rose seemed as different as chalk and cheese. But what was really going on here? Andy had grown up as the son of a Royal Air Force (RAF) officer and frequently had to move to different countries and air force bases when he was a young child, which meant that he often lost a lot of friends during these transitions. Andy's whole life changed when his father had an accident and was subsequently medically discharged from the RAF.

Looking back Andy realised that his father became very depressed and threw himself into working hard in a publishing company. His father worked long hours and spent little time at home, which left Andy feeling unwanted by him as a child. Unconsciously, from the model that his father had given him Andy learnt that as a man you do not express feelings of sadness, instead, you just get on with life and work hard.

There was a different, more obvious experience of depression in Rose's family. Rose's mother suffered from post-natal depression after Rose's younger brother was born and the sense of depression seemed to be a permanent fixture during her childhood.

When Andy and Rose got married, they had high hopes and no intention of being like their parents. Being missionaries inspired Rose and Andy and they felt free and enthused by living overseas. However, Rose became pregnant and their lives changed as Rose could no longer spend as much time with Andy working jointly on the projects they were involved in. Initially Rose was really happy being a mother and dedicated a lot of her time to looking after their baby. She wanted to give her children a different experience of mothering compared to what she had experienced as a child; she wanted to be happy, present and involved in her children's lives.

Andy, although he could not express it, felt somewhat pushed aside by the attention Rose paid to their baby. Consequently, he began to work harder and spent more time away from the home. At the same time a number of Andy's close friends finished their work contracts and moved away. This was hard for Andy, so he reacted the only way he knew how – he started up even more projects and became busier and busier. After their second child was born Andy became even more busy and absent, Rose became sadder and her feelings of depression started to get worse. By abandoning Rose through throwing himself into his work Andy had given his sense of abandonment and loneliness to her.

When Rose was a child her brother was sent away to live with his cousin during school term time so that he could attend the same school. This meant that she was deprived of a play mate and was left alone with her mother, who was often depressed. Rose's marriage to Andy was triggering some of her feelings of abandonment and sadness from her childhood, and she was also being given Andy's feelings of sadness and abandonment to express. In this way, Rose was being given a 'double dose' of sadness and to the outside world Andy did not seem to be sad at all.

Sadness was a difficult emotion for Andy to connect with because he had learnt that it was unacceptable to express feelings of depression as a man. Andy and Rose were able to use couples therapy to explore and understand why feelings of sadness had come to the fore in their marriage.

Andy began to own and express his emotions and became more emotionally and physically present in their marriage. He cut back on the number of hours of work that he did, and he started to decline requests from the church to help with evening events. Instead he began to prioritise spending quality time with Rose and their children.

This meant that he was able to listen properly to Rose and really tune in to her emotional needs. As Andy did this and started to express his feelings of sadness, Rose's sense of depression lifted. She also had the opportunity to process some of the difficult feelings she had experienced in her childhood and was then able to forgive her mother and let go of feelings of resentment that she had held towards her.

As Andy and Rose became more emotionally in tune other aspects of their lives started to grow as well. Their sex life started to develop and take on a new form of intimacy and openness. Rose felt a deeper urge to be spiritually connected and to deepen her relationship with God. In fact, the psychological healing of their relationship had a ripple effect and impacted many other areas of their lives.

In these two case examples we have seen clearly the process of individuation at work. Both couples were brave enough to take on the *burden of completeness* (Jung, 1978), and experienced significant moments of *self-realisation* (Jung, 1977) through integrating aspects of themselves that had been hidden in the unconscious. This was a gradual and often painful process, which in the end resulted in a transformation of their couple relationship.

'Couple fit' and transitions in marriage

Some of these dynamics and strong feelings arising from one's 'couple fit' may emerge early on in marriage. Other trigger points when strong emotions may surface are during transitions in marriage. A married couple may have settled into a comfortable emotional rhythm, only to be thrown unexpectedly into strong emotional states when they enter a new life stage.

For example, having children may cause both the husband and wife to reconnect with difficult emotions from when they were very young. They may not have had the emotional capabilities at the time when they were little to fully understand or express their feelings. The transition of having children may provide a link to one's emotional world as a child. So as an adult, a new space is provided for the unconscious to work through earlier difficult experiences. Alternatively, couples may unconsciously act out some of the emotional undercurrents that their parents experienced in their marriage during certain transitions. Growing up, Andy and Rose both experienced difficult emotions when their younger sibling was born. In their families of origin their parents were already stretched in terms of emotional resources, so the addition of a sibling meant they had to cope with even less parental support. Times of overwhelm were more frequent for their parents and in turn for Andy and Rose, after their siblings were born. Therefore, it's perhaps not surprising that after Andy and Rose went on to have their second child, some of these very early emotional states were triggered and intense feelings of overwhelm and stress cropped up in their relationship.

Because Rose and Andy felt overwhelmed after the birth of their second child, they had fewer resources and less support to give to one another. Of course, this replicated both of their very early experiences of not receiving the support that they needed from a loved one. So, the transition of having a second child reconnected Andy and Rose with a lot of raw, unprocessed emotions.

It's possible for couples to also experience a reactivation of emotions from their childhood when their child undergoes a developmental stage, or as their child reaches a certain age. Perry (2019) suggests that the size and form of our child's body can trigger unconscious feelings of what it was like for us at that age. For example, when Andy and Rose's second child turned five and started school, it was the age that Rose's younger brother was sent away to live with their cousin in order to attend the same prestigious school. This was a significant loss for Rose. There was no conscious recognition of this particular link at the time, but emotions surfaced from the unconscious and things became somewhat turbulent for Rose and Andy. Rose and Andy were able to make sense of these dynamics over time in their couples therapy sessions. Specifically, the links between the tensions they were experiencing as a couple and how these related to the feelings from their childhoods.

Generational transitions within the wider family

Another transition that occurs when couples have children is that the roles within the family system change. For example, the adult daughter becomes a mother, and the mother becomes a grandmother when a new generation is born. When this happened for Rose, she noticed that her mother could sometimes be critical of her choices as a parent, or somewhat distant and rejecting.

In Rosjke Hasseldine's (2017) book *'The Mother-Daughter Puzzle'* she highlights how adult daughters may lead very different lives to their mothers.

In fact, daughters may have increased opportunities, choices and freedoms open to them. It can be painful for a mother to see opportunities that have passed her by mirrored in her daughter's very different life, or her different experience of being a mother.

Andy was a different type of husband and father, compared with Rose's father. Despite Andy being busy sometimes with work, he was a loving, active father who enjoyed playing with his children. Rose and Andy travelled the world together for their work, whereas Rose's father was absent from the home on foreign business trips for long periods of time. Rose's mother often didn't have her husband by her side, and he wasn't a practical 'hands on' father like Andy.

Hasseldine (2017) points out that mothers can end up feeling jealous of their daughters, although it is hard for the mother and the daughter to recognise this emotion because society teaches us that it's shameful and not acceptable. Hasseldine (2017) tells us:

> *I also find that most mothers are unaware they're feeling jealous of their daughter. They hide it away beneath being critical of their daughter's beliefs, behaviors, and choices, or by being emotionally unavailable.*
>
> — p.15

Mother-in-laws may also feel jealous towards their daughter-in-law who has managed to cultivate a very different life and has different choices open to her. When a daughter is able to understand the grief and loss behind some of the confusing attitudes or hurtful behaviour of her mother, it can increase empathy, depersonalise the experience, and help the daughter understand that they are not responsible for making their mother happy (Hasseldine, 2017). This type of exploration can help daughters feel released to pursue opportunities for themselves and help them to circumnavigate sacrificing their needs for others and having the same restrictions that their mother had placed on her life (Hasseldine, 2017). When a mother can become more in tune with feelings of loss and jealousy towards her daughter and the understandable reasons for this, it can break down barriers and enable them to reconnect.

Similarly, when a husband and wife become parents, they may encounter criticism or silent disapproval about their choices from their parents or in-laws. This can place an additional strain on a marriage. However, it's also worth bearing in mind that this criticism or hurtful or confusing behaviour may also be related to an unrecognised sense of jealousy and loss. This may be because the couple present a painful mirror to their parents of the freedoms and opportunities that weren't open to them when they became parents a generation earlier. This can help to depersonalise the sense of disapproval, or criticism, and contextualise it in a helpful way.

Also, when we don't follow in our parents' footsteps and we do things differently, we are not providing them with a *reflected sense of self* (Schnarch, 2009), because we are choosing not to mirror their choices and preferences. This can generate conflict. I explore further the idea and problems related to being dependent on a *reflected sense of self* in Chapter 3: 'Encouraging intimacy through a balance of individuality and togetherness'. How to respond to the conflict created when you disturb another person's '*reflected sense of self*' is explained in greater detail in Chapter 8: 'Encountering conflict and being in your own boat'. Whilst the concepts have been described primarily in terms of how they apply to a marriage relationship, the same principles apply to our relationships with our parents, in-laws and other people too. The ideas are transferable, and the above chapters may be useful for you to read if the transition and choices that you are making in your marriage are generating conflict with other family members.

Understanding transitions in marriage

Other transition points may be entering different life stages, like retirement. For some individuals, retirement can be a fulfilling time where they feel liberated to explore new avenues and, overall, they enjoy the lack of constraints and demands. For others this period may require some adjustment of roles, and as well as gains, retirement may generate difficult emotions and feelings of loss.

Similar to other transition points, strong emotions from the past related to one's 'couple fit' could arise. Retirement has the potential to echo issues connected with adjustment, identity, or loss. This is something that you could try to explore and think about together during the genogram exercise at the end of this chapter. Drawing out your genograms (family trees) together can help you to explore repeating patterns across the generations and may help you to make sense of the particular transition that you are undergoing.

As a couple, the exercise may prompt you to reflect on similar transitions, adjustments or changes in role/identity that other family members experienced and how they may resonate with you in your marriage. It may be worth asking yourself if you are experiencing some strong emotions in your marriage, are you undergoing a period of transition? What is this connected to? Did your own parents undergo a similar transition and if so, what was that like for their marriage? You may need to hypothesise and guess the answers here if you're not sure. And in turn, how did you as a child experience the emotions surrounding this transition in your family of origin?

Once again, you may not be sure exactly how you felt as a child, but your adult self may be able to look back and make a fairly accurate guess. Another clue to how you may have felt as a child, if you continue to draw a blank, may be the feelings that you're currently experiencing in your marriage. For example, both Andy and Rose's sense of being overwhelmed and distressed and not feeling supported by one another were accurate reflections of how they felt as children in relation to their parents, following the arrival of their younger siblings.

The answers to these questions may help you to piece together and make sense of your current experience of transition in your marriage. It may also help you to understand that if your emotional reactions are very strong it may be because there's additional emotional load that is being triggered from the past. Once this is more conscious it can reduce the intensity of the feelings and the situation. When dynamics are more conscious this helps to resolve situations because you are able to place where the emotions are coming from. This in turn can reduce levels of distress.

As a caveat, it's of course natural for couples to experience stress and a range of emotions during a transition. This is likely to be very normal and requires time to process and work through. Periods of transition do not necessarily have anything to do with issues arising from one's 'couples fit' and emotions from the past. For example, becoming parents can naturally be an adjustment and stressful at times. The adjustment from having one child to two, can also be stressful. However, if you're experiencing very intense emotions that are difficult to process, or issues seem to keep flaring up rather than being gradually worked through, these may be clues that the period of transition is tapping into emotions from the past. If this is the case, then you may want to reflect on issues connected with your 'couple fit' either by using the 'Joint Reflection Points' below or through attending couples therapy.

If it's simply a transition with a normal level of stress attached to it, then supporting one another, seeking out additional support if needed from friends, family, your church, or professionals could be helpful. We all tend to cope better with transitions the more buffers and support that we have in place. You may more generally want to think about how you both individually cope with change and what you have learnt about 'doing change' from your family of origin. This too is something you could use the genogram exercise for and the details about how to do this are in the 'Joint Reflection Points' at the end of this chapter.

Changes in physical and mental health

Other transitions in marriage may relate to things like changes in physical and mental health. This can result in a reorganising of roles and shifts in identity. Feelings of loss may also come to the fore for both partners. When Andy's father sustained an injury and was medically discharged from the Royal Air Force, he suffered a dramatic loss. This loss was not merely related to his impaired physical capabilities, but a change in identity following the end of a career that he had so deeply valued. As a child Andy had observed and absorbed his father's emotions surrounding these changes. This was one of the reasons why Andy's work and identity as a missionary was very important for him to maintain. Andy gave work an elevated position because he was fearful of losing that identity like his father had. As we know, Andy's focus on work meant that Rose's and his children's needs were sometimes overlooked.

When individuals experience a change in mental or physical health, it can be hard to come to terms with. For some, it can be like an eternal transition that is never quite complete – where an individual sometimes briefly accepts that things have changed, only then to reject the altered version of themselves.

They may avoid or deny the reality of the changes. This may be problematic in terms of possible rejection of help, not seeking the support they need, and not being able to take on board medical advice or adhere to treatment/medication regimes. One's ability to relate to oneself, one's partner or children can be difficult if the individual hasn't accepted or adjusted to the changes they have experienced.

The 'empty nest' life stage transition

Another transition for couples that can generate a sense of loss is the 'empty nest' phenomenon when children leave the family home. When a mother or father goes through this transition it can take some readjustment. For some people the change may go relatively smoothly. There may be a natural grieving process for others as they come to terms with the absence of the children and subsequent change in parental duties.

For others, the loss of being a hands-on parent, without their children physically present at home may connect them with other losses. In particular, the loss of their own parent. This may be a literal loss through death or a sense of loss around a mother or father who may have been absent or neglectful in some way. They may feel like they weren't parented properly and that there was a lack of consistency in care when they were growing up. Sometimes becoming a parent can help people to override this sense of loss from the past. In fact, it may feel like an important opportunity to provide a different type of care compared to what they received as a child. In this way, parenting may help to fill a hole from their own childhood.

Therefore, when the children leave the home, this hole and sense of loss around not having the parent they needed for themselves may become exposed. When faced with this double loss (which may not be conscious) some people may enter a depression, try to become busy to manage feelings of sadness, or their body may react to the sense of loss and stress through different physical symptoms.

In addition, if a parent has ploughed all energies into caring for their children, then when the children leave the home this may bring into focus the lack of care that they provide for themselves. Their needs may have always ended up last on their priority list and others' needs came first. If their own parents were neglectful, they may have internalised this model of care and then self-neglect can be an unhealthy pattern that has followed them through life. Self-neglect may compound feelings of sadness as the individual may find it hard to look after themselves, so they don't seek out the support they need. They may also not prioritise things that would make them happy and give them pleasure. This is an important aspect of self-care and can be an antidote to depression.

When a parent is no longer needed in such an immediate way because their children have left home, this may have a significant impact on their sense of self-worth. For some individuals they need to feel needed and their sense of self-worth is closely linked to this. Individuals may require some time to reorient themselves and reinvest their energy in other relationships and in self-care. Having space to figure out what they need for a change may be a very helpful new experience.

Transitions and loss

There are many other types of transition that we can experience in marriage that can tap into themes of loss including things like: loss of a job; moving home and away from friends; loss of an actual loved one or family member when they die; the gradual loss of a parent through dementia; miscarriage and the loss of a baby; or the more ambiguous loss of infertility and the grief for the baby that fails to be conceived month after month, or year after year. It's important to allow time to process feelings of loss and allow one another the time and space that is needed to work through these feelings.

Thomas Moore (1992) in his book *Care of the Soul* points out that in some Renaissance gardens, historically there was a dedicated bower, a shaded, remote place under trees or climbing plants where people could go to sit with feelings of melancholy without fear of interruption. I think this presents a beautiful image of a sanctuary for reflection. This place was respected as well as the understanding that people sometimes needed to experience feelings of loss and low mood. Moore (1992) would argue that sometimes we are too quick to try and push away feelings of melancholy. Perhaps in modern society depression is difficult to tolerate, or we feel the need to fix things quickly rather than welcoming these feelings in and providing a space for them, just like the bower in the Renaissance garden. This idea may helpfully challenge us to find time and a space to stop still without interruption in order to connect with our emotions and allow them to be processed.

We can all at times struggle to find the healthy middle ground: at the other extreme there is the possibility of becoming overly immersed in feelings of loss. When this happens, we don't manage to work through these feelings, instead we may end up stuck. Loss has the potential to cause us to isolate ourselves and disconnect from others. Or we may disconnect from others by becoming manic and overly busy in order to avoid grief. Either way, this can be difficult in a marriage and a painful, distancing experience. If you feel overwhelmed by feelings of loss, it may be helpful to seek support from friends, family, or to seek support through your church and through prayer. You may wish to consider whether medication may help to provide the buffer that you need to lift your mood. Pausing to evaluate whether it's potentially the right time to call on the help of a trained therapist may also be beneficial. How themes of loss and change may have affected your marriage can be explored further in the genogram exercise at the end of this chapter.

Transitions and feminine and masculine ideals

Periods of transition may also challenge some of the ideals we hold around the ideal feminine or masculine role that we feel we should inhabit. For example, a man may feel that he needs to be strong and not show his emotions, and support his wife during transition points and times of stress. During retirement a man may experience a change in role, a challenge to rediscover a sense of purpose, but he may not feel able to express some of these difficult emotions openly. A woman too, may feel she should be happy as she enters retirement, with less work pressure, greater amounts of free time and grandchildren to enjoy. Yet it may be difficult to make sense of feelings of dissatisfaction.

A woman who becomes a mother or grandmother may feel overwhelmed with caring demands and unable to tap into her sensual side. She may also be pigeon-holed and viewed as 'mum' or 'grandmother' rather than as a sexy partner, almost as if both aspects of her identity cannot co-exist. Chapter 7 'Mountain and caves, Heaven and Earth, male and female' explores how we gain a greater sense of wholeness as men and women when we begin to integrate possibly overlooked aspects of ourselves. This chapter may be helpful for you to read if issues around your role as a man or woman may be having an impact on you during a transition. It may also help you think about the pressure that either yourself, others, or wider society places on you to live up to a feminine or masculine ideal.

Now there is an opportunity for you as a couple to 'lift the painted veil' and take a closer look at your couple relationship by working through the 'Joint Reflection Points'.

Joint Reflection Points

Working together to jointly reflect on the couple relationship can be very useful and interesting, but it can raise lots of difficult emotions and tensions. Try to work through the exercises below and take a step back to notice how you are both feeling in an accepting, non-judgemental way. However, if something important comes up and generates conflict that feels too difficult to manage, just make a note about what you were talking about and come back to it later. If you continue to find it difficult to discuss and hear each other, you may benefit from having a third person to help facilitate a reflective space for you both, like a trained couples therapist.

1. In your relationship does one of you hold a 'double dose' of some emotion? (For example: anger, anxiety, sadness.)

    ♥ Spend some time reflecting on and being curious about this possibility. Perhaps think about whether there is an aspect or emotion in your spouse that you particularly dislike or find difficult? Ask yourselves, have you identified a speck in your partner's eye when there is actually a log in your own?

    ♥ If you have identified something, explore together why it is an uncomfortable emotion for one of you and why the other person tends to hold a lot of that emotion. Consider the example of Mike and Jenny – are there any particular experiences from your respective childhoods and upbringings that may contribute towards this?

    ♥ If you have not been able to identify anything, drawing a genogram of your families may be helpful because it provides a visual map, so patterns of interaction can be seen more clearly.

    ♥ Remember, if you become more conscious about this dynamic – as opposed to it being unconscious and hidden in the dark – you will have a greater sense of control over it and can more easily choose to interact differently as a couple. However, this will take time and not necessarily be easy, so remember to be kind and patient towards each other as you go through this process.

2.   Drawing a genogram.

This could take a couple of hours to complete, so schedule this for when you have plenty of time and emotional energy. You may need to do this over two sessions.

    Genograms (family trees) are used as a visual way of making sense of family dynamics and repeating patterns across the generations. Throughout the following chapters I suggest that couples return to look at their genograms, so I would encourage you to find the time to do this exercise, as it is likely to help with other 'Joint Reflection Points'. If you like learning through visual means this is a great exercise for you. Genograms involve representing family members using symbols. The pages at the end of this chapter provide a key for the different symbols you can include on your genogram. Circles represent females in the family and squares represent males.

♥   Firstly, familiarise yourself with the symbols on the subsequent pages that are used in genograms. You can also look at the example of Mike and Jenny's genograms at the end of this chapter.

♥   Take it in turns to draw out each other's genogram together. So, the husband can draw the wife's genogram with the wife providing the guidance about the family members and the symbols that need to be drawn, and then swap over. You may wish to get a large piece of paper and you can use coloured pens if you feel like getting really creative (Remember you may need to do this exercise in two sessions.)

♥   Draw out three generations, which includes yourself at the bottom of the page and your siblings, including any of their spouses and children, your parents above you and your grandparents drawn out above them. See the example of Mike and Jenny's genograms at the end of this chapter as a guide.

♥   When you have drawn out the basics of the genogram, you can start
      adding other symbols, like a zig-zag line to denote conflict between
      two people, put a cross through a circle or square to denote that
      someone has died. Two parallel tram lines can be drawn from one
      person to another to denote particular closeness. Take a look at the
      key on the subsequent pages to see what you may like to include.

♥   Once you have completed each other's genograms, the next step is
      to ask each other questions about certain family patterns, cultures
      and values that may have been passed down through the
      generations and in turn have had an impact on your own marriage.
      Take turns interviewing each other, so for the husband's genogram
      the wife can ask the questions and help him to think about his
      family patterns and then swap over.

♥   Here are some example questions that you could ask each other
      whilst looking at the genograms. Please feel free to select the
      questions that feel most pressing and relevant for your couple
      relationship. You do not have to ask all of the questions below, just
      choose the ones that you think would be most helpful or to which
      you would be most interested to hear your partner's response. You
      also do not have to ask each other the same questions, although it
      may be interesting to compare your responses.

      –   What aspect of your family culture has the most
            positive/negative influence on your couple relationship?

      –   In what ways does your family tend to express emotion? Who
            expresses certain emotions most? Who expresses certain
            emotions least? How has this influenced your couple
            relationship?

      –   What is not talked about in your family? Are there any
            unspoken/no-go topics or emotions? How does this impact

your couple relationship? Does your partner express certain emotions for you?

–   How is/was disapproval expressed in your family? How is/was approval expressed? How is this potentially replayed in your couple relationship?

–   What have the significant losses been in your family? What has this meant for you? How has this impacted your couple relationship? Are you experiencing any transitions or events that tap into feelings of loss at the moment? What lessons have you learnt from your exploring themes of loss in your wider family? How could this help you in your marriage?

–   What does being 'separate' or 'together' mean in your family? How are/were times of separateness or togetherness managed? What influence does this have on your couple relationship?

–   What are the family stories that have had the most impact on you? Who tells them in your family? How do these stories influence your marriage?

–   What are the family stories of change? How do members of your family 'do' change? How do you do change? What does this mean for your couple relationship?

–   How does your family define weakness/strength? How does this influence your marriage?

–   How did your parents and wider family cope with particular transitions? Perhaps think about a transition that is relevant for you in your marriage. How do you think this may be having an impact on your marriage? Are there emotions surrounding transitions in your family of origin that are being echoed in your own marriage?

Spiritual Reflection Points

1. Thank God for the strengths that you both individually bring to the couple relationship.

2. Pray to God and ask Him to help reveal what emotions you may each be responsible for in the couple relationship:

    Search me, O God, and know my heart; test me and know my anxious thoughts. Point out anything in me that offends you, and lead me along the path of everlasting life.

    — Psalm 139:23–24

3. Thank God for the opportunity to grow as a couple through working through issues in your marriage. Ask for God's inspiration about how to interact differently with each other. Are there any particular fruits of the Spirit that you would like to ask God for more of right now?

    But the Holy Spirit produces this kind of fruit in our lives: love, joy, peace, patience, kindness, goodness, faithfulness, gentleness, and self-control. There is no law against these things!

    — Galatians 5:22–23

Symbols used for drawing genograms

The following symbols are commonly used in drawing a genogram. You can use these symbols to draw out each other's genograms as detailed in Joint Reflection Point 2.

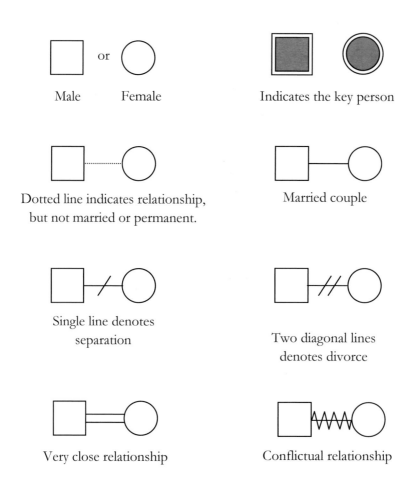

Male   Female   Indicates the key person

Dotted line indicates relationship,   Married couple
   but not married or permanent.

Single line denotes   Two diagonal lines
      separation   denotes divorce

Very close relationship   Conflictual relationship

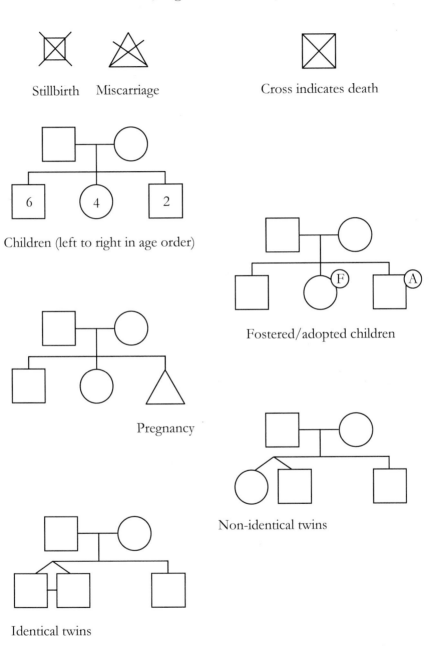

Stillbirth   Miscarriage

Cross indicates death

Children (left to right in age order)

Fostered/adopted children

Pregnancy

Non-identical twins

Identical twins

Examples of Mike and Jenny's genograms

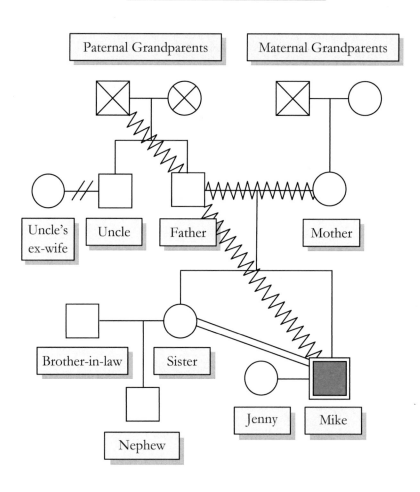

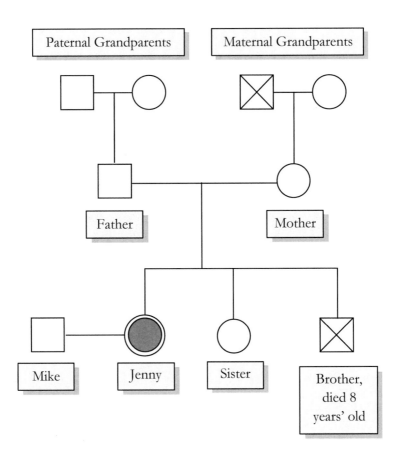

JENNY'S GENOGRAM

Paternal Grandparents

Maternal Grandparents

Father

Mother

Mike

Jenny

Sister

Brother, died 8 years' old

Chapter 2

The marital triangle:
parallels with the Trinity

A person standing alone can be attacked and defeated,
but two can stand back-to-back and conquer. Three are
even better, for a triple-braided cord is not easily broken.

Ecclesiastes 4:12

I have had the pleasure of reading a fascinating chapter on the 'marital triangle' by Stanley Ruszczynski (2004) and will attempt to summarise some of his points and link them to my own thoughts and connections with the psychological and the spiritual. Ultimately, I hope that this will provide you with a fresh and helpful angle on your couple relationship.

The configuration of the family triangle

The quotation at the beginning of this chapter highlights the importance of considering how three separate parts can form one whole:

> *... a triple-braided cord is not easily broken.*

— Ecclesiastes 4:12

So, we are going to spend some time exploring from a relational perspective how our ideas and experiences of being in a couple relationship can be affected by this valuable third position. We will be looking at several different trinities, depicted as triangles throughout this chapter, starting at the beginning with the individual's relationship with their parents.

Here we have the three positions of mother, father, and child. In psychoanalytic terms, the 'Oedipal stage', which is thought to be around age four to five years old. This signals the time when the child realises that their relationship with their mother is qualitatively different to the mother's relationship with the father. The child starts to realise that they are separate from their parents in this way – the child is small, and the parents are big, and they share a different type of intimacy. With this realisation can come a sense of loss and on some level a sense of being painfully excluded.

For example, often little girls say that they are going to marry their father when they grow up, but of course this is not a real possibility and with time this idea is discarded and seems to fade away, never to be mentioned again as the daughter passes through that stage. Being able to hold in mind the experience of the mother and father as a couple helps the individual to develop an internalised image of a couple relationship. Therefore, by working through the Oedipal position, the individual knows they are excluded from the parents' relationship, but still connected and loved. This means that the individual can bear the tension between separateness, yet togetherness. This is illustrated by the figure of the 'family triangle' below.

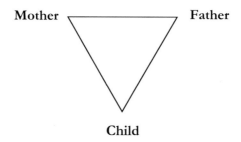

Figure 1: family triangle

As you can see in the figure above, the mother and father are united and linked together on the same level of relating, with the child connected to them below. So, although they all remain connected together, the child is somewhat excluded by being on a different level to the parents. However, sometimes the parental relationship can be dysfunctional. For example, a son can be inappropriately brought up to the same level as the mother, perhaps because the father is often absent and away on business and the mother relies on the son. Consequently, the father takes the place of the child at the bottom of the triangle and is somewhat excluded. Please see what I have referred to as the 'misaligned family triangle' in Figure 2 below.

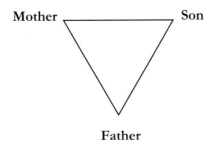

Figure 2: misaligned family triangle

This pattern of alignment can cause significant problems and as an adult, the son may find it extremely problematic entering an intimate couple relationship. What is likely to happen in this instance is that the son's own couple relationship may continue to have a parent–child quality about it, thus replicating his inappropriate childhood experience of what it meant to be part of a couple. For example, the son may be very passive and childlike with his wife and the wife may then feel forced to reciprocate in a nagging mother role.

You may wish to consider whether something similar happened to you as a child with one of your parents. Whether it was a father/daughter bond that became distorted or mother/son relationship that was unhelpful. In the case of a daughter and father becoming unhelpfully close, the mother may have become absent or excluded through circumstances like depression, disability, alcoholism, divorce or even death. Sometimes a daughter can then be subtly brought up to join the father and be expected to take on a mother role, look out for other siblings and perhaps the father as well. If you think that this triangle is relevant for you, it may be good to start thinking about the impact of this type of misalignment on your couple relationship.

I came across an interesting term, which expands upon the idea of the misaligned family triangle, in Jean Shinoda Bolen's brilliant book, *The Ring of Power* (1999). Shinoda Bolen refers to these types of relationships as 'emotionally incestuous'. The term shocked me to begin with and caused a certain degree of discomfort, but it made a lot of sense and helps to clarify how unhelpful these types of dynamics are. Here she details what can happen between a father and a daughter.

> *As a child, the daughter may love her father unconditionally and think he is wonderful, while his wife sees his flaws and failures. As she grows older, the daughter who adores him gives him emotional support. She may become his confidante, the person who shares his thoughts. If he turns to her for companionship and validation, the daughter replaces his wife as his central relationship (and is thereby in an emotionally incestuous relationship with him). She mirrors back a positive image to him, in contrast to his wife, who may be critical and angry or the voice of reality that he does not want to hear.*
>
> — Shinoda Bolen, 1999, p.76–77

So, the father inappropriately relies upon the daughter for affirmation and positive feedback, which can place a lot of pressure on the child. As I have already mentioned, something similar can happen between a mother and a son, whereby he is asked to become the source of emotional support. A daughter can also be called on to support her mother or a son to support his father as an emotional confidante if the other parent is absent in some way.

It is of course, a very disturbing position to be placed in as a child, in an 'emotionally incestuous' relationship with the parent. There is an inappropriate degree of closeness and a son or daughter cannot be a partner for their parent. On a conscious level, a child may to some extent feel special that they are wanted, sought after, or needed by their parent. Their self-esteem may be boosted, and they may rationalise that it is good that they are able to do so much for their parent who really needs them.

However, unconsciously this could feel like a precarious position to be in. Certainly, there may be unconscious fears about the blurring of boundaries and a fear that their parent is treating them like their adult partner instead of as their child. This does not have to be in very obvious ways, but there may be many subtle ways in which a parent can treat their child like an adult partner. For example, asking them to keep them company in their spouse's absence and sharing their innermost thoughts with their child – an emotionally intimate situation.

When the child grows up and is eventually in their own couple relationship, part of them may feel uncomfortable about the sexual side of their relationship with their partner. After all, the internalised image that they have of a couple relationship from their childhood is not of two sexual adults (their mother and father) but is of a parent and a child coupled together. Consequently, their internalised image of a couple relationship would be a non-sexual one. There may have been real fears for some individuals that the emotionally incestuous relationship could have tipped over into a physically incestuous relationship and resulted in sexual abuse. Indeed, in some cases there may have been some seductive undertones to the emotionally incestuous relationship and for some children being sexually abused as part of this misalignment may have been a traumatic reality.

So, as I have mentioned, children who have been forced or seduced into an emotionally incestuous relationship with one of their parents are likely to adopt a parent–child style of relating in their own couple relationship. Of course, this can kill off feelings of sexual desire and erotic playfulness because, let's face it, who wants to have a sexual encounter with someone who comes across like a 'parent' or a 'child'? That proposition isn't very sexy at all.

So, there may well be a certain degree of ambivalence about enjoying the erotic side of your relationship with your partner if you have experienced an emotionally incestuous relationship with a parent. Part of you is likely to still have a strong desire to express your sexual side and connect with your partner, but another part of you may inadvertently hold yourself back, in subtle or not so subtle ways. Just becoming more mindful of these dynamics and how you may have been inappropriately positioned as a child may help you to shift your way of relating with your spouse and help you to develop your own, healthier image of a couple relationship. Later on in the book, Chapter 10: 'Soulful sex' and Chapter 11: 'Control of couple intimacy: what's sex got to do with it?' will help you develop and understand the sexual dimensions of your relationship further.

Now putting issues around emotionally incestuous relationships to one side, there can be more generalised problems with misalignments with parents once married. This can occur when an adult daughter or son hasn't really left their original family unit. Instead, they may remain to a greater or lesser extent emotionally merged with their parents and not fully aligned with their spouse. This can create a whole host of problems in marriage. It may mean for example, that a husband or wife may allow their partner or family members to criticise or treat their spouse in a dismissive manner. This permission may be silently given when the spouse remains passive and fails to say anything in support of their partner. Perhaps due to a fear of upsetting others or because they are so merged with their family of origin that they don't see this negative pattern or recognise the impact on their spouse.

Other problems may include siding with one's parent's view or wishes, or plans for family celebrations, or other occasions over what their spouse wants. The individual may turn to their parents or other family members for guidance, or to discuss important matters before talking issues through with their partner. They may prioritise being available by phone or in person for their parents or other family members in ways that may inconvenience their spouse or own family unit.

It's important to be aware of any tendencies to remain merged with your family of origin. Then you can consciously try to prioritise and realign yourself with your spouse. Active efforts need to be made to emotionally and practically put your partner's needs first. You need to help create a more appropriate realignment with your husband or wife and for this to be clearly visible to your parents and other family members.

First and foremost, your emotional bond and responsibility to love, honour, and cherish lies with your husband or wife. Your parents or other family members can come a close second, but they should not take priority over your spouse. When a person in a marriage is struggling with their in-laws, examining what's going on in terms of alignments and trying to protect and uphold your spouse's needs, may help to improve the situation.

But I want my independence!

Ruszczynski (2004) points out that adolescence can be another significant time when we try to work through 'Oedipal' issues of separateness, yet togetherness with our parents. He points out that an illusion is often reached by the end of adolescence where we believe that we have finally become independent and no longer need any significant 'other'. As adults when we enter a couple relationship it can feel like our partner is making an attack and threatening our hard-won independence (Ruszczynski, 2004).

I think that this can be very common and losing the illusion of independence can feel like a bitter pill to swallow. However, the reality is that we have never been independent, as human beings we continually need to be in relationship with others. If you are struggling with the sense that you have lost your independence because you are in a couple relationship, then it may be helpful and comforting to remember that our independence has perhaps always been an illusion.

This illusion of independence is possibly further influenced by western culture that values independence over and above many other qualities. It is therefore important to face the reality that our partner has not taken away our hard-won independence because we need to be in relationship with others, and it is good to be in a relationship with our partner. How we navigate the tricky balance between separateness and togetherness in our couple relationships will be unpacked further in Chapter 3.

The marital triangle

We have now reached the all-important idea of the 'marital triangle', an idea that has been developed by Ruszczynski (2004). This triangle is made up of the two individuals and the third element is the couple relationship itself, which can be thought to have an identity and personality of its own. One of the most important aspects of being in an effective marriage is being able to create this reflective triangular space where you are both able to take a step back as individuals and reflect on the couple relationship. This is very important and may be something that you have not really thought about before.

You may find it interesting to ask yourself *'What does my couple relationship, as an entity in its own right, look like?'* almost as if it has a life and personality of its own.

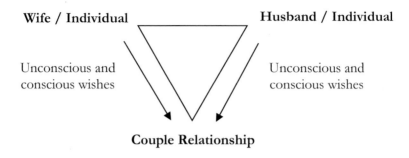

Figure 3: the marital triangle

Just like the first family triangle, the third position has been created by a coming together of the two individuals in order to create a third, which instead of the child is the couple relationship. The husband and wife, if you like, give birth to the couple relationship. The above triangle depicts each partner being able to take a step back in order to consider the couple relationship and its needs as if it were an entity in itself. From the triangle above, you can see how the entity of the couple relationship is positioned some distance away from the wife and husband at the bottom of the triangle, allowing them both to look at what sort of relationship they are creating together. However, it can take a lot of creative, sexual, emotional and spiritual energy to help achieve this reflective triangular space. Some couples may find it difficult to look at their couple relationship. They may be caught up in blaming one another for the 'wrongs' that they've done, or they may end up focusing on what they appreciate about their husband/wife, but not be able to peer beyond that, to reflect on what kind of couple relationship entity they are co-creating.

Your parents' ability to take up this position of reflection and symmetry as depicted in the triangle above, is likely to have had an impact on your own ability to take up this position in your couple relationship. For example, your parents may have functioned more as individuals in their couple relationship, each with their specific roles and duties, but they may have had little opportunity or capacity to take a step back and consider how their own demands and expectations impacted on their couple relationship.

Also, as a child you may have been encouraged to interact with your parents as separate individuals – having one type of relationship with your mother and another with your father, and very rarely relating to them, or having opportunities to see them together as a couple unit. The scene that we often see in movies is of a child with a specific question being told by their mother to *'Go and ask your father,'* which they do, only to be told by the father, *'You need to ask your mother.'* Here we see the child having very separate interactions with each parent and a joint couple response is lacking.

It may be helpful to ask yourself questions like: how many times do you remember seeing your parents kiss; go out on dates together; or having a conversation with them both sitting together and responding to you as a couple? The extent to which you were able to interact with your parents as a couple unit may influence how you are in your own couple relationship, perhaps seeing yourself more as an individual in the partnership and thinking about your needs instead of being able to take a step back to consider the needs of the couple relationship itself.

Sometimes there is the need to enter couples therapy and have the therapist as the third person in order to help facilitate joint reflections. The marital triangle highlights the need for symmetry and the capacity for two individual partners to recognise that there are two equal claimants to the benefits of the relationship *and* to the role of 'guardian' and 'protector' of the relationship (Ruszczynski, 2004).

Case example 3 – Lucy and Tom

A couple called Lucy and Tom found this point really helpful. The concept appealed to Tom in particular, who was an accountant, and this idea was grasped quickly by his keen business mind. He had never considered the idea of the couple relationship being an entity in its own right and how he had a duty to guard, protect and invest in it, as well as reap the dividends from it. This made Tom think about the intense arguments that he got embroiled in with Lucy and how his tendency to judge and be critical of her was chipping away at their marriage. He realised that he needed to take more responsibility for guarding and protecting their couple relationship instead of just expecting to take the benefits from it.

Tom pictured what he had been doing, criticising Lucy and eroding his couple relationship, as like rough waves crashing against a beautiful soft coastline covered with delicate flora and fauna. Tom started to realise that he needed to keep in check how rough and harsh he was with Lucy and that he actually wanted to build some wave barriers to protect his relationship from erosion. This imagery helped Tom in the heat of the moment reconsider what he was doing and not only focus on what he needed as an individual in that moment, but also on what the couple relationship needed.

As depicted in Figure 3: the marital triangle, Ruszczynski (2004) tells us that the conscious and unconscious wishes of each individual will make up the personality of the couple relationship. With both partners filling up the couple relationship with a wide variety of sometimes incompatible wishes. This will be a lot for the couple relationship to cope with. If we think of the couple relationship as an entity in its own right, there may be an awful lot of pressure and expectation weighing it down. With opposing individual wishes and expectations, the couple relationship may fragment, feel heavy, confused and uncertain about what to do. Of course, when wishes are incompatible, this can leave the individual feeling let down, betrayed, and failed by the couple relationship. This is an important point and can have drastic consequences. We will be looking at the ideals that individuals may bring to the couple relationship, alongside feelings of betrayal that can arise when these ideals are not met, later on in Chapter 4.

Parallels with the Holy Trinity

I think that it is helpful to compare the marital triangle with our understanding of another important spiritual triangle, the Holy Trinity. Obviously, the Holy Trinity is not the same as a couple relationship, but I am interested in exploring how each part of the Holy Trinity relates to the other and the lessons that can be applied to the couple relationship. I have been thinking about Jesus as the Son of God occupying the third position, particularly as he symbolises the marriage of two opposing qualities: divinity and humanity.

One of the most interesting things about Jesus is that he is able to effectively maintain the positions of being both Son of God and human. Moreover, his human nature never once seemed to overwhelm his godliness and his holiness did not seem to eliminate human feelings of tiredness, or hunger and pain. This seems to present us with an ideal image of the couple relationship, when two individuals are able to come together and tolerate their differences, even when they are quite extreme. There is a tendency in a couple relationship for one personality to try to dominate and overwhelm the other, yet Jesus showed us that it is possible for two opposites to co-exist in harmony.

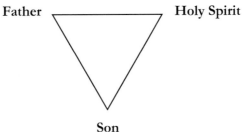

Figure 4: the Holy Trinity

The beauty of Jesus lies in the fact that he is present and entered into our human world rather than remain a distant God. Christians believe that he is God, yet he allowed himself to become vulnerable and be born into the world as a baby. He was King of Kings, yet he submitted to wearing a crown of thorns and being tortured on a cross. Strangely, he did not lose any sense of his godliness through doing this; instead his godliness seemed to stand out even more.

Perhaps this is what we are aiming for in our couple relationship: a way to compromise and be together without losing a sense of who we are. This also draws attention to a way in which our togetherness can help to highlight our individual strengths and celebrate our uniqueness.

The Holy Trinity: lessons on separateness and togetherness

Another important link regarding the Holy Trinity is the often problematic issue of separateness versus togetherness. The following quotation from Genesis 2:24 tells us:

> *... a man leaves his father and mother and is joined to his wife, and the two are united into one.*

This can sometimes be misinterpreted by couples to mean that there needs to be a complete merging in a couple relationship whereby one's individual identity is sacrificed. It is important to bear in mind that this is not the intention of the scripture and that the Holy Trinity demonstrates for us a very healthy depiction of separateness, yet togetherness when Jesus was on earth. Jesus was physically separate from the Godhead whilst living on earth, and yet was still connected as he drew on the power of the Holy Spirit and knowledge gained from the Father. Jesus' baptism is one of the few times in the Bible when we see and hear all three aspects of the Trinity together.

> *One day when the crowds were being baptised, Jesus himself was baptised. As he was praying, the heavens opened and the Holy Spirit, in bodily form, descended on him like a dove. And a voice from heaven said, 'You are my dearly loved Son, and you bring me great joy.'*
>
> — Luke 3:21–22

I would like to put forward the argument that being completely united and merged is not the norm in the couple relationship. It is perhaps only during times of sexual intercourse that the couple can momentarily feel merged, like they are one being. Particularly if this is a reciprocal, mutually giving and satisfying experience. However, when the climax of intercourse has been reached the couple must physically separate once more.

There have been many theological discussions about the meaning of the verse *'… two are united into one.'* (Genesis 2:24). I do not intend to provide a comprehensive answer but will attempt to summarise some of the ideas that have been put forward by theologians. One idea is that it may refer to the Biblical premise that woman was originally made from man, Eve was formed from part of Adam's body, thus the coming together of male and female reunites the body as one. Or that it may refer to the oneness achieved through sexual union. Alternatively, the verse is thought to highlight the monogamy and fidelity that marriage requires, the unity that cannot be broken by another. The verse may also present a variation on the commandment to *'love your neighbour as yourself'* (Mark 12:31) as some scholars believe it points to loving your spouse as much as you love yourself and holding their concerns in mind as if they were your own.

However, I do not believe that the verse is advocating that couples should be like emotional Siamese twins, fused in a very unhealthy way. Or that the only way of maintaining togetherness is to sacrifice one's individual identity for the sake of the marriage. Remember, Jesus' godliness was not undermined by his humanity and his humanity was not overpowered by his godliness: they managed to co-exist beautifully and neither aspect was sacrificed for the sake of the other. The image of the Holy Trinity reveals to us the right kind of balance between separateness and togetherness that Jesus experienced whilst on earth, alongside special moments of complete union.

For Christian couples there is a special sense of union with God in their marriage. Like the triple braided cord that cannot easily be broken, referred to at the start of this chapter God is the important third element that can help bond husband and wife together. See Figure 5: 'the spiritual marital triangle'. Spiritual activities like prayer and worship can help unite the wife and husband. They can draw on the spiritual resources available to them from God and be strengthened in their marriage. In the triangle below, we see the wife and husband in the position of being open and connected to one another in a reciprocal way. They are also jointly connected to God, who is positioned above them, supporting and helping to meet their needs.

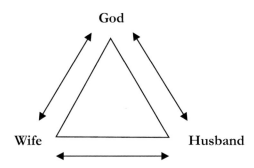

Figure 5: the spiritual marital triangle

Problematic merging and closeness in couples

Sometimes a couple is merged, perhaps because they unconsciously fear separateness – like Jenny and Mike following the tragic loss of her brother. This can cause couples to stick together and remain unhealthily close.

Similarly, Mike's experience of family life taught him that it is important to stay close and merge with other family members in order to protect them from getting hurt. The problem when couples are in a merged state is that it is hard for them to function as individuals. One partner more than the other may struggle to see the other partner as separate.

When this happens, the relationship can feel claustrophobic. If you have ever tried to look at your partner whilst hugging very closely you will know that you can end up with blurred, double vision because you are so close. You need to move away and create some distance in order to see them properly. The same thing can happen on an emotional level. When couples are very merged it can be confusing as to which emotion belongs to each person. Sometimes when couples become entangled like this, one person will end up talking on behalf of the other or completing their sentences for them. There are of course other indicators of a merged couple state, such as possessiveness or an inability to tolerate and appreciate a partner's separate ideas. There may be an underlying assumption that as a couple they should agree on everything and share the same views. When a couple is functioning on a merged level, it is difficult for them to gain any reflective triangular space. This may mean that there may be little space for reflection about individual needs or the needs of the couple relationship.

A couples therapist can help to provide a more reflective triangular space that can eventually help the couple to gain more symmetry and perspective on each other's individual needs and the needs of the couple relationship itself. See Figure 6 for the 'couples therapy triangle' below.

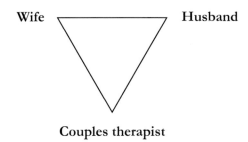

Wife   **Husband**

Couples therapist

Figure 6: couples therapy triangle

I hope the exploration of the family triangle, the marital triangle, and the links with the Holy Trinity has been useful and provided some food for thought for your own relationship. The development of reflective, triangular space can really energise a couple relationship and open up new opportunities for creativity and growth.

If we return to the Bible verse at the start of the chapter, we can see that it highlights for us the power and strength that can be gained from being able to incorporate that valuable third position:

> *A person standing alone can be attacked and defeated, but two can stand back-to-back and conquer. Three are even better, for a triple-braided cord is not easily broken.*
> — Ecclesiastes 4:12

Why not use the 'Joint Reflection Points' below to provide you with some reflective, triangular space, where you can take a step back and consider your couple relationship together? The 'Joint Reflection Points' may help you reflect upon how your parents' couple relationships have influenced your understanding of what it means to be in a couple relationship. They will also provide you with a space to consider the impact of each individual on the couple relationship and what your joint 'couple personality' may look like. There is also an opportunity to explore family alignments and the impact that these may have on your marriage.

Joint Reflection Points

1. Your parents' couple personality:

    ♥   What type of joint couple personality do you think your parents have or had?

    ♥   How do you think your parents' couple personality has affected your own couple relationship?

    ♥   Do you consciously or unconsciously expect your couple relationship to be similar to your parents?

2. To what extent have you been able to relate to your parents as a couple unit who are separate from you? Or did you relate to your parents as separate individuals and have one type of relationship with your mother and another with your father? Share with your partner how you think this may have influenced your own couple relationship.

3. Positions of symmetry and reflection in marriage:

    ♥   To what extent do you think your parents were able to take a step back and reflect both on their individual needs and the needs of their couple relationship?

    ♥   How has your parents' ability to reflect in this way affected your own couple relationship? (For example, did one partner tend to sacrifice their needs for the sake of the marriage? What could you have learned indirectly from your parents?)

4. Do you ever get into a cycle of competing with one another for control over the couple relationship, with one individual personality striving for more space than the other, or with one person wanting to be right? When does this tend to happen?

Follow up questions:

♥ How can you tolerate and accept your individual differences better in your couple relationship? You may need to consider what blocks you from doing this.

♥ How can your togetherness as a couple bring out your individual strengths? Set some small goals regarding how you could facilitate this.

5. Alignments with your spouse and children (if applicable). Discuss the following questions:

♥ What are the alignments with your spouse and children like? Do you sometimes align yourself with your children over your spouse?

♥ Do you ever seek out your children's company to help you feel good about yourself and boost your self-esteem instead of engaging emotionally with your partner?

♥ Are cuddles, physical affection, playing, and interaction with your children given more time and importance than physical touch and interaction with your spouse?

♥ Do you ever align yourself with your children and undermine your spouse by taking your child's side when it comes to discipline and decision making?

Try to be honest with your answers. Make a commitment to consciously prioritise your spouse and seek them out for emotional support and physical touch. This will help to strengthen your couple unit.

If you've answered yes to any of the above questions, discuss this with your spouse. Explore together in a non-blaming way to find practical solutions to redress any imbalance that you've identified. What areas are most important for you to change individually/together?

6. Being an emotional support for your parent:

    ♥ As a child do you think you were ever used by your mother/father
       as an emotional support because your other parent was absent
       emotionally/physically? If so, what impact do you think this has
       had on your own couple relationship? Is there an echo of child–
       parent relating in your marriage? (Remember if you were used as an
       emotional support for a parent, replacing your mother/father, your
       unconscious template of 'a couple' is that of a parent and child,
       rather than of two adults. This would have been a difficult
       experience for you as a child. It may mean that you may
       unconsciously replicate parent–child relating in your own
       marriage.)

    ♥ If you think this is an issue for you, it may be helpful to consider
       the following question: What would you need to do differently in
       order to adopt a more 'adult' as opposed to 'parent' or 'child'
       position in your marriage? Try to think about adopting the adult
       partner role in the following areas of your relationship:

       – decision making

       – level of responsibility that you take

       – your level of emotional/practical engagement in day-to-day
          matters

       – your level of emotional/practical engagement in lovemaking.

    ♥ Discuss this together in a compassionate, non-judging way and
       jointly make a list of any ideas that you think would help.

    ♥ Try to become more aware of this pattern of interaction when it
       emerges and then consciously step into the position of adult sexual
       partner, instead of a 'parent' or 'child' role.

7. The personality of your couple relationship:

♥ Try to think about your couple relationship as having its own personality or identity. Picture an image, perhaps from nature that you would compare it to. What would this look like?

♥ Try to imagine another image of how you would like your couple relationship to develop and be different in the future. What would this look like? What steps would you need to take to move towards that image?

Spiritual Reflection Points

1. Pray to God to help your couple relationship develop and grow in the
    direction that you would like. Use the verses below to visualise God's
    Holy Spirit flowing through your relationship like a river, bringing
    healing and new growth.

> *Then he said to me, 'This river flows east through the desert into the valley of
> the Dead Sea. The waters of this stream will make the salty waters of the Dead
> Sea fresh and pure. There will be swarms of living things wherever the water of
> this river flows... Fish will abound in the Dead Sea, for its waters will become
> fresh. Life will flourish wherever this water flows. Fruit trees of all kinds will
> grow along both sides of the river. The leaves of these trees will never turn brown
> and fall, and there will always be fruit on their branches. There will be a new
> crop every month, for they are watered by the river flowing from the Temple. The
> fruit will be for food and the leaves for healing.'*
>
> — Ezekiel 47:8–12

Chapter 3

Encouraging intimacy through a balance of individuality and togetherness

A portion of your soul has been entwined with mine.
A gentle kind of togetherness, while separate we stand.
As two trees deeply rooted in separate plots of ground,
while their topmost branches come together,
forming a miracle of lace against the heavens.

'Two Trees' by Janet Miles

Being differentiated

The above poem 'Two Trees' paints a beautiful image of what it means to be 'differentiated' in our marriage. It illustrates that when we are differentiated and able to uphold our sense of self, our separate ideas, yet still remain connected with our partner, then true intimacy can flourish. Being differentiated happens when we can embrace this unique balance between our sense of individuality and togetherness in marriage. You can see another echo of the poem 'Two Trees' when you look at the image on the front of this book. The two trees on the front cover highlight the beauty of what we might like to aspire to in our marriage: a healthy, differentiated form of togetherness. The book cover depicts two separate trees, in two separate plots of ground. Each with their own individual root system, yet still connected by their topmost branches. As the poem reminds us: *'A gentle kind of togetherness, while separate we stand.'*

Dr David Schnarch is a Clinical Psychologist and Sex Therapist and has written a brilliant book entitled *Passionate Marriage*. He introduced me to the concept of 'differentiation', which I would like to elaborate on and take some time to explore further. He describes differentiation as *'your ability to maintain your sense of self when you are emotionally and/or physically close to others – especially as they become increasingly important to you.'* (Schnarch, 2009, p.56). It is also about being able to remain true to yourself and what you feel is right despite pressure from family, friends or one's partner to conform to their wishes. Why is being 'differentiated' in couple relationships so important? Well, when we can stay connected with our spouse, yet feel able to be separate in lots of ways – like expressing opposing or conflicting ideas to our partner – then this can bring energy and growth to a relationship.

The opposite of being 'differentiated' is being 'merged' and this can create problems in a marriage and reduce levels of true intimacy. We started to explore the area of problematic merging and closeness for couples in Chapter 2. Dr Schnarch also refers to this as 'emotional fusion'. Merging with our partner and suppressing part of ourselves can slowly deaden a relationship – spiritually, emotionally, and sexually. We will take a look at what it takes to be 'differentiated' and some of the factors that can contribute towards us being 'merged' and emotionally fused with our partner. This should help you to circumnavigate some common pitfalls.

Being differentiated takes some work, so it is not surprising that it is easier to find examples of couples in the Bible who struggled to remain differentiated, than couples who were successful at it.

If we take the infamous Biblical couple Samson and Delilah, it is Samson who struggles to remain true to himself when he faces pressure from Delilah to disclose the secret of his great strength. Eventually, and with dire consequences, Samson caves in to her demands, reveals his secret, and he is betrayed. We will take a closer look at this fascinating couple in Chapter 4: 'The ideal couple and feelings of betrayal'.

Dr Schnarch (2009) points out that well-differentiated people are able express themselves and disagree with others without feeling that they have alienated themselves and this is really important. In couple relationships this can be very difficult. When we disagree with our spouse, we can lose our connection with them and may even feel that we need to leave the room in order to calm down and reduce the intensity of the situation. Being differentiated is about being able to disagree with our partner, or pursue an opposite way of thinking or course of action, whilst still being able to stay emotionally connected to them.

In the previous two chapters I have pointed out the difficulties that couples have finding the right balance between separateness and togetherness.

Dr Schnarch in his discussion of emotional fusion notes that it is common in our society for people to have 'fusion fantasies' and that our fascination with observing activities like synchronised swimming may be related to this. Dr Schnarch suggests that we are fascinated by the idea that two people can seem to share one mind and therefore be able to move their bodies in unison.

Sometimes people like the idea of emotional fusion as it falsely feels like a safe, secure position to be in with our spouse. However, when we are in a merged, fused state with our partner there is little space for different opinions and positions.

This means that it is difficult to fully relate to the other person because they are not seen as separate beings with their own wishes and desires. One of the dangers of this is that if our partner is not seen as separate to ourselves, then we can easily take them for granted. If we really did view our spouse as an extension of ourselves, perhaps invoking the idea of 'two shall become one', then we could end up like a pair of emotionally fused Siamese twins. From this position we have the potential to damage the other person as we push forward and prioritise our own individual emotional needs. All of this reduces our capacity to be truly intimate with our spouse.

Reflected sense of self

When couples are emotionally fused, they depend on what Dr Schnarch (2009) calls a 'reflected sense of self', so the individual relies on the validation, affirmation and consensus of opinion of their partner. If we are relying on our partner for affirmation or feedback that we have done the right thing it is hard to have a consistent sense of ourselves. Sometimes we want, or even demand, that our partner shares the same opinion as ourselves so that the reflected sense of self that we get from our partner is not disturbed. Furthermore, it may mean that we do not want our partner to develop or grow as their changing identity and views may threaten or destabilise our reflected sense of self.

Dr Schnarch points out that it is important for us to rely on 'self-validation' rather than 'other-validation' if we want to be differentiated in our couple relationship. Self-validating intimacy focuses on the individual maintaining their own sense of self-worth and understanding of who they are and what they want when disclosing their views to their partner, without expecting affirmation or acceptance in return. Other-validating intimacy focuses on receiving empathy, acceptance and mutual disclosure from one's partner. This is often mistaken for true intimacy. Other-validated intimacy is a bit like *'I'll scratch your back if you scratch mine'*, and when we function like this, we often do not really want to know our partner, who they are and what they think, we just *need* them to validate and accept us. When we *need* our partner rather than *want* them it is dangerous territory as it negates any true relating and intimacy.

The couple in case example 3, Lucy and Tom, were emotionally fused and had reached a place of emotional gridlock where they felt very stuck in their marriage. They had repeated arguments, followed by long periods of silence where they would emotionally withdraw from each other. Lucy felt that their marriage had reached crisis point and told Tom that she wanted them to go and see a couples therapist. Initially, Tom pretended to go along with the idea and provided Lucy with some superficial other-validated intimacy by saying that he would be happy to try this at some point.

The crux of it was that Tom did not really believe that Lucy would follow through with arranging for them to enter couples therapy. In fact, he was taken aback when Lucy showed him the emails from several couples therapists who could offer them sessions and had quoted their fees. Tom began to panic and feel really scared, he was aware that Lucy was serious about confronting their relationship and intimacy problems. Tom recognised that this could destabilise his reflected sense of self because he had always positioned himself as the victim in their relationship, which had enabled him to hold onto a sense of blame and superiority. Lucy was typically blamed for the things that went wrong in their relationship and on some level, this made Tom feel good about himself.

What happened next was that Lucy had to take a more differentiated stance in her relationship with Tom and rely on self-validation as Tom vigorously attacked her idea of going to couples therapy sessions and tried to pressurise her to give up on the idea. Tom wanted Lucy to remain emotionally fused and agree with his way of thinking and his decision. Lucy was able to listen to Tom's wishes, she did not enter into an intense argument, but was able to hold onto herself and communicate what she wanted. Tom tried everything he could to get Lucy to change her mind and attempted to make her feel guilty about the amount of money that they would be spending on couples therapy. He knew this was an area of weakness and anxiety for Lucy. She had to calm her fears, rely on self-validation, and she discussed ways that they could change their weekly budget to make money available for couples therapy. She then proceeded to book their first therapy session.

Tom resentfully agreed to go to therapy. Part of him knew that it would be good for them as a couple even though he liked to pretend everything was okay. Whilst he didn't really want to examine how he had been contributing to their difficulties, Tom also felt sad and confused at times in his marriage. Consequently, part of him was relieved that something was going to be done and action had been taken, even though he couldn't articulate this at the time. Lucy had sensed that Tom was also sad at times and this helped her to self-validate when he expressed his frustrations about going to couples therapy. She was able to remind herself that she was making a positive decision for her marriage by arranging couples therapy sessions for them.

Lucy knew that she was disturbing Tom's reflected sense of self when she spoke up about their difficulties in their marriage. Whilst she sensed that Tom was struggling too, she knew that he liked to try and keep up an image of them being a successful, happy couple. Lucy knew that by speaking out, and communicating that she wanted them to go to couples therapy, she would burst the illusion and reflected sense of self that Tom was trying to maintain. But for Lucy, she had reached a point of crisis in her marriage and she needed to adopt a differentiated stance with Tom. She knew that she needed to express her own separate thoughts and desires in order for their relationship to improve. At the start of couples therapy Tom *needed* Lucy to affirm and validate him by agreeing with his point of view. He didn't really *want* to know Lucy's own separate views and what she wanted: he thought intimacy was equated with agreeing with your partner and not having any conflict.

At certain points Tom experienced feelings of resentment about having to confront the problems that he was jointly responsible for during their couples therapy journey. However, at the end of a year's worth of sessions and a number of break-through moments in the therapy, Tom and Lucy's relationship was transformed. Numerous times Tom expressed how grateful he was that Lucy had ignored his pressurising demands not to enter couples therapy and how she had managed to hold on to what she knew she needed in order for their marriage to survive and grow.

Needing versus wanting our spouse

Another significant issue for couples who are not well-differentiated is what Dr Schnarch calls 'borrowed functioning', which is very different from offering one another mutual support. Sometimes in couple relationships one partner may help the other partner to identify and express their emotions. Helping our partner to be more emotionally literate could be seen as a positive thing, but this is often another example of borrowed functioning. This arises from the problem of wanting our partner to need us, rather than feeling comfortable enough to have a connection with our partner which is based on them wanting us. By encouraging our partner to 'borrow' some of our functioning it may seem like we are enabling them to be more autonomous. However, their functioning is in fact being suppressed, and their poor functioning is being perpetuated as they rely on their partner rather than developing the resources within themselves to grow.

From a Christian perspective, when we move towards a position of *wanting* our spouse rather than *needing* them, it reminds me of what theologian Neil Pembroke (2007) refers to (in his book *Moving Toward Spiritual Maturity: Psychological, Contemplative, and Moral Challenges in Christian Living*) as being in communion with our partner and being open to giving and receiving. We do not demand that our partner gives to us and that we are entitled to receive, but rather we display Christian love in its truest form as in a reciprocal way when we hold true to the Biblical guidance to: *'Give as freely as you have received'* (Matthew 10:8). So just as God freely gives His love to us, so we too give our love freely to our spouse, with no demands or expectations that our partner should respond in a certain way or pay us back. Note that this is the opposite of having your relationship based on other-validation – the *'I'll scratch your back if you scratch mine'* approach.

Similarly, God has admonished his people when they have offered sacrifices from a place of fear, anxiety, or habit, rather than from a position of *wanting* to have a relationship with him. Hosea 6:6 depicts God telling his people: *'I want you to show love, not offer sacrifices. I want you to know me more than I want burnt offerings.'* Likewise, in our couple relationship what we desire from our partner is to be known by them and loved, not needed or depended on, or clung to out of fear or even given expensive gifts in place of real interactions and genuine connection.

At the time of the prophet Hosea, God's people were getting on with their own lives and on a day-to-day basis they were ignoring God. They superficially kept up appearances and continued with important rituals by giving burnt offerings and sacrifices. In our couple relationship we may see something similar taking place with one or both partners continuing with their day-to-day life, bypassing any deep meaningful connection and superficially performing family rituals, falsely believing that they are doing enough.

If we think back to the couple in the case example in Chapter 1, it was Jenny who needed Mike to stay close to her and she did not necessarily want to know him and his feelings. Instead she needed him to soothe her anxiety and fears about loss and abandonment. Before going into couples therapy, she would argue that she needed Mike to stay close to her because she loved him so much and thought that's just what you do when you are married, invoking the Bible verse *'two shall become one'*. She would often say to Mike, *'You know it's just normal for a wife to want to have her husband by her side, what's wrong with that? I love you and that's what loving wives want, just to be together lots with their husband.'*

However, when Jenny told Mike that she missed him and that he should stay and spend Wednesday nights with her rather than meet up with his friends from church, it was not love, but rather a child-like need and demand. Dr Schnarch points out that when we cling onto and lean on our partners like this, *needing* them instead of *wanting* them, it can be very draining and subsequently reduces intimacy in the couple relationship.

Loving from a position of equal regard

One of the other significant points in Neil Pembroke's (2007) chapter 'The Agape response' is that in our relationships it is helpful when we start from a position of 'equal regard', so that we love ourselves just as much as the other person and not love ourselves less. This point is embodied by the Biblical command to *'Love your neighbour as yourself'* (Matthew 22:39). This verse suggests that it is important to love ourselves, as this sets the standard, and is the quality of love that we should be giving to others. When we love ourselves and dedicate enough time and energy to meeting our own needs, we are then more equipped to give out and love others and our spouse. This is important to hold in mind when trying to be differentiated in our couple relationship and not giving up on own our needs due to pressure to conform to our partner's wishes. Of course, it is natural to make compromises together and this may form part of a mutual giving and receiving. But it is also important to love ourselves and hold onto ourselves and our sense of integrity about what we want, and what is important to us. It's helpful to communicate our wishes, speak up, and not remain silent about key issues. We will explore this point further when we take a look at Queen Esther and King Xerxes' relationship from the Bible shortly.

Also, I think starting from a position of equal regard (where my needs are equally as important and valid as yours) may help us to avoid relying on a reflected sense of self from our partner. If we love ourselves as much as our spouse, not less, then I believe that it would perhaps be easier to self-validate. Then we would not depend so much on other-validation to feel that we have done the right thing. Whilst it's okay and positive to receive validation from our partner, being dependent on it or fearful of losing it can leave us in a precarious position.

For decisions, we may ideally like to reach a place of agreement with our spouse, but if we have a different idea, priority or desire for something to happen, being differentiated means that we can hold onto it, without feeling pressured to give up on something that is important to us. From this place, negotiation or a working through of the issues can take place, rather than being 'merged' and making a decision to ignore our own wishes for the sake of our partner and not wanting to 'rock the boat'. Being differentiated helps us to move towards a loving, open dialogue that is not driven by pressure, anxiety, fear of conflict, or thoughts that our own views or wishes are less important. Your partner is loved, and their wishes are respected. At the same time being differentiated means that you value your own wishes with a similar attitude of love and respect.

Sometimes we may review our priorities and feel happy to make a compromise, but it is better if this is done from a position of being differentiated. That it forms part of an active, conscious, freely made choice, rather than feeling compelled to adapt ourselves to our partner's needs due to a sense of pressure, fearing loss of approval, or fear of conflict or other reasons. Chapter 8 of this book 'Encountering conflict and being in your own boat' may be helpful for you to read if the fear of conflict makes it difficult to express your needs in your marriage.

Problematic lifetraps and equal regard

There are a couple of what Young and Klosko (1994) refer to as 'lifetraps' that can hinder our attempts to have real communion with our partner and stop us from relating from a position of equal regard. Firstly, let me describe the 'subjugation' lifetrap. Subjugation is based on the assumption that you must please others and strive to meet their needs (Young & Klosko, 1994). For those people who have a subjugation lifetrap, the focus of living life is not based on what you want or how you feel, it is based on what other people want and what you can do to make them happy (Young & Klosko, 1994).

The subjugation lifetrap is problematic in lots of ways, in particular because it is so demanding and exhausting and under the surface resentment can build up. People with this lifetrap can expend a lot of energy pleasing others and trying to avoid conflict at all costs. Young and Klosko (1994) highlight that: *'Subjugation robs you of a clear sense of what **you** want and need – of who you are.' (p.261).*

Furthermore, if we think back to the importance of the Biblical command to '*Love your neighbour as yourself*' (Matthew 22:39), subjugation means that you are loving others more than yourself. In fact, if you were to treat other people as you treated yourself then they would be pretty neglected, with their needs often overlooked and ignored.

Some people may think that it is women more than men who have a tendency to subjugate their needs. However, men can also experience problems with subjugation. For example, if we think back to the case of Mike, who had grown up learning to subjugate his needs in order to mediate conflict in his family of origin, and then in his couple relationship he prioritised Jenny's needs and often ignored his own. For a long time, Mike did not go out with his friends because Jenny could not bear to separate from him, but after a while Mike started to feel resentful about this arrangement. Resentment is a common feeling for partners who subjugate their needs. On the other hand, Jenny had a different type of lifetrap, one that often dovetails with that of subjugation: the 'entitlement lifetrap' (Young & Klosko, 1994) which will be explored next.

Entitlement relates to the belief that you should be able to have what *you* want and that other people in your life are primarily there to meet your needs. There are a number of reasons why people develop the entitlement lifetrap, which are described well by Young and Klosko in their book *Reinventing Your Life* (1994). I would recommend reading this book if you suspect that you may have entitlement or subjugation issues.

Jenny had developed a dependent type of entitlement where she felt entitled to depend on Mike and for him to be the strong one and take care of her emotional needs. After Jenny's brother died of leukaemia her parents tried to overcompensate for this loss and did lots of things for Jenny. In fact, they did too much for her, which meant that later on in life she continued to feel entitled to lots of emotional support, particularly from Mike. Entitlement is also problematic in terms of the Biblical command '*Love your neighbour as yourself*' (Matthew 22:39) because people with this type of lifetrap expect other people to put their needs to one side. In essence they are saying 'I come first' and so they are not treating their partner with equal regard, instead they are loving themselves more than their partner.

If we think back to the issue of being differentiated, both the subjugation and entitlement lifetraps promote a very merged, emotionally fused way of relating whereby the other person in the couple relationship is not really seen as separate. I'll explain briefly how this works. If you have the subjugation lifetrap you are not thinking of yourself and your own needs, recognising that you are a separate person who requires things in your own right. That you too have needs that are important to fulfil. Rather you focus your energy and efforts to please your spouse and let their needs overtake your own. You are merged with them, constantly thinking about how your actions, words, and choices affect your partner and you are always trying to accommodate their wishes.

On the other hand, if you have the entitlement lifetrap, then you are treating your spouse as an extension of yourself, and because of this you don't see them as really separate from you. And if your spouse is viewed as an appendage to yourself, this may give you a sense that you can use them and make demands when it suits you, without having to check in with them. As your partner almost feels like part of you, by default, you feel on some level that they are obliged to fall in line with your agenda. This may not be an entirely conscious process. Nevertheless, in this merged way of functioning, you take them for granted by expecting that they should be able to prioritise your wishes. This may mean them having to neglect their own needs and desires.

Christianity, subjugation, and equal regard

Neil Pembroke (2007) in his chapter 'The Agape Response' reflects on the historical tendency in the Christian world for women to prioritise their husband's needs. He writes:

> *The [women] saw it as their calling to give of themselves so that others – namely, the men of the family – could pursue their professional calling. On the model of mutuality, women are still called to give, but they are entitled to receive. Increasingly, we are seeing men prepared to make adjustments in order to help a partner pursue her goals. The men should not be asked to sacrifice their plans, but neither should they feel entitled to stick rigidly to what might be the ideal situation for them.*

— p.155

Here Neil Pembroke is advocating mutuality and equal regard in marriage and giving and receiving from one another. Previously, some wives may have felt that they needed to subjugate their needs. Subjugation is different from making compromises that we naturally need to do in our marriage. Subjugation goes beyond this: subjugation is where the person's needs are overlooked and ignored in order to ensure that someone else's needs are met, or so that conflict is avoided. Previously, I think that there may have been subtle messages given to wives that it is okay for them to overlook their needs for the sake of their husband. Whilst a wife may feel appropriately called to act in a self-sacrificial way, for some individuals there may be a danger of sacrificial giving tipping over into an unhealthy pattern of subjugation.

This is something really important to be aware of. A wife who has subjugation as one of her lifetraps, who feels driven to please others out of fear, anxiety and habit and is used to having her own needs overlooked could be badly affected by subtle messages that she should prioritise her husband's needs. By default, she may incorrectly assume that she needs to ignore her own. Such messages could unhelpfully reinforce an unhealthy pattern of subjugation. Someone with a subjugation lifetrap needs to spend more time thinking about their own needs in order to gain some balance and truly live out the Biblical command to *'Love your neighbour as yourself'* (Matthew 22:39) instead of worrying all the time about pleasing others. It is interesting that Neil Pembroke has noted that husbands are now much more likely than before to be open to making adjustments in their marriage so that a wife can pursue her goals.

However, Christian couples these days may still be influenced by messages that they have grown up with, or by the example of their parents or grandparents' marriages, whereby a pattern of subjugation may have been subtly encouraged. This type of role modelling may mean that even young Christian men of a different generation unconsciously expect their future wives to behave similarly to their mothers, despite being attracted to women who are independent, and to the idea of having a marriage based on equal regard.

Of course, something similar can happen to young Christian women who may have seen their mothers subjugate their needs in marriage –

although they do not intend to repeat this pattern once married they may find themselves unconsciously falling into a similar role. Or, alternatively they may try to rebel against this pattern, which could mean engaging in pseudo subjugation. Pseudo subjugation is where a wife may expend a lot of energy going along with the notion that they are going to overlook their needs and focus on what their husband wants, only to sabotage this and 'forget', or delay, or put off performing tasks that they have agreed to do. It is important to be mindful of these influences because it is only when we become more conscious of them, that we can choose a different path and a healthier way of relating in our marriage.

The Biblical story of Queen Esther, King Xerxes and differentiation

Queen Esther is a very prominent Biblical character who had to become differentiated in her couple relationship and we see how this ultimately brought her closer to her husband. If we take a closer look at her story through a psychological perspective, we can have the opportunity to learn more about being differentiated in our marriages. We know from the Bible that Esther was initially favoured by her husband King Xerxes, because of her beauty. After extensive beauty preparations Esther was presented to King Xerxes and we are told:

> *He was so delighted with her that he set the royal crown on her head and declared her queen...*
> — Esther 2:17

This may be similar to when we first fall in love and external factors, such as beauty, good looks, or the image of who we think the person is, draws us to our partner. These external factors may captivate us initially. It is only as the relationship develops and we take the risk of revealing more of ourselves, our needs, wishes and desires, that our relationship has a chance to really deepen. Being differentiated involves frequently exposing more of ourselves to our partner and taking the risk of communicating what we want even if this may be risky or could provoke displeasure. In the story of Esther and Xerxes this is the development that we see taking place.

In the past when I thought about the story of Esther, I didn't focus on her couple relationship or what it may have been like for her. My main recollection of Queen Esther was that she was a beautiful lady, she was courageous, and she helped to save the Jewish nation during a time of persecution. However, it is difficult to imagine what the start of Esther's couple relationship with Xerxes must have been like – to have been called to the palace and then to have become part of the king's harem. Whilst it was a great privilege for Esther, in the culture of her time, it may also have been a very daunting, overwhelming and lonely place to be. Similarly, when we get married, our whole way of life may change. Couples may live together for the first time and for Christian couples it may be the first time that they have sex together. This too can feel daunting and overwhelming, as well as being an exciting, new experience.

After the king declared Esther as queen there were a lot of celebrations. We are told:

> *To celebrate the occasion, he gave a great banquet in Esther's honour for all his nobles and officials, declaring a public holiday for the provinces and giving generous gifts to everyone.*
>
> — Esther 2:18

However, in the very next breath, after the excitement of declaring Esther queen we hear that the king orders a second lot of beautiful girls to be brought to the palace. Imagine how Esther may have felt hearing about this – the disappointment, feelings of betrayal, or even self-doubt, with thoughts running through her head like, '*I'm not good enough*'.

Similarly, in our own couple relationship, after the excitement of the wedding, the celebrations and initial honeymoon period, one or both spouses can lose interest and perhaps locate some of their erotic energy outside of the marriage. That erotic energy does not necessarily have to take the form of having an affair, but it can be ploughed into work or a passionate interest or hobby. It could be anything that captures your interest and means that your energy is deployed outside of your marriage. This can lead to feelings of disappointment and betrayal, which will be discussed in more detail in Chapter 4.

At this point in their marriage, the king does not really know Esther and neither has she revealed much of herself and her inner world to him. One of the key things that Esther has kept secret is that she is a Jewess. This becomes central when she learns of a plot to kill the Jews orchestrated by Haman, the prime minister. It is at this point that she needs to speak up and reveal more of herself to her husband in the hope of changing Haman's plans. At the time there were strict rules that forbade Esther from approaching her husband without invitation, but she courageously starts to form a plan:

> *... though it is against the law, I will go in to see the king. If I must die, I must die.*
> — Esther 4:16

Though less extreme in the modern couple relationship we may feel that there are unwritten rules that keep a distance between us and our partner; and a similar fear about approaching our partner with a need, or a question that they may not want to listen to. Sometimes we may think that it is important not to bother our partner, that we should not place too many demands on them, or continually ask for what we really want from our spouse. We may think there are some forbidden, no-go areas that we cannot broach with our partner.

For example, sex, and what we may want or fantasise about happening between ourselves and our spouse. We may not speak up due to fear of rejection. We may be brave enough to ask once or twice for what we want, but if our partner isn't as warm and receptive as we'd hoped, we may shut down and not speak up again. This may particularly be the case if the subjugation lifetrap is a significant issue in your life. We will take a look at how being differentiated impacts sexual intimacy alongside factors around who is the high desire or low desire partner when it comes to sex in Chapter 11: 'Control of couple intimacy: what's sex got to do with it?'.

Being differentiated means that we are willing to take the risk of communicating our needs because we want our partner to know us. It means that we are able to face our fears and use self-validation in order to help soothe any anxieties that we may have about our partner reacting negatively. We can see this in Esther's account as she faces her fear that her husband may be displeased and acknowledges the possible extreme outcome of approaching him without invitation: '... *If I must die, I must die.*' (Esther 4:16).

It is interesting that when we take the risk of being differentiated with our spouse and when we reveal more of ourselves and what we want, in the long-run it deepens the relationship. As we then see, Esther's bravery is rewarded, and she is welcomed by the king and asked:

What do you want Queen Esther? What is your request?...

— Esther 5:3

It is at this point in their couple relationship that we witness the opportunity for real dialogue to open up as Esther's husband Xerxes starts to show an interest in her that goes beyond her looks. Esther, in response, fosters continued dialogue by inviting him to dine with her at a banquet that she has prepared for him. And she then invites him to another banquet the day after. We can see that Esther is closing the distance between them in their marriage and bringing contact and closeness. She has in fact, initiated the equivalent of what modern-day couples would call date nights, in order to make quality time and to talk about issues that are important to her. Eventually she reveals to Xerxes that she is a Jewess and she also reveals the plot of Haman to destroy her and her people and then she makes her request:

... I ask that my life and the lives of my people will be spared.

— Esther 7:3

The fact that she is a Jewess is now no longer a secret. Now that her husband knows the truth, he chooses to protect Esther and her people and Haman is punished and hanged for his plot. In fact:

On that same day King Xerxes gave the property of Haman, the enemy of the Jews, to Queen Esther.

— Esther 8:1

Here we see that when we truly open up and reveal ourselves, even though this may feel risky, it gives our partner the opportunity to really know us and also gives our partner the chance to respond to us in a way that can deepen our relationship. I'm aware that for Esther the situation worked out well but sometimes when we reveal ourselves and what we want to our partner we do not always get a positive response. In fact, it can result in conflict, but holding onto your sense of self and what you want in the long-term can deepen intimacy in your marriage. Managing the conflict that arises out of being differentiated will be explored in more detail in Chapter 8: 'Encountering conflict and being in your own boat'.

If we think back to the case example of Lucy and Tom, initially she didn't get a positive response to her request to enter couples therapy, but due to Lucy's persistence and differentiated stance Tom made use of the opportunity he had to deepen their relationship. Eventually, he was grateful that they were able to get to know each other better through couples therapy and relate on a deeper, more satisfying level. Tom appreciated Lucy's risk-taking, despite it meaning that he had to confront himself and realise that he had often needed Lucy in the past but had not really wanted to know her and her needs.

We all have scope to develop our level of differentiation in our couple relationships and truly treat our partner with 'equal regard'. Moving away from *needing* our partner towards really *wanting* to know them is something for us to try and cultivate. Just as in our Christian life we may catch ourselves approaching God in a selfish way, praying to him to meet our needs rather than wanting to know him more and develop our relationship with him, so we also need to catch and correct ourselves when we treat our spouse in a similar way.

Being more differentiated in our marriage can be liberating, bring a sense of freedom and closeness. When we are not differentiated and therefore emotionally fused and merged with our partner, we are in essence trapped. We may feel that we need to keep certain things to ourselves and not speak up. When we feel brave enough, like Queen Esther, to open up to our spouse and reveal the truth about ourselves, our desires and our wishes, this is when transformation can take place. Being differentiated is about speaking the truth in a loving way and not withholding aspects of ourselves from our partner. In John 8:32 we are told *'And you will know the truth, and the truth will set you free.'* Whilst this is referring to the truth that we can find in Jesus that sets us free, we also know the overarching reality of this principle, and how God is a lover and an upholder of the truth. The truth that we can speak when we are able to open up, reveal more of ourselves and be differentiated has the power to set us free in our marriage.

Joint Reflection Points

1. Talk together and think about to what extent you are able to be differentiated and stay true to what you feel is right, despite facing pressure from your partner to conform to their wishes? Under what circumstances do you tend to put pressure on your partner and want them to conform to your way of thinking or doing something? Conversely, in what areas are you most likely to cave in to pressure from your partner?

2. To what extent do you rely on other-validation from your partner to help you feel that you have made the right decision for yourself? How could you both try to self-validate more?

3. How could you relate to your partner from a place of *wanting* them and *wanting* to know their needs and wishes more, rather than from a place of *needing* them?

4. To what extent is your couple relationship based on 'equal regard'? A mutual giving and receiving. How could you move towards this position more? What gets in the way?

5. If you think you may have subjugation or entitlement issues, then I would recommend that you buy Young and Klosko's book, *Reinventing your Life* (1994) and work through the 'Subjugation' and 'Entitlement' chapters. They are short and easy to digest. It is a relatively inexpensive book that can be purchased easily online. A few of the statements that may help you to identify whether you have the subjugation lifetrap include things like:

    'I feel guilty when I put myself first.'

    'I feel the pain of other people deeply, so I usually end up taking care of the people I'm close to.'

    'I am afraid that if I do not give in to other people's wishes they will retaliate, get angry, or reject me.'

    — Young & Klosko, 1994, p. 260

The entitlement statements below may help you to identify if this is one of your lifetraps, they include things like:

'I have trouble accepting "no" for an answer'

'I am special and should not have to accept normal constraints'

'I insist that people do things my way'
— Young & Klosko, 1994, p. 316–317

Even if just one of these statements resonates with you, this is an indicator that it may be an important lifetrap for you to explore further.

Spiritual Reflection Points

1.   Ask God how you can *Love your neighbour as yourself* (Matthew 22:39) in
      your marriage and be in communion with your partner, giving and
      receiving love in an equal way. After some time of prayer, share any
      thoughts or sense of what God may be saying to you as a couple about
      this.

2.   Reflecting on the verse below pray together and ask forgiveness for the
      times when you have bypassed real, genuine interactions with your
      spouse – when you have perhaps *needed* them, rather than *wanted* to know
      them and their desires.

> *'I want you to show love, not offer sacrifices. I want you to know me more than
> I want burnt offerings.'*
>
> — Hosea 6:6

Part Two

Standing in the light: every couple relationship casts a shadow

Chapter 4

The ideal couple and feelings of betrayal

Then Delilah pouted, 'How can you tell me,
"I love you," when you don't share your secrets with me?
You've made fun of me three times now, and you still
haven't told me what makes you so strong!'

Judges, 16:15

The story of Samson and Delilah

There could be no better Biblical example of couple betrayal than that of
Samson and Delilah. If you know this story you may be thinking that it has
little relevance to your life and your couple relationship. It is difficult to see
how you, or I, would allow ourselves to be betrayed as stupidly as Samson
was betrayed by Delilah time and time again. Yet, is this really the case? Maybe
it is too painful to see how our own couple relationship could be similar to
that of Samson and Delilah. As soon as Samson falls in love with Delilah, the
wheels are set in motion for betrayal to take place. We read in the Bible:

> *Some time later Samson fell in love with a woman named Delilah, who lived in the*
> *valley of Sorek. The rulers of the Philistines went to her and said, 'Entice Samson to*
> *tell you what makes him so strong and how he can be overpowered and tied up securely.*
> *Then each of us will give you 1,100 pieces of silver.' So Delilah said to Samson,*

'Please tell me what makes you so strong and what it would take to tie you up securely.'

— Judges 16:4–6

If this were a modern love story, then we could imagine Delilah as a foreign spy sent to obtain valuable secrets through seduction and pillow talk. I think what is difficult for the reader to grasp is that Delilah does not seem to hide her intentions or ask Samson to disclose his secret in a subtle way. So the question arises, how can he not realise that she is out to betray him? Yet, in many couple relationships one partner may promise to love, honour, and cherish the other, but can end up betraying that promise in a multitude of ways. For example, by continually prioritising work demands over investing time in the couple relationship or by passively allowing a partner to be treated in a dismissive way by their in-laws. Or time and time again 'forgetting' to make the effort to choose a gift that their partner would really appreciate. A general 'taking the other person for granted' and treating them as unimportant can also feel like a betrayal of the wedding vows that were made. And these types of betrayals can happen over and over again, just like Delilah's attempts to entrap Samson. The extract below depicts Delilah's first attempt at betraying Samson:

> *Samson replied, 'If I were tied up with seven new bowstrings that have not yet been dried, I would become as weak as anyone else.' So the Philistine rulers brought Delilah seven new bowstrings, and she tied Samson up with them. She had hidden some men in one of the inner rooms of her house, and she cried out, 'Samson! The Philistines have come to capture you!' But Samson snapped the bowstrings as a piece of string snaps when it is burned by a fire. So the secret of his strength was not discovered.*
>
> — Judges 16: 7–9

Delilah attempts to gain Samson's secret unsuccessfully twice more and we listen to him tell her: *'If I were tied up with brand-new ropes that had never been used, I would become as weak as anyone else.'* (Judges 16:11). So Delilah again ties Samson with new ropes whilst he is asleep and wakes him up with the warning that the Philistines are upon him. Delilah persists and asks for Samson's secret again and he tells her: *'If you weave the seven braids of my head into the fabric on your loom and tighten it with the loom shuttle, I would become as weak as anyone else.'* (Judges 16:13) and the same scenario happens again. So, it is difficult to understand why Samson finally caves in and tells Delilah the truth:

> *… If my head were shaved, my strength would leave me…*
>
> —Judges 16:17

Surely, Delilah's intention to betray him to the Philistines was crystal clear as each time she tried to deplete Samson's strength and awakens him with the cry: *'Samson! the Philistines have come to capture you!'* (Judges 16:9). However, as the reader of this Biblical story we have the privilege of being able to stand outside of the couple relationship and examine what takes place objectively. It is far harder to do this in our own marriage and identify unhelpful patterns of behaviour.

The story of Samson and Delilah is perhaps not too dissimilar to the modern couple relationship after all, as each individual may at times feel let down, disappointed or even betrayed by their partner in some way. The betrayals in your own couple relationship may seem less extreme when compared to Samson and Delilah's disastrous marriage, or the type of betrayals may just be subtler and less obvious in nature. However, they may still lead to intense feelings of disappointment, bitterness or resentment. Strong feelings of resentment can lead us into the dangerous territory of wanting to 'punish' our spouse for their betrayal and this may be done in a variety of subtle ways or may even be done on a more unconscious level if these feelings cannot be spoken about. This will be discussed later on in the chapter when we explore the couple dynamics depicted in the film *The Painted Veil.*

Couple ideals

Before returning to the story of Samson and Delilah let us take a closer look at how 'couple ideals' and feelings of betrayal are linked. It is normal in a couple for each individual to hold onto an ideal about their relationship and on some level, feel entitled to their partner meeting this ideal (Grier, 2006). However, it is likely that each of the individual's ideals for the relationship may not be shared or even openly talked about. For example, a wife may expect her husband to communicate how he feels and put emotional effort into maintaining the level of intimacy in their relationship. If the wife were able to have a really honest conversation with her husband, he may say that he does not think that it is necessary to be emotionally open and that he would feel too vulnerable if he were really to try to connect with his wife on a deep emotional level.

In couples therapy a common uniting ideal that often emerges is that the couple relationship should exist in perfect harmony at all times (Grier, 2006). However, this commonly held belief is not sustainable or realistic and can lead to intense feelings of betrayal for both partners (Grier, 2006). Interestingly, if a couple are able to step back and critically examine some of their ideals and the pressures these place on their relationship, then this can be a valuable turning point in their marriage (Grier, 2006). However, as mentioned in Chapter 2, creating some reflective triangular space can be difficult for couples as conversations can become tense. This is especially the case when we think about the ideals we hold as these may originate from strong sources of authority, such as the influence of our parents' relationship or guidance from the church. The wider Christian culture and popular culture may also contribute to our perceived ideals for couple relationships. Movies often present an idealised view of romance, relationships and sex. This can place a lot of pressure on couples as they attempt to live up to these ideals. Also, these ideals often deny any possibility of difficulties in couple relationships or sex, and consequently present a very one-sided view of what a romantic, fulfilling relationship looks like.

Grier (2006) states that when we start to look at ideals that we have grown up with, then sparks may fly for couples when they are explored further and challenged. When ideals are talked about in couples therapy they often seem far from ideal: in fact, objectively they may seem childishly demanding, have a self-serving quality to them, and ultimately may be aimed at controlling our partner and bending them to our will (Grier, 2006). As the ideals are examined more clearly difficult feelings of guilt, shame and anxiety may arise. It is important not to try and shy away from these emotions but allow them to be experienced as this can facilitate a journey towards greater acceptance within the couple relationship and help to develop more realistic ideals (Grier, 2006).

Being able to move away from a position of what is called 'all or nothing' thinking (that is, my relationship is only good if there are no arguments and by default inherently bad if there is conflict) towards a position of being able to tolerate some of the difficulties that are deemed 'unacceptable' in the marriage, is a positive step. However, a significant problem in our culture is intolerance: in particular, the tendency to judge others. We are often quick to see when something is not good enough and may judge ourselves and others harshly. This can happen in couple relationships when we somehow lose our way and our ideals may lead us to condemn our spouse. If we think back to Jenny's family, discussed in Chapter 1, her family's strong moral ethics brought the tendency to judge to the fore. Mike felt judged and condemned by Jenny when she withdrew from him after he had expressed his hurt and genuine anger. Being able to tolerate conflict and work through issues instead of withdrawing from our partner or punishing them in other subtle ways is an important developmental step in a couple relationship.

Ideals and feelings of betrayal

If we think about ideals in terms of the Biblical story of Samson, immediately we can see how Samson started his life with great expectations on his shoulders and how others may have hoped that he would be the 'ideal' hero figure that Israel so badly needed. Samson was an unusual example of a Judge of Israel because the other Judges were chosen for their role or their deeds, but Samson was appointed by God before he was even born. Samson's mother said,

> *A man from God appeared to me… he told me, 'You will become pregnant and give birth to a son… he will be dedicated to God as a Nazirite from the moment of his birth until the day of his death.'*
>
> — Judges 13: 6–7

Similarly, a Christian couple who have been dating often pray together and seriously consider whether their partner is 'the one' that God has chosen for them. This perhaps sets up the template and illusion of the possibility of finding the 'ideal couple' relationship.

Samson initially presents us with an ideal image of a strong heroic figure anointed by God, but in the end his uncontrollable rage and vengeful acts meant that he did not live up to other peoples' expectations. Christian couples can also feel let down when their expectations are not met by their marriage partner, the partner they believe God has helped them to choose and marry. Here we see the potential, when things go wrong, for the sense of betrayal to extend to God and possibly the church.

In the case example of Mike and Jenny, Mike felt very let down by the church as he noticed that it gave a great deal of support prior to getting married, with marriage preparation classes, but had very little interest in following up how he was coping in his marriage afterwards. Mike also felt that marriage had been idealised by the church and not enough time had been given to discussing the difficulties that people often encounter in marriage. In fact, with all the smiling faces of couples at church, he felt an increasing pressure that his marriage should be 'perfect', which made him feel even more isolated and alone.

Another interesting point in the story of Samson is that he does not seem able to learn from his mistakes. In fact, he actually seems compelled to repeat them. This raises an interesting point about how capable couples are at recognising unhelpful patterns of relating, learning from them and breaking free. More often than not, old arguments seem to repeat themselves and couples are faced with the same problematic dynamics over and over again.

If we take a closer look at Samson, it is interesting to note that he seems to be drawn to women who are likely to betray him (Kutz, 1989). First there was the young Philistine woman from Timnah (Judges 14:2), secondly the harlot of Gaza (Judges 16:1), and finally Delilah. All three women betrayed Samson to the Philistines. Delilah attempts to entrap Samson several times in very obvious ways and in the end succeeds and hands him over, a broken and humiliated man with his hair shorn and his power gone.

However, something that is often overlooked is that Samson betrays himself, as on some level he knows the outcome of revealing his secret to Delilah (that his hair must never be cut): that it will destroy him (Kutz, 1989). In couple relationships one partner may betray themselves and give in to the other person's demands in order to stop the arguments, have a quiet life and meet the ideal of having a harmonious couple relationship. However, like

Samson this may result in one partner feeling diminished or humiliated. The Bible reveals the following about Delilah: *'She tormented him with her nagging day after day until he was sick to death of it.'* (Judges 16:16).

So couples may not only feel betrayed by a partner who does not meet their expectations, but by themselves as they give up their desires, perhaps even a sense of their own integrity, in order to appease their partner. This underlines the importance of being differentiated in a couple relationship and maintaining one's individuality and paying attention to one's own needs as discussed in Chapter 3.

Feelings of betrayal and the dangerous territory of punishment

One of the outcomes of couple ideals being crushed, and the ensuing sense of betrayal, is that partners can end up punishing one another. Sometimes this is unconscious, and the punishment may take on subtle forms such as withdrawing or giving less affection or time to our partner, or deciding not to go out of our way to buy some special food that we know our partner would enjoy. If you take a minute to think about it, I wonder if there are some subtle ways in which you may have punished your partner after feeling let down by them?

It is important to become more conscious of any punishing dynamics as they can turn into a vicious cycle and slowly erode the foundations of a couple relationship. Being able to communicate our wishes, hurts and upsets to our partner is one way of ensuring that our feelings of resentment and betrayal are brought out into the open. If these feelings are pushed down or ignored they do not disappear, they are actually more likely to be 'acted out' on an unconscious level. This means that these repressed feelings may prompt a partner to behave or react in a particular way. For example, a partner may end up 'forgetting' important conversations because their feelings of resentment mean that it is sometimes hard for them to emotionally tune in to their partner and really listen to what they are saying.

The example of Kitty and Walter from the movie *The Painted Veil*

The film *The Painted Veil*, from the book of the same name by W. Somerset

Maugham, provides us with dramatic examples of couple ideals being betrayed, which lead the couple into the dangerous territory of punishing one another. The examples are extreme, but the story provides us with a mirror to examine our own relationships, the dynamics of betrayal and punishment, and how we can develop more realistic couple ideals. This can help to reduce the sense of betrayal and the need to punish our spouse.

The main character, Walter, marries Kitty because he falls in love, but later feels deeply betrayed by his wife's adultery. She marries him, hoping to be rescued from the clutches of her domineering mother. Kitty wishes to be kept amused, entertained, and to feel loved by her husband. She too feels betrayed as she finds herself isolated in a different culture with a husband who is only interested in his research post and not in socialising or playing cards with her during lonely nights in a foreign country.

Walter's decision to marry Kitty and the couple ideal he perhaps held seemed to be based on a fairly selfish need – he was attracted to Kitty and wanted a pretty wife who loved him. He makes no real effort to relate to her and find out who she is. Instead, Walter leaves her alone for long periods of time, abandoned with little to do.

After Kitty starts having an affair which is discovered by Walter, an interesting and, I believe, common dynamic emerges: both partners begin a campaign of punishing one another. Walter takes his wife on a long arduous journey to a remote outpost in the Chinese interior to help with the cholera epidemic and his wife discovers that he has purposely withheld the vaccine from her, thus increasing her risks of dying there. When Kitty arrives exhausted and visibly drained after the arduous journey by land, the local British government official is shocked and asks Walter why they did not take the far more comfortable and shorter route of travelling down the river. At this point realisation dawns on Kitty that her husband has chosen to take her on the arduous land journey as part of her punishment.

The punishment continues in other subtle ways. Walter ignores his wife and treats her in a cold, dismissive manner. She in turn, refuses his advice and begins eating food that has been washed with the local water, which may be contaminated. The audience quickly sees a destructive cycle emerging, which gathers pace.

However, bored and feeling even more isolated, Kitty offers to help the nuns at the local orphanage and plays the piano for the children. This is the turning point in their relationship as she is able to see her husband at work in the adjoining hospital and begins to appreciate his kindness and the dedication that he shows to his patients. He too begins to see another side to his wife as he stumbles across her playing the piano for the orphans. The nuns subtly point out the strengths of the husband to his wife and vice-versa. Hope is gained from a new perspective and a new appreciation of one another. Finally, they begin to truly relate to each other because they have been able to recognise and accept their failings, but also see their strengths as individuals and as a couple.

The dynamic of couples punishing one another is referred to by Dr Schnarch in his book *A Passionate Marriage* as 'normal marital sadism,' highlighting that it is a dynamic that most couples get caught up in. However, it is important to become more conscious of the ways that we may subtly punish our husband or wife. Some of the subtler forms of punishment may include withdrawing affection, being cold or distant or forgetful, choosing to spend less time with our spouse and devoting our energies to our work or agreeing to do something for our spouse, but then not following through or prioritising the request.

A lot of this type of behaviour could be termed 'passive aggressive' as the person's upset is not expressed directly, but through indirect passive means. It is vital that this passive aggressive behaviour is brought out into the open and real attempts are made for couples to communicate and express their feelings. Otherwise, the destructive cycle of interaction continues in an almost compulsive manner, as seen in the film *The Painted Veil* and in the story of Samson and Delilah.

Concluding thoughts

The film, *The Painted Veil,* draws to our attention the feelings of betrayal that can surface in a marriage. Perhaps the example of the affair is a rather obvious betrayal as is the series of betrayals of Samson by Delilah. However, there are many ways that individuals in a couple relationship can feel betrayed by each other. Western culture places a great deal of emphasis on romantic love and finding the perfect partner. This too, is perhaps reflected in the Christian culture. In fact, as Christians often pray and try to consider very carefully whether the person they are dating is 'the one' God had in mind for them, there is perhaps even greater pressure to have the ideal couple relationship. So when things become difficult, the sense of betrayal, disappointment or feeling let down may be even greater. Rather than dismissing the story of Samson and Delilah as having nothing to do with our own marriage, take some time using the 'Joint Reflection Points' below to consider the ideals that you each have for your relationship and where you may have felt let down, disappointed or betrayed.

Joint Reflection Points

1. Spend some time thinking about your couple ideals: where do they come from? Maybe look at your genograms and the couple ideals that your parents/grandparents may have communicated either directly or indirectly. For example, the way they may have modelled these ideals. *(If you have not completed your genograms and would like to, please see the end of Chapter 1 for instructions and guidance.)*

    ♥   How have these couple ideals impacted your couple relationship?

    ♥   What couple ideals do you hold for your marriage? What couple ideals would be helpful to let go of? And what would be a more realistic expectation for you and your couple relationship?

2. Take some time thinking about times when you have felt let down or betrayed by your spouse. Try using the following Nonviolent Communication (NVC) technique to express your hurt. The NVC communication technique is also referred to as Giraffe language because Giraffe's have one of the largest hearts and the technique is about speaking from the heart.

    Decide on an issue you want to share with your spouse and go through the following steps:

    a)   I noticed that… (give the example of what your spouse may have said/done in a non-judgemental, factual, objective way).

    b)   It made me feel… (really describe the emotions of how this made you feel, again in a non-blaming way).

    c)   I'd like you to… (say what you would generally prefer in the future or how you would like things to be different).

    d)   End with making a specific request to your spouse. (For example, next time this happens, I'd like you to…).

Take turns using the NVC technique. This is an effective way of communicating that you can come back to and use for different problem areas. It helps to reduce heated arguments as you are focusing on your feelings and conversation is structured to help you to problem-solve and make requests of one another.

4.   Punishment: what subtle or not so subtle ways do you think you may use to punish your partner when you feel let down by them? (Try to be as honest as you can with each other.)

Follow up exercise:

♥   Discuss together how you would like things to be different. Perhaps try using the NVC technique again, focusing on one example each.

Spiritual Reflection Points

1. Often when we have felt betrayed or let down, we can end up feeling crushed and low in spirit. Spend some time meditating on the following verse and ask God to help you with these feelings. At the end of this time of prayer/meditation share with each other any feelings or promptings from the Holy Spirit.

    > *The Lord is close to the broken hearted; he rescues those whose spirits are crushed.*
    >
    > — Psalm 34:18

2. Take turns praying for each other and ask God to heal any feelings of disappointment or betrayal that you may have experienced as a couple.

3. If you have felt let down by the church or by God during difficult times in your marriage, use this opportunity to pray about this and ask God to heal these painful feelings.

Chapter 5

Resentment and forgiveness

'Forgiveness requires us to recognise the coexistence of good and bad feelings...'

John Steiner

The process of forgiveness

The process of forgiveness is complex and Christian couples in particular may feel the pressure to keep up the appearance of being in a marriage in which arguments and feelings of resentment are rare. As previously mentioned, Biblical guidance to dwell on positive rather than negative influences can sometimes be misunderstood and add to this sense of pressure:

> *And now, dear brothers and sisters, one final thing. Fix your thoughts on what is true, and honourable, and right, and pure, and lovely, and admirable. Think about things that are excellent and worthy of praise.*
>
> — Philippians 4:8

This advice can make some people, like Jenny in our first case example in Chapter 1, feel guilty when feelings of anger, resentment or annoyance crop up. Non-Christian couples can also experience pressure to have a happy, satisfying marriage in which arguments and feelings of resentment shouldn't be present or dominate. We all probably have an image of what the perfect relationship or perfect marriage looks like, and when anger and feelings of resentment raise their ugly heads this can feel difficult. However, it is important to explore our emotions in order to make them more fully conscious and understand where the anger is coming from. When we understand the roots of our emotions, it can help us to feel freer and more in control of them. Sometimes there is a desire to bypass this exploration and ignore what Jung referred to as the 'shadow' aspect of our unconscious. If we think of the unconscious as a backpack in which lots of feelings get repressed and hidden away, we can understand that this is perhaps where some of what we judge to be unacceptable emotions, like anger and resentment, get placed.

What can happen for some Christians is that feelings of guilt about being angry or having an argument may result in the knee-jerk reaction of quickly saying 'sorry' to God and their spouse. This may not allow space for emotions such as anger and resentment to be fully processed.

Thinking back to the quotation at the start of the chapter: *'Forgiveness requires us to recognise the coexistence of good and bad feelings.'* (Steiner, 1993, p.85), it is almost as if we don't want to dwell on the existence of the 'bad feelings' and perhaps we move on too quickly to the positive again. As Christians we may want or feel we ought to move quickly away from feelings of resentment in order to reconnect to the goodness we find in God: the forgiveness that He can offer us and our spouse. Although there is nothing wrong in this, it can mean that the shift from feeling resentful to wanting to forgive may at times be rushed. Or we may feel pressure to forgive, because it is the right thing to do, before we have really dealt with the cause of the resentment. Very little attention may be paid to feelings of resentment and the process of forgiveness, as some couples, whether Christian or not, struggle to talk openly about any of these feelings.

Some partners may keep the feelings of resentment to themselves and try to pretend that everything is alright. This may mean that the resentment remains pushed down in their unconscious, in the backpack of unwanted feelings. This is a dangerous place to leave feelings of resentment because they tend to leak out and surface in unexpected ways.

In Chapter 4 we discussed the dangerous territory of punishment following feeling let down and betrayed. Similarly, if resentment is not dealt with, then partners can end up expressing it in more unconscious, punitive ways such as: withdrawing emotionally; not giving so much of themselves in conversation; not showing as much interest in what their spouse has been doing; or not bothering to contact their partner during the day. These types of behaviours are subtle, silent ways in which resentment can be 'acted out' instead of being spoken about openly and processed in a healthier way.

In order for a place of forgiveness to be reached and for feelings of resentment to be released, we sometimes need to really grapple with them. Figuring out why feelings of resentment are so strong may be quite a process in itself and Jesus provides us with some valuable guidance about forgiveness and how it can be an ongoing process:

> *Then Peter came to him and asked, 'Lord, how often should I forgive someone who sins against me? Seven times?' 'No, not seven times,' Jesus replied, 'but seventy times seven!'*
>
> — Matthew 18:21–22

Interestingly, Jesus is communicating that forgiveness needs to be continually offered. It's revealing that the number seven in the Bible is thought by theologians to represent wholeness, completion and perfection. By multiplying seven by seventy Jesus may have been trying to tell us that we have to keep working at the process of forgiveness until we reach that sense of completion and wholeness. Jesus may be cautioning us to try to stay with the uncomfortable process of working through feelings of resentment. It may not necessarily be achieved in one fell swoop or by offering one quick prayer. Of course, sometimes the process of forgiveness can be resolved more quickly, but for more complex situations we may need to spend more time exploring these emotions.

If we have only managed to partially figure out what has grieved us, we can only forgive that part. This may mean that the process of forgiveness is not complete, perfect or whole. Instead forgiveness remains partial, just as the resentment remains partially intact. This is where psychology can complement the spiritual process of forgiveness because it can help us to reflect on issues that remain unprocessed and understand the emotions that may be feeding the resentment and keeping it alive.

The roots of resentment

If we think back to the case example of Mike and Jenny from Chapter 1, we will remember that Mike often felt a lot of resentment towards Jenny because she was so absorbed in her work as a lawyer that she was often emotionally unavailable and not able to pay attention to Mike's needs. Mike often tried to communicate important things to her, like special moments in his day when he had helped one of his students achieve the grades that they needed to go to university. However, Jenny would sometimes have a distracted look on her face and Mike instinctively knew that she had not been listening properly. She was often caught up thinking about an important court case.

From their couples therapy sessions Mike began to understand why his feelings of resentment were so strong towards Jenny. Jenny's lack of emotional availability echoed Mike's experiences as a child of not being listened to and his needs being overlooked. As Mike began to realise why feelings of resentment were being triggered, he was able to mourn not being listened to as a child and also let go of his resentment towards Jenny. This was a slow, gradual process for Mike and meant that he had to confront himself and think about where the feelings of pain and resentment had originated from. However, after some period of time Mike managed to resolve his feelings of resentment and he was able to achieve a more complete sense of forgiveness.

When we react strongly to something our partner does, and the experience resonates so much that we feel taken over by the emotion and upset, it is likely that the situation may have triggered similar feelings from earlier experiences in our life that have caused us pain. You may not be conscious of this or the connection to the past experiences, but if this is happening to you in your couple relationship, it may be a clue that your interactions with your partner are triggering unresolved emotional pain from the past. This is something for you to bear in mind, especially as becoming more aware of this could help you in the process of forgiving one another and letting go of resentment.

Lucy and Tom, whose case was first discussed in Chapter 2, had problems with repetitive arguments and feelings of resentment that would build up. Tom was often very critical and resentful of Lucy, particularly about what she chose to spend their money on. This was frustrating for Lucy because she worked hard as a nurse and sometimes wanted to treat herself by buying herself something nice. Overall, Lucy was more spontaneous than Tom who took pride in planning everything in advance and was very cautious with money.

Tom always wanted to save their money to buy the very best version of everything. He would argue that this just made sense. Lucy sometimes felt anxious about money, but she had recently been given some money from her aunt, so she decided to buy a second-hand car so that they could travel easily out of the city to visit her parents. However, Tom was really angry that Lucy had bought a second-hand car rather than a new one. All of the rationales that Lucy put forward about the car having low mileage and the fact that it was economical to run were dismissed by Tom – he was fuming and withdrew from Lucy in stony silence.

The anger and resentment that Tom felt about this was intense, he felt betrayed and let-down by Lucy. Lucy had talked to him about buying a second-hand car, but Tom couldn't understand how his last noncommittal response had been misinterpreted as agreement to purchase the car. There were other reasons why Tom's emotional reaction was so dramatic, and this emerged during their couples therapy.

Tom came to realise that his experiences as a child growing up in a large family where they had to make do, meant that he had often felt extremely embarrassed. Memories came back to him about the second-hand clothing he was forced to wear and the house that his family lived in. As an adult he strived to fit in and he put a lot of effort into overcoming his family's perceived deficiencies by becoming highly educated, earning good money as an accountant and buying material possessions that were of the best quality. He had what Young and Klosko (1994) refer to as the 'social exclusion lifetrap'. When Lucy bought the second-hand car, it triggered a lot of difficult emotions for Tom from his past. As a child he had felt excluded and different from his peers due to poor housing conditions and personal belongings that were second-hand. However, Tom was not aware of this link to his past at the time of his argument with Lucy.

As Tom became more aware of this connection during couples therapy, he was able to understand the anger and resentment that he felt towards Lucy and this helped to reduce the intensity of his resentment. It also enabled him to forgive Lucy more fully. Afterwards, they both noticed that Tom was less critical of Lucy about things that she wanted to buy. Similarly, this new understanding enabled Lucy to be more sensitive towards Tom and so she took the time to discuss purchases with him. Ultimately, because there had been a more complete understanding of the roots of the resentment, a more complete sense of forgiveness was reached.

The story of Hosea and Gomer

Let us take a look at the story of Hosea and Gomer from the Bible and think about what their couple relationship can teach us about resentment and forgiveness. The following verses describe the unusual circumstances that prompted Hosea to marry Gomer:

> *...the Lord said to [Hosea], 'Go and marry a prostitute, so that some of her children will be conceived in prostitution. This will illustrate how Israel has acted like a prostitute by turning against the Lord and worshipping other gods.' So Hosea married Gomer...*
>
> — Hosea 1:2–3

Who knows how Hosea felt when God gave him these instructions? As a prophet his role was to communicate God's views to the people of Israel – perhaps Hosea wished that God had simply asked him to tell the nation to stop being unfaithful and stop worshipping other gods. Marrying a prostitute may have felt like an extreme way for Hosea to get God's message across. It is likely that Gomer did not fit his ideal image of what a marriage partner should be.

What I think is interesting here is that simply telling the nation of Israel of God's disappointment in them was not enough. Hosea was symbolically asked to live out the betrayal and adultery of the nation by marrying Gomer. God was asking Hosea to experience the betrayal and the feelings of resentment and anger first-hand. Applying this to our own couple relationship, the example of Hosea and Gomer underlines the importance of allowing ourselves to fully experience and understand why we feel resentment towards our spouse. Hosea had to go through this experience and understand it in order to communicate its meaning to the nation of Israel.

God submerged Hosea in the experience of betrayal, being let down and abandoned; his whole life and the lives of his children were impacted by his marriage to Gomer. However, eventually God asks Hosea to welcome his wife back and to forgive her:

> *Then the Lord said to me, 'Go and love your wife again, even though she commits adultery with another lover. This will illustrate that the Lord still loves Israel, even though the people have turned to other gods and love to worship them.'*
>
> — Hosea 3:1

Hosea had to go through the experience of betrayal with Gomer and the pain and hurt that accompanied that – God didn't spare Hosea any of those feelings or experiences. Like Hosea, we may also need to open ourselves up to fully experiencing, processing and understanding some of the pain and resentment that we experience in our marriage. It is perhaps only when we have gone through this experience that we can reach a place where complete forgiveness can take place.

Subjugation and resentment

I have already talked in Chapter 3 about how the problem of subjugation can stir up feelings of resentment, but I think it is worth exploring further as we try to unpick how understanding our resentment can facilitate the process of forgiveness.

Having a subjugation 'lifetrap' can be exhausting because it tends to involve the following: continually feeling compelled to please others; striving to avoid conflict; putting others' needs first; and overlooking one's own needs. This soon wears thin and resentment can start to build up. The classic example of this in the Bible is the story of Martha and Mary:

> *As Jesus and the disciples continued on their way to Jerusalem, they came to a certain village where a woman named Martha welcomed him into her home. Her sister, Mary, sat at the Lord's feet, listening to what he taught. But Martha was distracted by the*

big dinner she was preparing. She came to Jesus and said, 'Lord, doesn't it seem unfair to you that my sister just sits here while I do all the work? Tell her to come and help me.'

— Luke 10:38–40

It is clear that Martha feels frustrated and annoyed that she is expending all of this effort to please everyone – she has in fact subjugated her own needs and not followed her sister's example of stopping, resting and listening to Jesus. In the end Martha approaches Jesus and asks Him to reprimand Mary and tell her to help out. However, Jesus highlights how Mary's approach is healthier. This story underlines the importance of taking the time to nourish ourselves and make sure that our needs are met, whether they are spiritual, emotional or physical needs. This was Jesus' response:

But the Lord said to her, 'My dear Martha, you are worried and upset over all these details! There is only one thing worth being concerned about. Mary has discovered it, and it will not be taken away from her.'

— Luke 10:41–42

In essence Jesus is saying to Martha that Mary was doing the right thing by focusing on her spiritual needs instead of feeling overloaded with the demands of caring for others. If you tend to subjugate your needs, then withdrawing some of the energy that you put into compulsively giving to others in order to look after your own needs may be something that you need to do. If you do this, it may resolve feelings of resentment in your marriage.

Practically putting your needs first for a change in your marriage could take many forms. Mike, who had problems with subjugation, needed to let Jenny know that he was going to prioritise his need for social contact and friendship, and he started to meet up with some of his male friends from church. This gave Mike opportunities for meaningful conversation and the social support that he needed. This was hard for Jenny at first, but she came to realise from their couples therapy sessions that she needed to stop clinging on to Mike and expecting him to be at home to meet her needs. She knew that it was good for them to have some time apart, meeting up with friends.

In your own marriage creating time for yourself may mean asking your spouse to clear up after dinner and look after the children whilst you take the opportunity to call a close friend or take a relaxing bath. It may be important to schedule in time for yourself regularly to do whatever you need to do, whether that is to spend some time in prayer and meditation, or to look after your body and go to the gym and do some exercise. It may also mean prioritising some money for yourself to meet your needs if you tend to save your money and spend it on your spouse, children, or grandchildren.

If you would like to gain a more comprehensive understanding of subjugation and how you can address this lifetrap and the resentment it generates, I would recommend reading Young and Klosko's (1994) chapter on subjugation from their book *Reinventing your Life*.

Visiting and holidaying on the island of resentment

John Steiner has written a lot about the subject of resentment. He suggests that people can have retreats – places where we go in our mind to try to escape from anxiety, emotional pain, and felt wounds that we have experienced. From reading his book, I conjured up the image of resentment as being like a small island in our mind that we can take ourselves off to; resentment can be a place that we withdraw or retreat to. In fact, if we are not careful, it can become like an island that we are shipwrecked on and if resentment builds up or is kept alive, it may be hard for us to find our way back from this island. The retreat of resentment becomes our home, where more often than not we find ourselves isolated and stranded in our marriage.

In your marriage you may just visit the island of resentment from time to time, rather than take a whole vacation there. For example, when you have felt wronged by your partner you may take yourself off for a short while and say to yourself: 'I can't believe that s/he's done this to me again!' You may go over the scenario in your head several times before getting over it and attempting to move on. If the resentment is triggering some deeper pain, as in Tom's case, you may find yourself packing a bag and going to stay on the island of resentment for a while. Tom's emotional withdrawal and the wall of silence that he put up against Lucy meant that he had marooned himself on the island of resentment for some time. It was the sharks under the water that were circling the island that kept Tom trapped there – namely the deeper pain, stemming from bad memories and feelings of resentment from his childhood.

Sometimes we may convince ourselves in a self-righteous manner that it is good to stay on the island of resentment, to take a long vacation there and punish our spouse. We may even convince ourselves that it feels good to be on this little island on our own – at least here we may feel that our anger and resentment protects us from further pain and let-downs. The island of resentment may in this sense feel falsely like a safe haven to withdraw to.

Resentment can be likened to a cat toying with a half-dead mouse. As the cat continues to paw at the mouse, the mouse is kept partially alive, just as our resentment is kept alive by our constantly revisiting in our mind the wrongdoings of our partner. If the cat were simply to let the mouse die, the death of the mouse – that is, the resentment – would have to be recognised and acknowledged. We would perhaps no longer feel in control of the situation or protected by our self-righteous anger. It is possible that toying with the half-dead mouse and keeping the resentment alive may provide a sense of satisfaction at some level.

Steiner (1993) tells us that when we let go of resentment we have to come to terms with emotional pain and the loss that needs to be mourned. As previously mentioned, in the case of Mike and Jenny, Mike needed to let go of his resentment towards Jenny for all the times that she had prioritised her work and had dismissed his needs. For Mike, letting go of the resentment towards Jenny meant that he also became aware of the pain of his needs being ignored by his alcoholic father and his fearful mother when he was a child. For Mike, this hit him quite hard – it was the full realisation that the extent of his resentment was not just limited to Jenny, but that it went much further back to his childhood. Mike had to get more in touch with the pain that he had experienced but had not been aware of at the time because as a child he expended most of his energy trying to prevent and diffuse arguments.

It can take great courage to venture forth and leave the island of resentment and allow ourselves to come into contact with the pain and loss connected with letting go of these feelings. In order to fully move forward in our couple relationship, it is necessary to mourn any let-downs or experiences of betrayal and come to terms with experiences from which resentment stems. Acceptance, mourning and moving forward in order to cultivate greater couple unity will be explored in more detail in the next chapter.

Joint Reflection Points

1. Sit together and individually write down one or two areas where you tend to feel resentment towards your partner. (Please note: the idea here is to start to be curious about what triggers feelings of resentment, so try to adopt a non-judgemental, compassionate attitude towards your partner as you write your list.)

   Follow up questions:

   ♥ Now take turns looking at each other's lists and try to explore whether the resentment you feel towards your partner may be triggering feelings of resentment and pain from your past. Perhaps ask each other: do the feelings of resentment and related situations echo any experiences that you had earlier on in your life? Try to be curious about why certain situations or actions may trigger feelings of resentment.

   ♥ You could also look back at your genograms and think about feelings of resentment in your family of origin and the types of situations that tended to trigger strong feelings of resentment – how is this possibly replayed in your couple relationship? *(See Chapter 1 'Joint Reflection Points' for the genogram exercise if you haven't already completed this and would like to.)*

2. How can you help each other with feelings of resentment? For example, how could you let go of feelings of resentment and stop visiting or holidaying on the island of resentment? And if your actions are triggering feelings of resentment in your partner, what could you do differently? How could you be more sensitive to your partner's needs in order to prevent feelings of resentment flaring up?

Spiritual Reflection Points

1. Pray to God and ask for His wisdom and guidance on how you can better understand the feelings of resentment that arise in your marriage and how you can offer each other a more complete sense of forgiveness.

    Then Peter came to him and asked, 'Lord, how often should I forgive someone who sins against me? Seven times?' 'No, not seven times,' Jesus replied, 'but seventy times seven!'

    — Matthew 18:21–22

2. In your couple relationship, do you sometimes end up like Martha, rushing around instead of stopping to find the spiritual, emotional, or physical nourishment that you need? Pray to God to find the right balance between nourishing yourself and giving to one another in your marriage.

Chapter 6

Cultivating couple unity: acceptance, mourning and moving forward

'... this task requires a capacity to face reality
in order that mourning can proceed.'

John Steiner

One important way of moving forward in general, and in couple relationships in particular, is the ability to face, mourn and accept the reality of the situation. We do not have to look far for some poignant Biblical examples of this. The story of Saul/Paul in the book of Acts helps us to understand the importance of coming to terms with our actions in order to move forward. In Saul's case, moving forward resulted in him using his Roman name, Paul, in place of his former Jewish name, Saul: the change in name symbolised the dramatic shift that had taken place in his life. In this chapter we will take a look at the ways in which we too can make dramatic shifts in our efforts to move forward in our marriage.

Moving forward: the scales fell from my eyes

Focusing on the Biblical story of Saul, the first account we come across depicts him expressing murderous intentions towards those he disagreed with:

… Saul was uttering threats with every breath and he was eager to destroy the Lord's followers. So he went to the high priest…

— Acts 9:1

However, God intervened in Saul's plan to kill Christian believers. On the road to Damascus Saul was struck and blinded by a bright light. When he recovered, he not only stopped persecuting Christians, he joined them. The Bible tells us:

As he was approaching Damascus on this mission, a light from heaven suddenly shone down upon him. He fell to the ground and heard a voice saying to him, 'Saul! Saul! Why are you persecuting me?' … Saul picked himself up off the ground, but when he opened his eyes he was blind.

— Acts 9:3–4, 8

In couple relationships feelings of anger or betrayal may result in wanting to persecute our spouse, and like Saul we may set off on a path that may lead to destruction and a lot of harm. If we have felt betrayed or let down by our spouse, feelings of resentment may fuel a desire to attack them, whether this is verbally or passively, through withdrawing the affection, time and energy that we devote to our relationship.

Saul originally thought he was doing the right thing as his actions had been sanctioned by the High Priest. We too, in our marriage, may self-righteously feel that our behaviour is justifiable, that we have been doing the right thing and responding to our spouse in the way that they deserve. It is only when we encounter the blinding light of self-realisation that we can recognise that we have been at fault and are given a second chance to make amends and alter our course of action.

If we think back to the missionary couple, Andy and Rose – introduced in Chapter 1 – Andy did not think that there was anything wrong in the way he had been behaving in his marriage. After all, Andy had been working as a missionary and had committed a lot of his time to working for the church, what was wrong with that? Surely, this was a godly and appropriate way to spend his time. This was how Andy justified his workaholic lifestyle and periods of absence from his wife and children.

It was during couples therapy that Andy had several 'road to Damascus' moments as he came to realise that he had felt very depressed and somewhat pushed aside by the arrival of their first child. As other team mates left the country Andy's sense of abandonment increased, which resulted in him throwing himself into his work even more. This was a pattern that Andy had internalised from his father, who had immersed himself in work as a way of managing feelings of depression. This had left Andy feeling rejected and unwanted as a child. Andy realised that his actions resulted in Rose being left increasingly on her own and he had in fact given his sense of abandonment and depression to her.

This was an incredibly painful moment of self-realisation for Andy because he had not been conscious of these dynamics. He needed to face the reality of what had been happening in his marriage and accept responsibility for the part he had played. In addition, this realisation also required Andy to come into contact with the painful feelings of abandonment from his father, accept these feelings and mourn the loss of time spent with his father during his childhood.

Andy also had to accept and mourn the fact that he had been absent from his own children and had unwittingly repeated the mistake that his father had made. This was a lot for Andy to take on board. However, eventually it meant that Andy and Rose freed themselves from these unhelpful patterns of relating and this brought them closer together as a couple. It also brought a greater sense of unity to their relationship.

Rose also had a lot of work to do with regards to acceptance, mourning and moving forward. She had felt abandoned when Andy put his work first and then found it hard to re-connect with him when he was around. In subtle ways Rose would push Andy aside as she felt she had been pushed aside. For example, when Andy would approach Rose for a hug, she would shrug him off, move away and pick one of the children up. This was something that Rose came to recognise as a pattern of behaviour that she engaged in and she saw how she kept the cycle of rejection going. When Rose accepted her part in the dynamic it helped them to move forward as a couple.

During couples therapy Rose also had to accept and recognise some painful feelings of rejection and abandonment from her childhood. This was mainly related to her mother who had suffered from post-natal depression after her younger brother was born. But she had also felt abandoned when her brother, who she was close to, was sent away to attend the same school as their cousin. This meant that during term time she had been left alone with her depressed mother.

Rose came to understand how angry she had felt towards her mother for the lack of attention and care that she had given. She also felt angry towards her mother for taking the decision to send her brother away. She realised that underneath her sadness she felt angry towards Andy for leaving her for long periods of time because of his work. However, Rose found it very difficult to voice her feelings of anger and resentment because Andy's work was focused on helping to improve peoples' poor housing conditions.

Rose had learnt from an early age that she should subjugate her needs and so kept doing so in her marriage. Just as in her childhood, she kept these resentful feelings inside, which only added to her depression and low mood. In order to move forward in her couple relationship with Andy, Rose needed to face the reality of what had happened to her as a child and how that had contributed to feelings of resentment.

She also needed to mourn the care and attention that she had not received from her mother as a young child. When Rose did this, although she felt very sad, she also felt freed from past hurts and closer to Andy. From this position both Andy and Rose were able to move forward in their couple relationship in a healthy way.

Couples therapy enabled Andy and Rose to confront themselves with the reality of what had been going on in their marriage. When God intervened in Saul's life we are told:

> *Instantly something like scales fell from Saul's eyes, and he regained his sight. Then he got up and was baptised.*

> — Acts 9:18

The phrase 'the scales fell from my eyes' is often used to denote a sudden understanding of the truth or the reality of a situation. I think that this is important in couple relationships; the capacity to face the reality of what has been going on. As we have seen in the case example of Andy and Rose, it was crucial and allowed them to mourn and move forward.

Moments of self-realisation – the cock crows

Another Bible story that deals with facing the reality of betrayal, mourning, and moving forward is the poignant account of Peter and his denial of Jesus. Peter loved Jesus and was one of his closest followers. He had no intention of betraying Jesus or letting him down. Similarly, in couple relationships, even when there is a deep sense of love and a strong bond of commitment, betrayals can unwittingly happen.

Peter expects to prove his faithfulness to Jesus. It is inconceivable to him that he would deny Jesus and let him down:

> *Peter declared, 'Even if everyone else deserts you, I will never desert you.' Jesus replied, 'I tell you the truth, Peter – this very night, before the rooster crows, you will deny three times that you even know me.' 'No!' Peter insisted … 'Even if I have to die with you, I will never deny you!'*
>
> — Matthew 26:33–35

It can sometimes be very hard to face the reality that we may make mistakes in our couple relationships. In case example 3, Tom initially did not want to enter couples therapy. He could not understand that he had done anything wrong; in his mind Lucy was largely to blame for their difficulties. He certainly did not want to go and see a couples therapist: a stranger who would ask him to take a closer look at his own behaviour. All too often we may find ourselves in denial, like Peter, not believing that we have the potential to be in the wrong.

Peter's denial of Jesus, as we see it unfold and culminate, is very moving:

> *Peter swore, 'A curse on me if I'm lying – I don't know the man!' And immediately the rooster crowed. Suddenly, Jesus' words flashed through Peter's mind: 'Before the rooster crows, you will deny three times that you even know me.' And then he went away, weeping bitterly.*
>
> — Matthew 26:74–75

Peter shows us that it can be very difficult to face up to the reality and pain of recognising our errors. Peter's bitter weeping was perhaps not only because he had compromised his integrity and broken his promise, it was also probably related to the pain of letting Jesus down. It was the sound of the cock crowing that brought Peter to his senses and there are often similar moments of self-realisation in therapy, where an individual comes to realise how their choices and actions have impacted their marriage.

It is important to note that in the cases of both Paul and Peter they did not hold on to a sense of regret, pain, or sadness about their mistakes. In fact, the moments of self-realisation spurred them on to live their lives differently. Similarly, in couples therapy, it is important to mourn mistakes or losses from the past, but then to learn from them and move forward.

Shame and hiding from reality

We have seen how important it is to be able to mourn and move forward in couple relationships but for this to happen we have to be able to face reality. One of the significant emotions that can get in the way of this is shame. In fact, the fear of shame often propels couples to hide from reality. In his book, *From Impasse to Intimacy* David Shaddock (1998) informs us that:

> *Since shame is such a painful emotion, most of us want to avoid it at all costs. And since shame involves a fear of being exposed, intimate relationships pose a great threat…*
>
> — p.39

The Bible can help illuminate what shame does to relationships in the story of Adam and Eve and their experience in the Garden of Eden. After they ate the forbidden fruit, we see how feelings of shame quickly come to the surface:

> *At that moment their eyes were opened, and they suddenly felt shame at their nakedness. So they sewed fig leaves together to cover themselves.*
>
> — Genesis 3:7

Both Adam and Eve suddenly realised that they were naked and wanted to cover up, they did not want to feel so exposed and they wanted to hide their nakedness, perhaps from themselves and each other, as well as from God.

When the cool evening breezes were blowing, the man and his wife heard the Lord God walking about in the garden. So they hid from the Lord God among the trees. Then the Lord God called to the man, 'Where are you?' He replied, 'I heard you walking in the garden, so I hid. I was afraid because I was naked.'

— Genesis 3:8–10

It is interesting to note how feelings of shame result in so much hiding and covering up, first with the fig leaves and then Adam and Eve hide themselves away from God in the trees. Adam and Eve seemed to fear that God would see the reality of their nakedness and would discern that they had disobeyed Him by eating the forbidden fruit. I wonder if Adam and Eve may also have been concerned about being judged by God.

When something goes wrong in couple relationships, individuals may go to great lengths to hide their misdemeanours, potentially from themselves as well as their spouse. Shame, embarrassment, avoiding reality and judgement may result in individuals not wanting to accept and face some of the difficulties in their marriage. Therefore, shame may present a barrier to facing reality, mourning past hurts and moving forward in couple relationships.

David Shaddock (1998) states that couples can do a range of things in response to feelings of shame. These coping strategies often fall into 'fight or flight' responses. Both responses are ways of avoiding the reality of what has been going on in the couple relationship as well as avoiding feelings of shame. Adam and Eve clearly undertook a 'flight' response by hiding beneath the fig leaves and in the trees, but let's consider how the couples in our case examples responded to feelings of shame.

In the case of Andy and Rose, they engaged in 'flight' coping strategies. Andy took flight and tried to escape feelings of sadness that he felt ashamed of, by working compulsively and staying away from the family home for periods of time. Rose took flight from the feelings of anger and resentment that she wanted to disown, by withdrawing her emotional energies from the world and becoming depressed. It is possible that Rose was given a 'double dose' of shame to hold in the marriage because to the outside world Andy seemed like a hard-working, almost heroic, figure, whereas Rose seemed like a weak wife, who was depressed and not coping. So, Rose could be seen as holding the sense of embarrassment of not coping for both of them.

Fight responses can either be direct or indirect. Direct fight responses include arguing and attacking a spouse in order to avoid shameful feelings. Indirect fight responses may have a passive aggressive quality, for example, a spouse may passively agree to do something whilst secretly resisting and not following through with the task. If we think about Tom's response to Lucy's request to go to couples therapy, he engaged in both direct and indirect forms of the 'fight' response. Initially, Tom passively agreed to go along with Lucy's idea of starting couples therapy, although secretly he had no intention of following through and did not believe that Lucy would either. Tom did not do any research on couples therapy as Lucy had suggested. So when Lucy showed him her email correspondence with potential couples therapists Tom initiated a more direct fight response, arguing with Lucy and criticising her for the amount of money that she wanted to 'throw away' on therapy.

Tom was desperate to avoid having to face the reality of their problems and he was equally desperate to avoid any feelings of shame and embarrassment. He had grown up feeling painfully embarrassed about his family's lack of wealth, poor housing conditions and the second-hand clothing that he had to wear as a child. As an adult he worked extremely hard to be successful and he wanted to avoid any form of social embarrassment at all costs. So, avoiding shame was a highly motivating factor for Tom and initially presented a huge barrier to facing the reality of the problems in their marriage.

Over time Tom began to welcome couples therapy sessions as he realised that they brought him closer to Lucy and made them both feel happier in their marriage. Tom was extremely sensitive towards feelings of shame, but as Lucy learnt more about her husband and the reasons for this, she was able to be more empathic and supportive of Tom.

Feelings of shame can also crop up during significant transitions in marriage particularly if we judge ourselves not to be coping as well as we think we ought to be. Entering new life stages can be challenging, like parenthood or retirement. In order to disconnect from feelings of shame, a spouse may sometimes take flight, go inward and withdraw their energy from the world. As a result, one of the things that might happen is they could become depressed. In this sense they may unintentionally hide themselves away from the world. When feeling low and experiencing shame due to not coping with a transition, it can be helpful to share these emotions with one's spouse if that feels possible. Alternatively, seeking help like Tom and Lucy did by going to therapy can support couples undergoing transitions that are challenging.

Another important thing to bear in mind is that it's helpful to try and remove the fear of being judged when we're encountering an area that may tap into feelings of shame. Truly wanting to understand each other often helps to minimise any concerns about negative judgement. Understanding is far removed from judgement; it sheds new meaning on behaviours and increases warmth and connection between spouses. It is also important not to judge ourselves too harshly either – sometimes we can feel shame and embarrassment unnecessarily when we criticise ourselves and judge ourselves badly for what has happened or the mistakes that we have made. Being kind and compassionate towards ourselves is something to work towards. We are all human and we do not always get it right, but I believe that is okay and there is enough grace for everyone, even ourselves.

Metaphorically speaking, we cannot hide behind our fig leaves or in the bushes like Adam and Eve forever. The shame that we sometimes may feel needs to be confronted as that is the only way that reality can be faced, and healing can occur. In the classic game 'hide and seek', the purpose is for people to be found. The idea of being able to hide, be safe and not be discovered is tantalising, but I think part of the thrill is the possibility and pleasure of someone finding you in your secret hiding place. When we manage to truly find each other in our couple relationship and unearth the secrets, mistakes, or problems we have hidden, we have the opportunity to reconnect and discover each other anew. This, I believe, is a golden opportunity not to be missed.

Being present-focused and letting go of anger

Two significant things that can stop us from moving forward in our couple relationships are: constantly focusing on the past and holding on to anger. It is helpful to take the time to explore these two areas in depth.

In the Bible, Lot was warned about the dangers of looking back and angels gave him the following instructions:

'Run for your lives! And don't look back or stop anywhere in the valley! Escape to the mountains, or you will be swept away!' … But Lot's wife looked back as she was following along behind him, and she turned into a pillar of salt.

— Genesis 19:17 and 26

Lot was advised to head for the mountains, figuratively a place from which we can gain perspective on life. In our couple relationships it can be helpful to try and reach a place where we can gain a better perspective on what has been happening. However, it can be unhelpful to constantly look back and dwell on grievances, mistakes and bad memories.

Lot was warned not to look back, but his wife (Jewish traditions suggest that she was called Edith, although her actual name is not mentioned in the Bible) could not help herself and glanced back. It can be all too tempting to look back and dwell on past mistakes but, like Lot's wife, it can cause us to become paralysed – metaphorically turned into a pillar of salt – and consequently unable to move forward in our marriage. We may never reach the mountain, a place where we can gain some perspective on our couple relationship if we are constantly looking back.

If you notice your thoughts filling with assumptions based on past resentments during interactions with your spouse, then try to pay attention to this. Before you respond to your partner, catch yourself thinking about any assumptions and try to place them to one side. For example, you may automatically think something like, *'You always try to make me feel responsible for everything'* when your partner makes a request. Instead, respond in the present moment letting go of any assumptions and hurtful memories. Your partner's request may not be about trying to make you *feel responsible* for example, although this has happened in the past. Try to take the request at face value in the present moment, with no past memories or grievances attached to it. Your response is likely to be less emotionally loaded if you are able to do this. If you think this is an issue for you, why not experiment with this new approach and try to catch any assumptions and place them to one side when you interact with your partner. Notice how your response is less emotionally charged and try to adopt this approach each time assumptions from past resentments come to the fore.

Focusing on the present and mindfully tuning into the 'here and now' can be an antidote to looking back. Jon Kabat-Zinn (1994) talks about the importance of dying to the present and stopping all thinking and busyness in order to focus on and enjoy what you are doing and where you are. This is helpful advice for our couple relationship; to stop and enjoy where we are. He says:

> *By dying now in this way, you actually become more alive now. This is what stopping can do. There is nothing passive about it. And when you decide to go, it's a different type of going because you stopped. The stopping actually makes the going, more vivid, richer, more textured. It helps keep all things that we worry about and feel inadequate about in perspective. It gives us guidance.*
>
> — Kabat-Zinn, 1994, p.12

Prayer and meditation can be helpful ways of stopping, focusing on the here and now, and on the needs of our marriage. Letting go of the past in order for healing to take place in our couple relationship can be very important. Letting go leads us towards acceptance. Jon Kabat-Zinn (1994) describes the process of 'letting go' eloquently:

> *It is a conscious decision to release with full acceptance into the stream of present moments as they are unfolding. To let go means to give up coercing, resisting, or struggling, in exchange for something more powerful and wholesome which comes out of allowing things to be as they are without getting caught up in your attraction to or rejection of them, in the intrinsic wanting, of liking and disliking. It's akin to letting your palm open to unhand something you have been holding on to.*
>
> — p.53

In our couple relationships it is important to open our palms and 'let go' of things that we have been holding on to – past hurts or self-blame for mistakes that have perhaps hurt our partner. If we cannot do this, then we cannot move forward, and we become stuck as we cling on to the past.

Another thing that we can unhelpfully hold on to is anger. Jon Kabat-Zinn (1994) describes anger as: *'the strong energy of not wanting things to be the way they are and blaming someone (often yourself) or something for it'* (p.48). As anger is often linked to feelings of not wanting things to be the way that they are, it can take us away from acceptance. Acceptance is important in terms of facing the reality of our own mistakes and of our spouse in order to move forward.

It is important to underline that not expressing anger, and keeping angry feelings bottled up, is very unhealthy and may add to feelings of low mood and can have other negative consequences on our mental and physical health. Being able to assertively express feelings of anger or upset in a conscious, adult way, perhaps using the Nonviolent Communication technique outlined at the end of Chapter 4, can be a very positive way of moving forward in our couple relationship. However, venting angry feelings whilst in a state of agitation, or continually flaring up in anger out of habit, can be just as unhelpful as bottling up feelings of anger.

Jon Kabat-Zinn (1994) elaborates on the potential toxicity of anger:

> *You can feel it cloud the mind. It breeds feelings of aggression and violence – even if anger is in the service of righting a wrong or getting something important to happen – and thus intrinsically warps what is, whether you are in the right or not. You can feel this even when you can't stop yourself sometimes.*

— p.77

Therefore, it is necessary to think twice about anger, even if in our marriage we feel self-righteous about being angry, as it has the potential to be toxic for ourselves as well as our spouse.

For Christians the desire is to follow God's example:

> *The LORD is compassionate and merciful, slow to get angry and filled with unfailing love.*

— Psalm 103:8

Taking the time to stop, focus on the 'here and now', and become aware of how we are feeling may help us to take a step back and prevent feelings of anger over-taking us. It can also help us to refocus on the guiding principles of love and compassion that we need for ourselves and our spouse. Love is the unifying principle that can guide us and ultimately help cultivate unity in our marriage.

Joint Reflection Points

1. Spend some time exploring together whether feelings of shame stop you from facing reality in your couple relationship. Does part of you shy away from admitting mistakes and do you automatically try to cover up your errors like Adam and Eve? Or do you react in a defensive way? Are there any particular fight/flight responses that you tend to engage in to protect yourself from feelings of shame? What would be a more helpful response for your couple relationship instead of a fight/flight reaction when feelings of shame come to the fore?

2. Facing reality, mourning and moving forward can be significant in a marriage. This exercise will help you to experience this process together in the form of a symbolic walk. This is an experiential exercise that provides you with space to be creative. It's perhaps a bit more adventurous than some of the other exercises, but I'm hoping some couples will be adventurous enough to try it out. As this chapter is all about moving forward, I thought a symbolic walk would be a helpful exercise for you as a couple. If you read the following six bullet points below, this will provide you with a guide to the process.

    Note: You may not feel that you have reached a place yet in your couple relationship where you have begun to understand feelings of resentment, or where you feel you have reached a place of acceptance in order to mourn issues from the past. If this is the case, this exercise may be difficult for you to engage in, so you may want to skip this or come back to it at a later date.

    ♥   Find a space where you can do this symbolic walk together. This could be in a meadow, some woods or any other outdoor space. If you have small children, doing this exercise in your house after they have gone to bed would be equally good. The amount of space doesn't matter, just use your imagination and be creative with the space you have.

    ♥   You may want to allot a certain amount of time for the facing reality, acceptance and mourning part of the exercise (5, 10, 15 minutes or more). Then agree a joint meeting place where you can come together and spend a further allotted amount of time (5, 10, 15 minutes or more) on the moving forward together aspect of the walk. This exercise can be as short or as long as you want it to be.

♥   Use the space for you both individually to explore the process of facing reality, mourning and moving forward as a couple. You can think together creatively about how you'd like to symbolise moments of self-realisation on your walk, like Paul had on the road to Damascus. You may want to start your walks off as individuals at polar positions in your chosen space and gradually draw closer. Or your experience may be that of being very close, yet confused, and disconnected. You can decide together on how you'd like to use the space before you start.

♥   The process of facing reality may be a long meandering journey, where you go around in circles through different rooms in your house, or through woods. Or it may be a sharp, sudden, painful experience for you both. Think about how you would show this in your walk. You may also want to think about how you would allow for a period of mourning and how you would represent this. You may want a period of stillness on your walk or to go to a place where it feels peaceful to stop and feel sad.

♥   Finally, think about how you want to show that your journey ends with moving forward together in unity. This may simply be by holding hands and walking side by side through an outdoor space or until you reach a specific space in your house. There is no right or wrong way to do this walk, it will be your walk, and it will evolve in your own unique way. Try not to judge anything and just accept the feelings that arise along the way.

♥   Before you start, decide together on a time, a room, or place that will signal that you have reached the end of this exercise. When you start your walk, my advice would be to let your instincts guide you and don't try to over-think this too much. You don't have to talk to each other during the exercise unless you want to – it's more about allowing yourself to experience what it has been like in your relationship through actions, movements or stillness. At the end of the walk you could share how you felt at different stages:

a) What was it like when you were walking close/far away from each other?

b) What was it like when you allowed yourself to mourn?

c) What emotions arose when you moved forward together in unity at the end of your walk?

For people with mobility issues: If you cannot walk, why don't you try putting on some relaxing music or music that you think fits the theme of accepting reality, mourning and moving forward. Then close your eyes and visualise your walk. Whilst you are visualising the facing reality, mourning, and moving forward part of the walk, your partner can do this physically if they would like to, or like you, they can do this sitting, using their imagination. When you get to the point of moving forward in unity with your partner, agree a time to meet to do this part of the walk together. Then talk them through the process with eyes closed, seeing in your mind's eye you both moving forward together on your walk. Use your imagination to tell the story of what you'd do, what you'd see on your walk, the physical touch between you, if you'd like that. As you're using your imagination, it doesn't necessarily have to be a walk, it can be a swim, a hot-air balloon ride, any type of movement that you'd like to use to symbolise your moving forward together. Afterwards, let your partner describe to you with eyes closed, their visualisation of you both moving together in unity and what that joint walk would look like for them. Use the bullet points above as a rough guide and adapt them as you see fit if you'd like to do the visualisation exercise instead of an actual physical walk.

Spiritual Reflection Points

1.   God has often moved his people forward on journeys – for example, leading Moses and the people of Israel out of slavery and into the promised land:

> *...He guided them during the day with a pillar of cloud, and he provided light at night with a pillar of fire...*
>
> — Exodus 13:21

Another example of being guided on a journey by a visible sign was when the wise men followed a star which led them to the infant Jesus. As a couple pray together and ask God to guide you on your marital journey. Pray and ask God to give you a direction or sign to follow that will point you in the right direction and show you the way that you can move forward together in your marriage. Be open over the coming days or weeks to God revealing a sign, perhaps through your daily devotions, a sermon, a word from a friend or through the circumstances of your daily life. Write this down and share it with one another.

2.   Pray to God and ask for his help in mourning and letting go of past mistakes. Ask Him to help you to move forward afresh in your marriage each day.

> *The faithful love of the LORD never ends! His mercies never cease. Great is his faithfulness; his mercies begin afresh each morning.*
>
> — Lamentations 3:22–23

Part Three

Mutual regard and embracing difference

Chapter 7

Mountains and caves, Heaven and Earth, male and female

*'We believe in God above us, maker and
sustainer of all life, of sun and moon, of
water and earth, of male and female.'*

Iona Creed[1]

Feminine and masculine in couple relationships

In this chapter we will take some time to explore what it means to be male
and female and what impact this has on our couple relationship. I would like
us to consider one of the important foundations of the Christian faith – that
both men and women are made in the image of God. Consequently, it is
perhaps not surprising that God is sometimes referred to in feminine as well
as masculine terms, as denoted by some Bibles verses that we will look at
shortly. From a psychological perspective, I would like us to explore the

---

[1] The Iona Creed comes from the well-known Iona Christian community based in Scotland.
A creed is a statement of beliefs shared by a religious community and is sometimes used as
part of the church service whereby the group of believers read out the creed together in
unison. For more information about the Iona Community please see www.iona.org.uk

Jungian concepts of *Anima* and *Animus,* the role they play in relationships and in a man's and woman's personal development respectively.

In order for each person in a couple to develop more fully I believe that it is important for the man to develop what Jung would refer to as their *Anima* and the woman to develop their *Animus*. The *Anima* is not feminine, and the *Animus* is not masculine in the sense of how we define that in everyday life, but rather they form a natural, inherent, complementary opposite aspect of ourselves. According to Jung, the *Anima* for the man and the *Animus* for the woman are the corresponding contra sexual elements in the unconscious. On a conscious level, women for the most part take on a feminine role and persona and men typically take on a masculine role and persona. Integrating the contra sexual element from our unconscious, for men it's the *Anima* and women the *Animus,* can help to bring a sense of balance and wholeness.

I would like to point out that this is about each person in the couple relationship realising their full potential and it is not about men becoming more like women or vice versa, and it is not about denying that there is any difference between the sexes. There are unique differences which bring great joy and can be celebrated. In fact, I believe there is scope for women to experience a deeper sense of their femininity and men to experience a deeper sense of their masculinity. However, what I would like to focus on in this chapter is our complementary opposites and how the inner workings of *Anima* and *Animus* can impact our couple relationship.

Jung believed that a man's *Anima* initially remains in the unconscious waiting patiently (or not so patiently in some cases) to be recognised and play a part in the man's conscious life. Whereas for a woman it is her *Animus* that initially remains in the unconscious and is waiting for the chance to play a role in her life. As previously mentioned, it is typical for a man to consciously function through his masculine side and a woman through her feminine side – what we are talking about here is integrating one's *Anima/Animus* qualities respectively in order to utilise the strengths and sense of wholeness that they can bring.

However, both men and women can be wary of their *Anima/Animus,* because it is not their primary way of functioning, so it often feels foreign and hard to relate to. One of the ways that individuals may try to deal with this 'problem' is that a husband may project his *Anima* onto his wife and may, for example, expect his wife to take a lead on issues to do with relating and emotions. Similarly, a wife may project her *Animus* onto her husband and, for example, expect him to take a lead on being strategic, organising finances and making decisions about their future. In this sense each spouse has perhaps unconsciously given up their ability to do this and located it in their partner, which deprives each individual from developing and growing in this area. It is also a way for each spouse to try to get rid of an aspect of themselves that they feel uncomfortable about by giving it to their partner. Of course, we don't always project our feminine or masculine ideals onto our partner, if tempted, we can project them onto other men and women outside of our marriage and this can lead to affairs. I believe that this is another important reason to try and get to grips with *Anima/Animus* and the idealised feminine/masculine images that we may hold.

I found the idea of *Anima/Animus* hard to understand to begin with, so I'm aware that these concepts may initially be puzzling for you. However, the explanation of *Anima/Animus* has been invaluable to me and it has shed so much light and understanding on couple relationships that I would like to share it with you step by step. My hope is that you will gain a lot from these concepts too.

Male and Female – reflecting the image of God

Before exploring *Anima/Animus* in more depth, let's go back to the beginning of the book of Genesis to see what the Bible has to say about the origins of being male and female:

> *So God created human beings in his own image. In the image of God he created them; male and female he created them.*
> — Genesis 1:27

Here we see that foundational to the Christian faith is the idea that both men and women reflect the image of God. It is interesting that the original Hebrew text refers to Adam as having a neutral gender and he is assigned a generic term for 'human' and is not referred to as male (Tverberg, 2006). It is only after Eve is created that Adam is distinguished as man by the term 'ish' and Eve is referred to as woman 'ishah' (Tverberg, 2006). This means that God did not necessarily create man first and woman second. The text suggests that a 'human' was created first and gender was only assigned after Eve came into being. The following verses tell of the creation of Eve:

> *So the LORD God caused the man to fall into a deep sleep. While the man slept, the LORD God took out one of the man's ribs and closed up the opening. Then the LORD God made a woman from the rib, and he brought her to the man.*
> — Genesis 2:21–22

Lois Tverberg (2006), in her article 'To Be the Image of God', tells us that the Hebrew word that is translated as rib 'tzela' is not used in the same way throughout the rest of the Bible, it means 'side'. And other verses show us that the meaning pertains to one half or one face of a building or object Exodus 26:26, Exodus 37:3 (Tverberg, 2006). So Tverberg suggests that it is as if God has made Eve out of one of his sides, or that Eve was formed from one half of Adam. This underlines that together, as a whole, both male and female equally reflect the image of God. As Christians, we are also individually encouraged to reflect the image of God – so I would like to suggest that this points towards men integrating *Anima* qualities and women integrating *Animus* qualities.

God is often viewed as male and he is referred to as *'Father'* (Matthew 6:9) in the Bible. However, we have read that both male and female reflect the image of God. So it is not surprising that there are also Bible verses that use imagery to depict God's *Anima* side as a mother figure, such as:

> *I will comfort you there in Jerusalem as a mother comforts her child.*
> — Isaiah 66:13

Jesus also used motherly, nurturing images:

> *O Jerusalem, Jerusalem, the city that kills the prophets and stones God's messengers! How often I have wanted to gather your children together as a hen protects her chicks beneath her wings, but you wouldn't let me.*
> — Luke 13:34

In her book, *Liberating Tradition: Women's Identity and Vocation in Christian Perspective* (2008), Kristina LaCelle-Peterson points out that there are also verses that highlight God as both father and mother. For example, when God asks Job where he was during creation:

> *Does the rain have a father? Who gives birth to the dew? Who is the mother of the ice? Who gives birth to the frost from the heavens?*
>
> — Job 38:28–29

These verses highlight the capacity for God to be both paternal and maternal and that he is not restricted by gender but can encompass both male and female qualities as the author of creation.

I think this point is significant with regards to husbands striving to welcome and integrate their *Anima* and wives striving to integrate their *Animus*, because this integration means that we can more closely reflect the image of God. I also believe that God's character is such that he continually desires to see the people he loves develop and grow and reach their full potential. Then they can make full use of their talents and gifts.

So, when a man realises the potential that his *Anima* has to offer, and a woman harnesses the strengths of her *Animus* they can grow and more fully reflect the image of God. It also means that we may stop putting pressure on our husband/wife to do certain things or be a certain way as we come to realise that we can do this for ourselves. In short, I believe that integrating our *Anima/Animus* can help not only with our spiritual development but can release blockages in our couple relationship and foster greater intimacy.

Anima and *Animus* – complementary opposites

I would like to take some time now to outline the differences between the *Anima* and the *Animus* before going into more depth about this concept. The title and quotation at the start of this chapter are filled with images and complementary opposites, such as sun and moon, heaven and earth, mountains and caves. These images help to illustrate some of the complementary opposites that we find in feminine/masculine qualities and in *Anima/Animus*.

Anima qualities are thought to be linked to feelings of relatedness and are associated with an openness to love, emotions and intuition. When a woman predicts something may happen and it does, the common phrase you hear people say is, 'that's female intuition for you'. Being receptive and open is also thought to be an *Anima* quality. Receptivity is needed for relating and connecting to oneself, others and God. When a person is good at listening they are being receptive and open to what the other person has to say. If we think about the female reproductive system, physiologically it is the woman who is the receptive person in sexual intercourse. She receives the man inside her body and the womb provides the space for the egg and the sperm to meet, and for the baby to grow.

Animus qualities are the complementary opposites of *Anima* qualities and are thought to be linked with objectivity, goal-directedness, rationale and the mind. The assertiveness that is linked with *Animus* qualities can be seen in a man's role during sexual intercourse, as it is the man who thrusts forward and takes up the space, whilst the woman receives him.

Other images of womb-like spaces, such as caves, are associated with the *Anima* whereas contrasting images of mountains thrusting upwards into the sky are connected with the *Animus*. The sun is often thought to be a masculine *Animus* image, perhaps because it is strong and distant; whereas, the earth (Mother Earth) is often thought to be a feminine *Anima* image. We are much more closely connected to the earth and have a stronger emotional tie and relationship with the earth compared to the sun. Here we could think about parallels with the stereotypical mother/father relationship, with the mother traditionally being closely involved with the emotional lives of the children, whilst the father may be a strong, distant figure, who may be less available.

Of course, a Biblical symbolic image of *Anima* and *Animus* joining together and finding balance is the sacred marriage between Christ and his bride, the Church. Christ representing 'logos', the word, the way, the truth *(Animus* qualities*)* and the Church encompassing individual followers, the community and relationships *(Anima* qualities*)*.

There will be times in our life and couple relationship when we will need to strive to find the right balance of *Anima/Animus*. The Biblical story of Mary of Bethany anointing Jesus with expensive perfume highlights a tension between the *Anima* act of demonstrating love and devotion, versus Judas' logic-driven criticism and concern about the cost of the perfume. Judas' comments could be seen as a typical *Animus* reaction with practicalities and concern about cost coming to the fore and trying to dominate. Let's take a look at the story.

Mary anointing Jesus' feet is a very moving scene and a touching expression of her devotion, as we are told:

> *Then Mary took a twelve-ounce jar of expensive perfume made from essence of nard, and she anointed Jesus' feet with it, wiping his feet with her hair. The house was filled with the fragrance.*
>
> — John 12:3

In the culture of the time, Mary's act of devotion may well have been viewed as improper by onlookers, as Jewish women did not let down their hair in public, let alone use it to wipe another's feet. We get the sense that she is oblivious to propriety as she humbles herself and kneels at Jesus' feet. She gives extravagantly of herself in this act of love as well as giving extravagantly with regards to the cost of the perfume.

However, Judas is the polar opposite of Mary and he puts forward his rational, logical argument as to why Mary shouldn't have done it:

> *But Judas Iscariot, the disciple who would soon betray him [Jesus], said, 'That perfume was worth a year's wages. It should have been sold and the money given to the poor.' Not that he cared for the poor—he was a thief, and since he was in charge of the disciples' money, he often stole some for himself.*
>
> — John 12:4–6

Jesus knew this and said,

> *Leave her alone. She did this in preparation for my burial. You will always have the poor among you, but you will not always have me.*
>
> — John 12:7

Jesus was aware that he would be crucified soon, although his disciples did not fully understand what was going to happen to him. Perhaps Mary, with her female intuition, had a stronger sense of what was to come, and this may have prompted her public yet intimate display of love.

Ultimately, we see that Jesus upholds Mary's actions as fitting and honourable – the demonstration of love and worship were more important than the practicalities of cost in that situation. If we think about our couple relationship there may be times when demonstrations of love, generosity, passion and devotion need to come to the fore (the *Anima* side). Just as Mary broke open the jar of costly perfume, we too, may need to open our hearts to our partner, set aside time, money and energy to express our love to them.

However, there may also be times when practicalities need to be considered and unlike Judas we may have a genuine, authentic need to focus on practical arrangements, like spending/saving money or organising childcare arrangements (the *Animus* side). Both the desire for love and relating and the desire to focus on practicalities are equally valid – we just need to find the right balance in our couple relationship. We'll be able to spend some more time exploring the importance of focusing on practicalities in Chapter 10: 'Kitchen sink dilemmas and the soulful care of the household'.

Recognising *Anima* and *Animus* projections

Jung first stumbled across the idea of *Anima* when he was treating a female patient and became aware that he felt very annoyed with her – this led him to ask himself why he felt so annoyed. Jung came to realise that he had certain unconscious expectations of this patient because she was a woman and being a woman, he expected her to behave and react in a certain way. So when she did not conform to his expectations he felt frustrated and angry. Jung realised that he had inner images of women and how they should be.

Jung also believed that our culture: religious stories; history; myths; films; and folklore, influence our understanding of what it means to be a 'woman' or a 'man'. In fairy tales for example, there are lots of archetypal images of men and women, such as 'the princess' and 'the hero'. Jung believed that these cultural influences are stored in the 'collective unconscious' and have the potential to influence our 'personal unconscious'.

In the Bible there are two strong, yet very different images of women: Eve, the temptress, and the opposing image of the Virgin Mary. In our society (particularly in movies) we often witness these two polarised images of *Anima* women being portrayed. For example, Marilyn Monroe took up the *Anima* projection of the sexy temptress, whereas Jackie Kennedy was assigned the opposing role of faithful, pure wife.

One of the dangers of a man projecting his *Anima* images (ideal feminine image) onto a woman and the woman going along with this projection, is that no real relating can take place. The man becomes infatuated and attempts to relate to the image that he has projected and so fails to relate to the real woman beneath.

A stereotypical example of this is the male artist and his female muse, who he becomes infatuated with, and places on a pedestal as he paints her. However, he doesn't really relate to his muse, or know her. She represents something to the artist, but this has nothing to do with who she really is. In fact, the artist's muse often has to sit in position, not move or speak for hours, whilst her image is painted – her role is to remain silent. Sometimes, this can be the case in marriage, with a husband wanting his ideal image of a wife to sit before him and not speak up and reveal who she truly is.

It is also dangerous for the woman who goes along with the projection because despite being worshipped and adored, she often ends up sad and lonely. She is not known and loved for her true self, but for this *Anima* image which does not fully represent who she is. Princess Diana was an *Anima* woman on whom lots of idealised images and expectations were projected. Publicly, she went along with these projections, although privately there was a sense that she may have been sad and lonely at times. In the case of Marilyn Monroe, she was publicly adored, although privately it is likely that she was sad and in the end she committed suicide.

Every couple relationship has *Anima/Animus* projections to a greater or lesser extent. Therefore, becoming aware of them is important because *Anima/Animus* projections stop us from relating to our spouse. These projections can give rise to feelings of loneliness in our marriage. There is also increased potential for misunderstanding one another and becoming annoyed that our spouse is not meeting our ideal image of a 'man' or 'woman'.

Anima and *Animus* projections may also play a role in disillusionment and affairs because when our husband or wife is not able to live up to this idealised image that has been projected onto them, then some individuals may look elsewhere for a figure or a substitute to become their ideal lover. In addition, there is an idea out there in society that once married, your wife is no longer the sexy temptress Eve figure, she becomes the faithful Virgin Mary figure. The image of the wife is often polarised and distorted in our society so that being faithful for some reason is not naturally paired with being sexy and tempting. But of course a wife can be very sexy and tempting in her husband's eyes and it is a positive thing to be sexy and alluring to our partner.

Similarly, when a woman transitions into the role of mother or grandmother, she may unintentionally become aligned with the Virgin Mother Mary feminine ideal, leaving little space for the husband and wife to explore her sexy side. It's helpful to integrate one's motherly or grandmotherly caring role with the sensual side of life and reclaim this aspect if it's somehow got lost along the way.

Once married, your husband too may seem less and less able to be the *Animus* man of your dreams, unable to hold the projection of the 'hero' figure who can sweep you off your feet, like Lois Lane and Clark Kent in the movie 'Superman'. This can potentially leave a woman thinking, where has my 'hero' gone? Perhaps he is elsewhere? This can make some people look outside of their marriage for the sexy, tempting 'other'. This dynamic will be discussed in Chapter 12, which explores 'Disillusionment and adultery' further.

If we think back to the case example of Tom and Lucy, Tom had projected a very strong, idealised *Anima* image onto Lucy of a caring, nurturing wife. Lucy was a nurse, and this was part of her disposition, so she had a natural hook for Tom to hang his projection on. Lucy was very nurturing, but she was also a forthright, determined woman who wanted a marriage based on 'equal regard'.

Tom unconsciously expected Lucy to be this perfect, pure, wife, so was often very disappointed and critical of her when he felt let down by her. Even though part of Tom knew that he too wanted a marriage based on 'equal regard', he unconsciously held this expectation that Lucy should nurture him and strive to meet his needs. For example, despite Lucy doing a long nursing shift at work, part of Tom still wanted her to cook him a meal and wait on him. This was part of Tom's *Anima* projection of what a woman should be like and therefore what Lucy should be like. Of course Lucy could not go along with this and be the *Anima* woman that Tom desired. She was simply too tired and exhausted to try and meet this ideal.

When this was explored further in couples therapy, Tom acknowledged that he quite liked cooking and was in fact pretty good at it – it was a challenge for him to accept that this was something nurturing that he could do and bring to the marriage, because he associated it with something a wife should do. Tom in general found it difficult to nurture himself and others, he was very cut off from his *Anima* side and his capacity to nurture because he had grown up in a deprived household where his needs were overlooked and not nurtured. One of the reasons that he had initially been so attracted to Lucy was because at the start of their relationship she was able to hold his *Anima* projection of an ideal, nurturing woman. However, there was more to Lucy than her caring side and she required some nurturing too.

Throughout the course of couples therapy, Tom tried to nurture himself more and take care of his needs and he also tried to become more in tune with Lucy's needs. Over time he was far less critical of Lucy and he encouraged and affirmed her more. In essence, Tom was gradually able to take his *Anima* projection back from Lucy and integrate his own *Anima* strengths, bringing his capacity to nurture to the fore. Interestingly, from a spiritual perspective, Tom also started to become more comfortable with the nurturing aspect of God and more frequently felt encouraged during moments of worship and prayer.

The story of Abigail's *Animus* saving the day

A lesser known story in the Bible is that of Abigail and how she harnessed her *Animus* qualities of being decisive and strategic. In the account we see how Abigail managed to rescue herself and save her family and servants – she did not wait for her husband to reconsider, make the right decision and rescue her. Abigail's husband, Nabal, was rude to David's men (the David who killed Goliath) and refused to give them provisions when they asked for them. Abigail soon learns of this disastrous interaction:

> *Meanwhile, one of Nabal's servants went to Abigail and told her, 'David sent messengers from the wilderness to greet our master, but he [Nabal] screamed insults at them … You need to know this and figure out what to do, for there is going to be*

trouble for our master and his whole family. He's so ill-tempered that no one can even talk to him! Abigail wasted no time. She quickly gathered 200 loaves of bread, two wineskins full of wine, five sheep that had been slaughtered, nearly a bushel of roasted grain, 100 clusters of raisins, and 200 fig cakes. She packed them on donkeys and said to her servants, 'Go on ahead. I will follow you shortly.' But she didn't tell her husband Nabal what she was doing.

— 1 Samuel 25: 14–19

David's men had approached Nabal for bread and provisions but had been rudely refused. On learning this Abigail takes matters into her own hands and rides out to meet David and his men with the provisions that were requested. She pleads with David not to take vengeance against her husband.

David replied to Abigail, 'Praise the LORD, the God of Israel, who has sent you to meet me today! Thank God for your good sense! Bless you for keeping me from murder and from carrying out vengeance with my own hands. For I swear by the LORD, the God of Israel, who has kept me from hurting you, that if you had not hurried out to meet me, not one of Nabal's men would still be alive tomorrow morning.' Then David accepted her present and told her, 'Return home in peace. I have heard what you said. We will not kill your husband.'

— 1 Samuel 25: 32–35

We can see here how decisive Abigail was and how David praised her for her logical good sense. If Abigail had waited for her husband to come to his senses and take action, she may have been killed. Abigail did not project her *Animus* qualities onto her husband and expect him to be the only one to make decisions. Because she harnessed her *Animus* qualities and was not afraid to strike out and go forth on her own she saved the lives of her family and servants.

Sometimes women can be very wary of being decisive and striking out on their own, being strategic and actively pursuing their goals and ideas. However, as we can see from Abigail's example, when a woman welcomes and uses her *Animus* qualities the results and the rewards are often substantial. In fact, shortly after this event, Abigail's husband Nabal has a stroke and then dies. On hearing this, David asks Abigail to marry him.

King David embraces his *Anima*

In the Old Testament it seems to have been common practice to have more than one wife and before marrying Abigail, David had been married to King Saul's daughter, Michal. David was described by God as '*...a man after his [God's] own heart*' (1 Samuel 13:14) and interestingly David often seemed very in touch with his *Anima* side. However, we are shown how Michal looks down on David and despises him when he dances and praises God in the streets and openly demonstrates his love for God. We get the impression that she does not believe this to be very fitting behaviour for someone of his position or status:

> *But as the Ark of the* LORD *entered the City of David, Michal, the daughter of Saul, looked down from her window. When she saw King David leaping and dancing before the* LORD, *she was filled with contempt for him.*
> — 2 Samuel 6:16

and

> *When David returned home to bless his own family, Michal, the daughter of Saul, came out to meet him. She said in disgust, 'How distinguished the king of Israel looked today, shamelessly exposing himself to the servant girls like any vulgar person might do!'*
> — 2 Samuel 6:20

It is almost as if Michal disapproved of David being in touch with his *Anima* side, perhaps she did not think the openness of his dancing and demonstration of love for God to be very manly or very kingly. This raises an important point because it is often other people who do not want us to develop or show certain aspects of ourselves and this can include our spouse. Expectations from our partner, our family, and our culture may mean that we repress certain sides of ourselves because we may fear that other people will disapprove.

Certain transition points for men like entering marriage or becoming a father may be prompting men to get in touch with their *Anima* side. When feelings of stress arise around transitions, it's important for men not to dismiss their feelings, push them to one side, or look down on them like Michal despised David's display of emotions. When a husband can open up and place value on his emotional realm, just like King David, it can draw him closer to his wife.

If we think back to the case example of Mike and Jenny, Mike's father was very upset that he went into the teaching profession. He didn't see it as a particularly manly job, and he had hoped that Mike would have become a car mechanic like him. Mike fortunately stuck to the career that he wanted; he had a strong nurturing side that was suited to teaching and he had a real gift for bringing out the best in his pupils.

Jung wrote a lot about how our culture and family can influence and prevent natural talents, or sides of our personality from developing. For example, if we think back to Tom, he was often told by his father: *'men don't cry'* and *'you need to toughen up in this world if you're going to survive'.* Tom soon picked up the idea that it was not good for him to be in touch with his emotions or to express them. In subtle and not so subtle ways, he was encouraged to fear his *Anima* qualities and his emotions. However, it is important for men to feel able to connect with their *Anima* qualities and, like King David, feel free to express themselves. As previously mentioned, Tom gradually learned to do this and saw not only his relationship with Lucy develop, but his emotional connection with God too.

The role of *Anima* and *Animus* in arguments

Anima/Animus plays a particular role in arguments between couples. When I first heard about this, I realised straightaway how true it was. Often when couples argue, the woman's negative *Animus* may raise its ugly head and go into overdrive. She may become very logical, almost dogmatic in the way that she expresses her frustrations, arguing, and repeating the rationale behind why she feels upset, driving her point home, not letting up, hoping that at some point her husband will hear her pain and see sense. What actually tends to happen is that the man's negative *Anima* is often provoked, and you may notice that he tends to become sensitive, sulky, and withdrawn in response. He may seem almost offended by his partner's brutal, thrusting assertions that he is in the wrong. During the heat of the argument, the woman can be seen to be in the grip of her negative *Animus* and the man appears to be in the grip of his negative *Anima* – this basically means that they cannot hear each other.

Before Tom and Lucy entered couples therapy, this tended to happen quite a lot. Tom often withdrew from Lucy in a sulky manner if she argued with him or expressed her frustrations. Lucy noticed that Tom would often become offended and walk off in a hurt silence. On one occasion Lucy had enough of Tom not doing chores around the home. She had asked him to take out the garbage the night before, but he said that he had 'forgotten'. Lucy was very logical arguing her point, highlighting that the chore was easier for Tom because he got home before it was dark, so it was easier for him to sort out the items for recycling and find the right boxes in the shed. Lucy went on to list all the other practical things that she had done around the home that week and how Tom had done little to help. She went on to tell Tom that if he hadn't really wanted to do it, he should have said so, instead of promising her that he would do it.

Here we can see how Lucy was gripped by her negative *Animus* and was very logical and dogmatic in her unrelenting debate with Tom. Tom felt hurt and to him it seemed like all the other efforts he had made to help support Lucy were being dismissed. Tom felt overwhelmed by Lucy's long list of how he had failed to help her, so he withdrew. He felt wounded and sensitive about Lucy's onslaught, so went off to his study in a sulk.

It can be helpful for couples to become aware of this unhelpful dynamic. If you catch yourselves doing this, take a pause and try using the Nonviolent Communication (NVC) technique outlined at the end of Chapter 4. The NVC technique helps the couple to refocus on each other's emotions, which ultimately increases our empathy and ability to be receptive and listen to one another's point of view.

The dangers of ignoring the *Anima* and *Animus*

I have mentioned briefly the idea of the negative side of the *Anima/Animus* and like all qualities and attributes, there is the potential for a negative – what Jung would call a 'shadow side' – to show itself. One of the dangers of ignoring the *Anima* (if you are a man) and *Animus* (if you are a woman) is that it remains in the unconscious, so we do not have control over it. Furthermore, if one's *Anima/Animus* is not embraced, welcomed and integrated, it is more likely to show itself in its negative form. It also means that there is more potential for it to wreak havoc or grip us and take over our emotional mood for example, during arguments.

For a woman, her negative *Animus* can become like a critical father's voice, telling her she's not good enough, she's not competent, she can't achieve things. She may also project her negative *Animus* out onto men and potential husbands, picking the man who is no good, believing that her love will make him a better man. In this way, she may be attempting to redeem her negative *Animus* through this type of relationship.

Of course, a man too may fall in love with the wrong sort of woman, who is troubled, leading a chaotic life. This may also be an attempt to connect with his negative *Anima* and redeem it.

Another issue for a man who has trouble connecting with his *Anima* side is that he may project his negative *Anima* onto his wife. He may find it difficult to nurture his family and follow through on tasks that would be supportive and nurturing for his wife. He may 'forget' repeatedly or be too busy with work to prioritise the nurturing that his wife or his family needs. When he's not at work and at home, he may just wish to collapse and not have to put any effort into relating or nurturing with his family.

His wife as a consequence may become angry, harassed, upset, and driven 'crazy'. When this happens, his wife reflects back to him, his negative disowned *Anima*, which he has projected onto her. The husband, not liking what he sees may then turn away from his wife and go find a nice, comforting feminine elsewhere in the form of an affair. And so the pattern can repeat if the husband leaves his wife, the mistress will then be confronted with the man's lack of nurturing and she will become the angry, harassed female and an affair may happen again. The man of course may not have an affair, but stay in his marriage. Both partners are then tormented by this dynamic stemming from the man's difficulty to integrate the positive, nurturing *Anima* qualities for himself, his wife, and family.

To the outside world the pattern of interaction may seem like that of 'the Hag and the Hero' (Young-Eisendrath, 1984). With the hard-working emotionally absent husband appearing like the hero, even more so because the wife who has been driven 'crazy' by the husband's lack of emotional nurturance comes across as the hag. The husband, a false hero, may promise a lot and pay 'lip service' to his wife's requests, but not follow through. She is left harassed, nagging, angry, and full of complaints. Her emotional disposition is ugly, holding all of the negative. In comparison, the husband having projected his negative *Anima* onto his wife may appear gentle, stoic, and forbearing with his 'difficult' wife. Individuals outside of the couple relationship may be taken in by the face value of this polarised dynamic and not understand how the roles of 'Hag and Hero' have been formed.

Of course, there may be many reasons why a man may struggle to connect with his *Anima* side and the feminine. He may have had a very good mother, perhaps too good a mother who did everything for him. A smothering mother: psychologically a very uncomfortable experience. A mother who provided very little opportunity and space for him to learn how to nurture himself. This could be just one of the reasons why a man may find it difficult to welcome and utilise the strengths that his *Anima* has to offer.

To resolve this dynamic, firstly it is helpful for the man to recognise that this is an issue for him. That he is triggering his wife by projecting his negative *Anima* onto her and driving her 'crazy'. If he can welcome his *Anima* in its positive form and become more comfortable in adopting more of a nurturing and relational presence at home, then these types of dynamics are likely to subside. This will take a conscious, purposeful effort. Therapy can help with this process.

If you have had a particularly negative or difficult relationship with one of your parents, this can give rise to ignoring, or finding it difficult to associate oneself with, the *Anima/Animus*. In the case example of Lucy and Tom, Lucy had a very difficult relationship with her father. Consequently, she unconsciously wanted to associate herself with the feminine, hence her decision to develop her nurturing side and take up nursing as a career. She found it extremely difficult to integrate *Animus* qualities of being logical and assertive because she associated them with her father who was a domineering, unpleasant man. Being logical had been prized by her father and was a guiding principle in his life.

Lucy's reluctance to welcome and utilise her *Animus* qualities meant that she had not put herself forward for several promotions at work – it was difficult for Lucy to be assertive in the workplace, so she let these opportunities pass her by. It also meant that she projected her *Animus* qualities onto Tom, the logical accountant. Lucy didn't really like to have anything to do with the household finances and so she stepped back and let Tom take charge. However, this meant that Tom sometimes reminded Lucy of her domineering father because he typically took control and made financial decisions for both of them.

Furthermore, Lucy's unwillingness to welcome her *Animus* meant that her negative *Animus* often raised its ugly head and her critical inner father's voice told her she wasn't really that good a nurse, there were other nurses more competent than her and she didn't deserve to be promoted. It took a while for Lucy to recognise this unhelpful pattern and to stop projecting her *Animus* strengths onto Tom and to use them for herself. After a while Lucy began to jointly take on board household budgeting and financial decisions with Tom. The more she integrated her *Animus* qualities, the more confident she felt and the strength of her critical inner voice (her negative *Animus*) diminished.

Thinking back to the Biblical story of Abigail; if she had ignored her *Animus* and had remained passive, waiting for her husband Nabal to take action, the consequences would have been disastrous. It is likely that Abigail and her household would have died. Similarly, the consequences can be disastrous for women who get stuck in a passive mode of functioning for most of their life – these women may at some point feel resentful that they have not struck out and achieved the things that they wanted to in life. They may feel like a part of themselves has been suppressed and important opportunities have passed them by.

This may result in a wife pushing her husband to be more ambitious or nagging him to take action in certain areas because she has felt unable to do this for herself. It could also result in projecting her desires and goals onto a child and encouraging them to go forth and undertake adventures (unconsciously) on her behalf. It is also a worry, because such women may secretly or unconsciously resent their life, which has been focused too much on the feminine side. A son is likely to unconsciously pick up a mother's resentment arising from having to adhere to an overly stereotypical, feminine role. This in turn may make it more difficult for him to have a relationship with his *Anima* and integrate it in his life.

There are, of course, women who have traditional roles that are extremely fulfilling for them, but at the same time these women may also end up pursuing opportunities to develop their *Animus* side. In the case of Andy and Rose, Rose had a very traditional role of housewife and stay-at-home mother. However, later on Rose felt called to lead and develop an area of prayer ministry for their church. Rose still spent a lot of time at home nurturing and raising the children with Andy, but taking a lead on the prayer ministry also provided the opportunity for her to integrate and utilise her *Animus* qualities. This was very fulfilling for Rose and brought an additional sense of direction and purpose to her life. As Rose started to feel less depressed she began to reconnect with her musical side and started to help arrange songs for the church choir. She played an instrumental role in shaping the worship music for church services. All of this resulted in a deepening of her faith and spiritual growth. So, it is possible to have a traditional feminine role, yet still find the time and space to develop *Animus* qualities: they are not mutually exclusive.

In its positive form, a woman's *Animus* can help lend direction to her life, help her be strategic and pursue her goals. It can also help her find spiritual direction and act as a source of strength that she can fall back on. It can help her follow the path she needs to take in life instead of being swept along a less rewarding one that focuses on other peoples' needs and subjugates her own. Being direct, assertive and able to say 'no,' are also *Animus* qualities and these can be of great assistance if, as a woman, you have a tendency to subjugate your needs.

Earlier on in the chapter we talked about how a man may attempt to avoid integrating his *Anima* by projecting it onto his wife, and the trouble that can arise from this. Another way a man may try to avoid having to integrate *Anima* qualities, is by focusing on a stereotypical masculine role. Adopting a workaholic lifestyle and striving to be the breadwinner for the family may be one way that a man may try to avoid issues to do with relating and connecting properly with his wife and children. If a man ploughs all of his energies into the objective world of work and is overly focused on work-related goals, then this may leave little time and energy for emotional connection and intimacy.

This attitude may become particularly problematic when a man enters retirement and the world of work is no longer able to contain all of his energies. Without this structure and less connected to his *Anima* side, he may not feel so well equipped at emotionally supporting and orienting himself through this transition. There are some women for whom the world of work has been a primary interest and family life has held less importance. They too may struggle during the transition into retirement. Some women may have become overly focused on their work role as a way of avoiding falling into the subservient, stereotypical feminine role that they may have seen their own mother adopt. So retirement, and a forced reduction in activity may well feel unsettling for them. They may well experience a loss of identity, feel trapped, or helpless without work-related achievements or income. It may be difficult for them to tune into what they need or how best to nurture themselves, and discover new areas that would give them pleasure and enjoyment.

In case example 2, Andy's workaholic lifestyle certainly meant that he kept busy, and avoided having to acknowledge that he was depressed and having to relate to the emotional world of his wife and children. Couples therapy helped Andy get in touch with these feelings and start to integrate his *Anima* side more. Eventually, this prompted Andy to re-evaluate his work–life balance and he reduced his work commitments, which allowed him to spend more quality time with Rose and his children.

It may not just be work that a man ploughs his energies into, it could be a particular hobby that he feels passionate about, which takes up a significant amount of time and energy. It is important to have hobbies and interests, but if the amount of time and energy spent on a hobby is disproportionate to the amount of time and energy given to cultivating emotional connection in your marriage, then this is a sign that there needs to be more balance.

Interestingly, with *Anima* and *Animus* projections, the way that we may wish our spouse to change is probably an indication of how we may need to change. For example, if a wife is wanting her husband to be more ambitious and have a clearer sense of direction about future plans, it may well be that there is part of her that wants or needs to develop a greater level of ambition and direction in her own life (develop her *Animus* side).

Sometimes we hear of the stereotypical tale of a husband wanting his wife to wear sexy, lacy, red and black lingerie, which is often not to the wife's taste at all. Clearly it is what the husband, not the wife desires. Here, we could speculate that this may be a sign that the husband wants or needs to develop his sensual, sexual side – this could mean buying items of clothing in which he feels sexy or attractive in. Or it could be interpreted to mean that he needs to invest more time connecting with his own 'sexy' side and spending the time and effort creating opportunities to be sensual with his wife. Whether this is buying some appetising food and organising a romantic picnic, or connecting with his wife in an erotic way. In this way the man can cultivate his sensual side instead of locating it in his wife.

The other important issue to mention, which Jung refers to, is the phenomenon of the 'puer aeternus' Latin for the eternal boy. Peter Pan, who never wanted to grow up, is an archetypal image of 'puer aeternus'. He just wanted to go off on adventures with the 'lost boys' leaving Wendy to worry and try to look after them.

Sometimes this type of dynamic can happen in a couple relationship. If the husband has never really left his mother then he may try and find a replacement mother in his wife, whom he expects to look after him. In such couple relationships, the wife can feel very worn out, looking after herself and her husband, who in some respects remains child-like. The husband may be very proactive in work, almost seeing it like an adventure for himself, but this type of 'puer' man is not very grown-up in the realm of relationships and emotionally he may not pull his weight. He may expect his wife to do all of the organising for him, similar to a mother who may facilitate her son's social life.

In some respects, Mike had found it very difficult to grow up and become a man, because he associated being a man with his verbally abusive father. Consequently, this meant that he often presented as a 'puer aeternus', an eternal boy, and he would lean on Jenny sometimes for strategic decision making and practical things, whereas Jenny would lean on Mike for emotional support. This made the perfect marital fit for them both because after Jenny's brother died, she learnt that she needed to take on the hopes that her parents had for her brother's future as well the hopes that they had for her future. There was a pressure on Jenny to be everything for her parents; the perfect daughter and the perfect son they had lost. This meant that Jenny was used to identifying herself with the masculine, which Mike was wary of, as well as having to uphold the feminine aspects of herself.

Jenny's brother had been bright, and her parents had thought that he would have a brilliant career. This was part of the reason why Jenny was driven to succeed in her career as a lawyer – she was trying to be both son and daughter for her parents and identify with both masculine and feminine qualities. Initially this worked quite well in her marriage because Mike felt uncomfortable with his masculine side. Unconsciously he had taken on the nurturing role of a teacher because it helped to put some distance between himself and his father, who had expected him to be a 'manly' car mechanic.

However, Jenny soon became tired and worn out managing practical affairs for Mike, who was finding it difficult to associate himself with the masculine. This meant that Mike was clinging to his Peter Pan-like persona and he hoped that he wouldn't really have to grow up. Part of him hoped that Jenny, the lawyer, would make all the difficult practical decisions for them both as a couple.

In our society we seem to value the idea of remaining childlike and not growing up. People spend huge amounts of money on plastic surgery to look young and we are almost obsessed with being youthful in our western culture. In other countries, ageing is seen as a valuable and worthwhile experience. In addition, many other cultures help men to transition from being a boy to becoming a man through rituals and ceremonies, which involve leaving the mother and identifying with the group of men. Moore and Gillette (1990) have written a lot about this and about the difference between boy psychology and man psychology. This may be helpful for you to explore further if this is an issue for you.

There have been lots of important dimensions to think about in terms of the impact of *Anima/Animus* projections on our marriage. Hopefully this chapter has helped to show that by integrating one's *Anima/Animus* we can develop a more whole sense of ourselves and achieve what Jung referred to as a *greater personality* (Jung, 1977). I believe that this can also help us to reflect the image of God more fully as we embrace the masculine and feminine qualities that we possess.

When we stop projecting our *Animus/Anima* onto our husband or wife and integrate these qualities for ourselves, then we open up the opportunity to relate to our spouse for who they truly are. Ultimately, integrating one's *Anima* or *Animus* can help us to have a deeper connection with ourselves, our partner and from a spiritual perspective, God. It can bring a greater sense of balance for ourselves and our couple relationship. The 'Joint Reflection Points' below will help you to start exploring this together in greater depth and to see how the complementary opposites of *Anima/Animus* may influence your couple relationship.

Joint Reflection Points

1. Take turns discussing the following:

    ♥   Do you have an ideal *Anima* image of a woman that you sometimes
        project onto your wife?

    ♥   Do you have an ideal *Animus* image of a man that you sometimes
        project onto your husband?

    ♥   How have these projections affected your relationship and the way
        that you interact? What would be more helpful for your marriage?

2. Discuss and share how you feel about developing aspects of your *Anima*
    if you are a man. And if you are a woman, discuss how you feel about
    developing aspects of your *Animus*? How do you think your relationship
    would be different if you were both able to do this more?

3. How has the family that you have grown up in influenced your ability to
    integrate your *Anima/Animus*? For example, to what extent do you think
    your mother (or another close female relative) was able to integrate her
    Animus? What do you think you may have learnt or internalised
    unconsciously from this role model? To what extent do you think your
    father (or another close male relative) was able to integrate or be
    comfortable with his *Anima*? What do you think you may have learnt or
    internalised unconsciously from this role model? It may be helpful to
    take a look at your genograms together to help spark conversations *(See
    Chapter 1 'Joint Reflection Points' for the genogram exercise if you haven't already
    completed this.)*

4. Explore together whether there are areas where you would like your
    partner to change or be different? Could this be an aspect of yourself
    that would actually be good for you to try and integrate and develop?
    Dwell on this idea for a moment and reflect on whether there is some
    truth in this possibility.

5. What do you think some of the dangers are for you personally with regards to ignoring and not developing aspects of your *Anima* (for the man) and *Animus* (for the woman)? Did anything from the chapter stand out for you in relation to this? What impact do you think this potentially has on your marriage?

6. Are you going through a period of transition in your marriage at the moment? If so, how do you think welcoming and utilising your *Anima* side could help (for the man)? And how could welcoming and utilising your *Animus* side could help (for the woman)? Are there any particular areas in your life where you would benefit from more balance?

Spiritual Reflection Points

1. Praise God and thank Him for the way that men and women are
    uniquely different, yet both equal and of value in His sight.

    > *There is no longer Jew or Gentile, slave or free, male and female. For you are*
    > *all one in Christ Jesus.*
    >
    > — Galatians 3:28

2. Pray for forgiveness for the times you may have wanted your partner to
    meet your idealised image of what you thought a man or woman should
    be. Ask God to help you to relate to your spouse for who they truly are
    and who God has made them to be.

3. Pray together and ask God if there are any ways in which He would like
    you to make opportunities to embrace your *Animus*, like Abigail (for the
    woman) or to embrace your *Anima*, like King David (for the man). Try
    to be open and receptive to God speaking to you, perhaps play a piece
    of worship music that you like as you ask God to shed light on this aspect
    of your lives.

Chapter 8

Encountering conflict and being in your own boat

To know what you prefer instead of humbly saying
Amen to what the world tells you you ought to prefer,
is to have kept your soul alive.

Robert Louis Stevenson,
Scottish author, 1850–1894

'Being in your own boat' is a phrase that stands out in the book *Passionate Marriage* by Dr Schnarch (2009), and there are times in marriage when it is really useful to summon up this image of being in one's own boat. This tends to be most helpful when there are points of contention between a wife and husband. During these times differences of opinion are often not going to be easily resolved and the emotional tension in the conversation is usually going up a notch or two.

When couples notice this happening, they can say, *'It's okay, I'm in my boat and you're in yours.'* Sometimes, summoning this phrase can stop couples in their tracks and help them to accept that they have different views. This phrase reminds us about both parties being separate individuals even though they are married. It also brings home that it is not helpful for either one to pressurise the other to get out of their boat (I tend to picture a canoe) and clamber into yours.

Metaphorically, this is like trying to force someone to change their view and share your opinion. But as you can imagine, feeling pressured to clamber out of your own canoe and attempt to step across into someone else's canoe could be a precarious, destabilising move. As the quotation at the start of the chapter suggests, remaining in our own boat, instead of humbly accepting what another person tells us we should think, is a way of being 'differentiated' and keeping our soul alive. Ideally, we want to be paddling in our boats side-by-side, even if we disagree.

Essentially, this is what the majority of this chapter is about, and we will be revisiting some of Dr Schnarch's terminology that was introduced in Chapter 3, as well as some other valuable concepts. Towards the end of the chapter I will take some time to explore how conflict is sometimes used as a substitute for intimacy, and how unhelpful patterns of pursuit and avoidance can generate conflict. Ultimately, I hope that this will provide you with a new perspective on what you can do when you encounter conflict in your couple relationship.

Holding on to yourself and encountering conflict

Dr Schnarch's opinion is that it is still possible to remain connected and intimate with our spouse even when we encounter conflict. Sometimes couples struggle with this because they fear conflict and they want to remain emotionally fused with their partner, so they do not feel able to disagree. Alternatively, an individual may feel overwhelmed by being in such a close intimate relationship perhaps because they feel unable to be 'differentiated'. They unconsciously seek out conflict as a way of pushing their partner away and moderating the level of closeness.

In both these situations the individuals are sharing one canoe – the argument and resulting silence or withdrawal may help to provide some temporary relief from being cooped up in the same boat. However, this is not a valid long-term solution. You may not think either situation applies to you, but just hold any judgement as you go ahead and read the rest of the chapter: you may end up feeling surprised as certain scenarios start to resonate with you.

Dr Schnarch points out that when we hold on to ourselves – our sense of identity, and what we want – without expecting our partner to validate us (relying on self-validation*)* then this can help us to develop our level of differentiation in our marriage. As we saw in Chapter 3, this is a good thing.

Holding on to ourselves and what we want, trying to soothe ourselves about any potential displeasure that our wishes may stir up in our partner, can help us to stay in our own boat.

When we encounter conflict in couple relationships, anxiety levels can go up, particularly if we are concerned about trying to express something which may make our partner feel upset, or may be difficult for them to hear. Another crucial factor is that anxiety is often contagious and as you both encounter a point of conflict, one way to try to quickly get rid of this anxiety is for you to both agree and say, *'Okay then, let's forget about this, we'll agree, or we'll just stop discussing this. Come on, we're better off being in one boat together, even if it's a bit cramped and we're unhappy, it's far less anxiety-provoking than this conflict.'* However, what tends to happen is that at least one person may need to disconnect from the other, or one individual may end up feeling controlled by the other person who has pressurised them to agree or forget the issue.

Ultimately, this wears down levels of intimacy and, according to Dr Schnarch, what can happen is that couples may reach a place of emotional gridlock. Life becomes more and more unsatisfactory, the problems are temporarily ignored, but issues flare up with increasing frequency. Neither person is able to use self-validation and self-soothe when they encounter a partner's negative reaction and neither person knows how to move forward.

If we think back to Andy and Rose's relationship, Rose was very fearful of conflict and so was Andy. If Rose started to try and open up a difficult topic, Andy would typically start talking about a stressful work project and would look distracted, giving Rose very limited eye contact. Many times Rose wanted to speak up and tell Andy how sad she felt – how being a missionary couple no longer felt like the right thing for her. She longed to return to the UK where she would be less isolated, would have friendships and feel connected again. Rose had really tried to stick it out living overseas, but things were just getting worse.

However, Rose was used to being 'emotionally fused' with Andy and being stuck in an unhappy situation, just as she had been as a child. It was difficult for Rose to self-validate and at a deeper level she felt anxious about Andy getting upset and withdrawing from her. This anxiety kept Rose from telling Andy how she really felt and what she wanted.

Eventually Rose couldn't cope any longer, so she had to confront herself and face her anxieties and tell Andy that she needed to move back to the UK. Rose had to hold on to her sense of self and self-validate that this was the right thing for her. On some level Rose knew a change needed to happen in order for her to feel better and for their relationship to get better too.

As well as confronting her fears about being abandoned, Rose also had to confront herself and tackle her tendency to subjugate her needs and neglect herself. When Rose eventually told Andy how she felt, he was shocked and surprised. He then reacted quite negatively about going back to the UK, viewing it as them 'giving up': for Andy it felt like a personal failure.

When we encounter conflict and self-validate, not expecting or demanding that our partner agrees with us, but simply expressing our view, it can feel quite threatening for the other person. Essentially, we have got into our own boat and our partner may react saying, *'Hold on a minute, get back here into my boat!'*

This is what happened with Andy and Rose; Rose's request to go back to the UK threatened Andy's 'reflected sense of self'. Andy saw them as a successful, pioneering missionary couple and Rose was basically highlighting that that wasn't how she had been experiencing life overseas. Andy tried to order Rose to get back into the same boat as him, pointing out that this was where God had called them to be.

When couples encounter conflict and one partner is threatening the other's reflected sense of self, then the 'reptilian' part of our brain (as Dr Schnarch refers to it) can get activated. We can lash out in an attempt to revert the situation back to the normal status quo, forcing the other person to agree with our way of thinking. This happened with Andy as his whole sense of identity was wrapped up in being a missionary, so he went on the attack and tried to place an enormous sense of pressure and guilt on Rose.

In couple relationships, because there is a deep, emotional attachment, we often know what type of things trigger a response from our partner and how we can 'push their buttons'. Andy knew what would upset Rose the most, so he attacked her with this and pressurised her to change her mind. Feeling guilty would often make Rose want to comply and please others, so Andy berated her and told her how she would be letting God down, letting the people he was helping down, and letting her husband down too.

Andy actually hadn't stopped to ask God what He wanted them to do or consider that his wife's distress was a sign from God that things needed to be different. Unlike Andy and Rose, other missionary couples who are struggling may pray and feel called to stay in their posting – seeking support for their marriage whilst remaining overseas. A useful book to read if you're wanting to reflect on the issue of God's vocation and what God's will may be not only for the husband, but for his wife and family too is: '*Good Christians, Good Husbands? Leaving a Legacy in Marriage and Ministry*' (Moore, 2004). This is a helpful book for Christian couples even if you are not in full-time ministry.

To Andy's surprise, Rose didn't react to the pressure and guilt-inducing accusations in her usual way. In fact, she said that she didn't care and as the intensity of the argument increased, she suddenly left the house. By the time Rose returned Andy knew that she meant business and he would have to take her request seriously.

Interestingly, Dr Schnarch outlines that the more differentiated we are in our couple relationship, the more likely it is that we will be able to stay in the same room and not leave during an argument. In *Passionate Marriage,* Dr Schnarch details six levels of self-soothing when conflict occurs, which I will summarise below, starting from the point of least differentiation through to being highly differentiated (the position we'd ideally like to be in when encountering conflict). The least differentiated strategies are focused on trying to self-regulate and re-establish a sense of well-being through withdrawing contact from your partner. Alternatively, the most differentiated strategy involves trying to maintain your sense of equilibrium whilst still being in close physical proximity to your partner and eventually re-establishing a connection.

1. You are greatly affected by the conflict that has taken place and it is difficult for you to cope following the disconnection from your partner. You find it difficult to re-establish connection with your partner and you also find it difficult to distract yourself and direct your energies into activities that you would normally enjoy *(Least differentiated stance)*.

2. You don't want to speak to your partner. You may withdraw from them or actively avoid them following the conflict. You reject your partner's attempts to re-establish connection with you.

3.   Following the conflict, you do not attempt to re-establish connection with your partner, rather the emotional and physical activities that you engage in are focused on minimising negative interactions.

4.   Attempts to initiate a re-connection with your partner happen less frequently. Instead, you withdraw into yourself and activities that help give you enjoyment and may help to fill the gap of your needs not being met by your partner.

5.   Temporarily, you may break contact with your partner in order to self-soothe and/or focus on other interests that help to give you energy and meet your needs, before then attempting to re-establish connection with your partner.

6.   You have developed the ability to self-soothe whilst disagreeing with your partner and you are able to remain with them whilst trying to problem-solve and re-establish a connection *(Most differentiated stance)*.

Of course, if you need to leave the room when you are encountering conflict with your partner, that's okay and it may be the only way that you feel able to cope with the situation at the moment. Over time you may see this begin to change, just like Andy and Rose did through the course of their couples therapy. By the end of their therapy, they sometimes needed to break contact briefly when encountering conflict but were then often able to re-establish connection fairly quickly.

People may wrongly assume that leaving a room and breaking contact is a differentiated stance, but it actually highlights that the couple is still emotionally fused and merged. The conflict may feel too difficult to bear because they are too close (in the same boat), so the intensity can feel overwhelming. Also, if we think back to Chapter 1, if you are merged and projecting difficult feelings onto one another, then this is likely to create intense situations which you may feel that you need to walk away from. Recognising and owning your own emotions, instead of projecting them onto your spouse, and being more differentiated will help you when you encounter conflict.

High toleration for pain and low toleration of anxiety

Interestingly Dr Schnarch (2009) tells us that emotionally fused couples often have a high toleration for pain (for example, staying in difficult situations that make both partners unhappy) and a low toleration for anxiety. So basically, when couples are emotionally merged it feels safer for them to continue with the status quo and make sure that they 'don't rock the boat', rather than face the anxiety of trying to do something new that is out of their comfort zone – such as broaching topics that could generate conflict.

If we consider Andy and Rose, this was definitely the case for them. They were both unhappy in their marriage and really Andy was also struggling with being isolated overseas, no matter how hard he worked. However, Andy and Rose had learnt as children that you just have to put up with painful, difficult situations that you don't like. Rose was forced to cope with her mother's post-natal depression and the decision to send her brother away to live with their cousin during term time so they could attend the same school. Andy also had to cope with his father's absence, workaholic lifestyle, and depressed mood when he was at home. Andy and Rose were unfortunately both very good at putting up with situations that caused a lot of pain. In Jean Shinoda Bolen's brilliant book, *Ring of Power* (1999), she says:

> *In all dysfunctional families, there are agreements to remain silent about some subjects and emotions: these are the binding agreements that co-dependents enter...*
> — p.126

Some of you may be familiar with the term 'co-dependent', which is the same as being emotionally fused or merged. In Rose and Andy's respective families of origin, they had both learnt that they needed to remain silent about certain subjects. Andy knew that he wasn't allowed to mention the injury that precipitated his father's discharge from the Air Force and the related change in his father's behaviour. Furthermore, Andy certainly knew that he had entered a silent agreement with his mother and father not to express any of his own sadness about these changes. Andy was silently asked not to speak up and as a child he became emotionally fused and co-dependent with his parents. He had picked up the message that he needed to help look after them both by going along with the silence.

This type of agreement to remain silent also impacted another couple that we met in Chapter 1, Jenny and Mike. Jenny also received strong messages that she wasn't supposed to speak about the distress of her brother dying and she also wasn't supposed to express other strong emotions, such as anger or frustration. Jenny's family seemed perfect on the surface, but the lack of space to talk about difficult emotions was unhelpful. This meant that being differentiated, expressing her own frustrations and encountering conflict felt very scary for Jenny.

Returning to the case example of Andy and Rose, it is easy to see how their childhoods resulted in a pattern of being emotionally fused with each other. They were both used to being cramped and unhappy in the same boat. They knew how to put up with pain and dissatisfaction, and remain silent about it all. However, as the situation got worse and worse the problems in their marriage reached the point of what Dr Schnarch would call 'critical mass'. The amount of pressure and strain that Rose felt, propelled her into breaking her silence. This pivotal moment started Rose and Andy down a new path, moving away from tolerating high levels of pain towards tolerating new and uncomfortable levels of anxiety. Without toleration for anxiety, there was no potential for growth and development in their couple relationship.

Rose needed to confront herself and her anxiety that Andy might distance himself further if she spoke up. She also needed to confront herself and prepare herself for the possibility that Andy may not like what she had to say, and that they may have to encounter conflict. Rose's decision to speak up meant that she had to 'let go' of Andy, get into her own boat, and hold on to herself. Rose had to focus on her own integrity and hold firm to what she knew she needed, and what their couple relationship needed. This was scary for Rose, but because she had reached a point of 'critical mass', where she could no longer tolerate the situation and subjugate her needs, there was an urgency and a huge amount of energy propelling her forward in a new direction.

Dr Schnarch points out that all couples reach a point of emotional gridlock, where Rose and Andy were, where they can no longer tolerate the situation that their couple relationship is in, but it may be difficult to know how to move forward. When couples fall in love they speak to each other, try to find out commonalities and shared interests, and they agree with each other. During the falling-in-love stage, the positive feedback and glow from one's 'reflected sense of self' is huge. You may hear someone gush about their partner during this stage, saying things like, *'Oh, he's perfect for me!'*

Society falsely leads us to believe that this is how it should always be, that the falling-in-love (or honeymoon) period should last forever. That is often why individuals feel shocked, betrayed, or let down when they encounter conflict and growing levels of dissatisfaction in their couple relationship. When couples reach a place of emotional gridlock they may think – 'I've married the wrong person,' or if they are a Christian, they may question God's guidance for getting married and blame themselves for not praying enough. In fact, some individuals may think that they need to have an affair or get divorced in order to recapture the euphoria related to the falling-in-love stage and recover a positive reflected sense of self.

However, Dr Schnarch points out that this is a normal process, and all couples will at some point reach a place of emotional gridlock, where the urge to differentiate and get into your own boat is being stimulated. When this happens it can bring a truer, deeper sense of intimacy and opportunities to really know each other, instead of insisting that your partner agrees with you and provides you with a reflected sense of self to make you feel good.

The 'Saturday phase' following Friday's crucifixion

It can be daunting to step across into our own boat because, like Rose and Andy, we may not have done this before, and we don't really know what it will be like or what will happen. Jean Shinoda Bolen (1999) points out:

> *When we decide to do what is true, or speak up about it, our efforts may be greeted with hostility, denigration, and efforts to humiliate us; we may feel ourselves being crucified, abandoned by others or even the certainty that got us there. Once we have declared ourselves we cannot go back to our former position or role; we cannot go back to who we were.*

— p.193

This reminds me of Dr Schnarch's warning that the reptilian part of our brain may get activated when our spouse speaks up and takes a differentiated stance. We saw that with Andy and Rose, when Rose spoke the truth about how she was feeling and what she wanted, Andy panicked and switched into a type of bullying mode. He ended up berating Rose for her feelings and tried to place a huge amount of pressure on her by making her feel guilty.

After a partner has taken a differentiated stance and spoken up, perhaps for the first time, they may enter what Jean Shinoda Bolen calls the 'Saturday' phase, referring to the day after the crucifixion of Jesus, where the world is in limbo and Easter Sunday is yet to come. During the 'Saturday' phase we may feel uncertain about what may happen to us and our couple relationship. Jean Shinoda Bolen (1999) writes about the 'Saturday' phase:

> *On Friday the crucifixion takes place. On Saturday, we do not know there will be a resurrection. So it is in life. Once we declare ourselves, we step beyond our known world into the void, into the fire, or onto the cross. We make an irrevocable break with the past and go into a period of uncertainty in between that is like the Saturday after the crucifixion. Following the initial reaction … we usually find ourselves in the 'Saturday' phase. Our old life and old identity are dead; and we go for a time into the underworld or underground: not knowing whether this will be a tomb or a womb, a burial of all promise or the beginning of a new life; not knowing whether this will be the end of us, or whether Sunday will come and with it resurrection and transformation.*
>
> — p.193–194

I believe something similar occurs in couple relationships when one partner speaks up and makes a break for it, trying to find and get into their own boat. The night that Rose stormed out of the house neither she nor Andy knew what was going to happen; they had entered their 'Saturday' phase. In reality, their 'Saturday' phase didn't just last that evening, their couple relationship issues weren't resolved in the morning when they started talking to each other again. Rose didn't know if she had done the right thing, whether her push to move back to the UK would result in the death of their relationship or whether it would help to bring new life.

Their 'Saturday' phase continued throughout the different stages of their couples therapy as well. Increasingly, they had to confront themselves and their own individual anxieties around exposing their true feelings and thoughts to themselves and each other. Talking about these issues in couples therapy brought some level of containment, but at times Rose and Andy felt anxious and uncertain about what was going to come out of their 'Saturday' phase and what would greet them on Sunday morning – an empty tomb or new life.

Holding on to the hope and tolerating the anxiety and uncertainty was important for them both as they discussed their feelings and encountered conflict. Andy made a significant reflection during couples therapy. He drew attention to the verse that is well-known, and he had often heard being read at weddings.

> *Three things will last forever – faith, hope, and love – and the greatest of these is love.*
>
> — 1 Corinthians 13:13

Andy reflected that hope seemed to get a bit lost and overlooked sandwiched between faith and love, but to him it seemed pretty important. For Andy and Rose it was the hope of Sunday morning and the transformation of their couple relationship that kept them going through their 'Saturday' phase.

Joseph and Potiphar's wife – get into my boat or else!

Let us turn our attention to Joseph, yes, the same Joseph on which the musical, *Joseph and the Amazing Technicolour Dreamcoat* is based. After being betrayed by his brothers, Joseph finds himself being purchased as a slave for Potiphar, one of Pharaoh's officials. He does well in Potiphar's house and soon rises to become his master's personal attendant. We are told some interesting information in verse 6 of Genesis 39, namely that '… *Joseph was a very handsome and well-built man.*'. We may wonder why this is so important for us to know and then we are told that '… *Potiphar's wife soon began to look at him lustfully. "Come and sleep with me," she demanded.*' (Genesis 39:7). Joseph and Potiphar's wife are not in a relationship, but here we see how she attempts to get him into her boat and succumb to her demands.

Joseph is decisive and expresses his own different view, saying:

'Look,' he told her, 'my master trusts me with everything in his entire household. No one here has more authority than I do. He has held back nothing from me except you, because you are his wife. How could I do such a wicked thing? It would be a great sin against God.

— Genesis 39:8–9

As a slave Joseph was in a very vulnerable position and it could have been easier for him to just go along with what Potiphar's wife wanted. Instead, Joseph faces his own anxiety and manages to say 'No' to Potiphar's wife. However, that is not the end of it; Potiphar's wife will not be dissuaded:

She kept putting pressure on Joseph day after day, but he refused to sleep with her, and he kept out of her way as much as possible. One day, however, no one else was around when he went in to do his work. She came and grabbed him by his cloak, demanding, 'Come on, sleep with me!' Joseph tore himself away, but he left his cloak in her hand as he ran from the house.

— Genesis 39:10–12

Similarly, in our marriage, we may try to take a differentiated stance, hold on to our integrity, knowing what is right, but that does not mean that our partner will willingly acknowledge what we want and accommodate our needs. Often, when we try to get into our own boat it can create a reaction in our partner and they may, like Potiphar's wife, put up a fight.

So what does Potiphar's wife do following this dramatic struggle with Joseph? Yes, you may have guessed what happens, the reptilian part of her brain takes over. Feeling humiliated and rejected by Joseph's refusal she lies in order to punish him.

When she saw that she was holding his cloak and he had fled, she called out to her servants. Soon all the men came running. 'Look!' she said. 'My husband has brought this Hebrew slave here to make fools of us! He came into my room to rape me, but I screamed. When he heard me scream, he ran outside and got away, but he left his cloak behind with me.

— Genesis 39:13–15

I have a book entitled *Great Couples of the Bible* (Haag, Chungel-Straumann, Wetzel, Elliger, Grohmann & Soelle, 2006) and it is filled with beautiful paintings of couples in the Bible that have been painted at different points in history. There are lots of almost amusing portrayals of Potiphar's wife desperately clinging on to Joseph's cloak as he is trying to run away from her. It can be like this in modern-day couple relationships.

One party may be attempting to be differentiated, trying to step into their own boat, whilst the other person is desperately clinging on to them and forcing them to remain cooped up in a boat with them. We can see this clearly in the example of Andy and Rose, as Andy attacked Rose, he berated her for expressing her views and hoped that by making her feel guilty she would get back in the boat and agree with him.

As we have seen with Joseph and Potiphar's wife's attempts to force him into a relationship with her, when we take a differentiated stance the outcome is not always positive for us and the other person may react negatively. Joseph held on to his integrity, but when Potiphar hears of his wife's false accusations of rape, he throws Joseph into prison.

However, those of you who are familiar with Joseph's story know that whilst he is in prison, he interprets the dream of Pharaoh's cup bearer. Eventually he is released from prison and is asked to interpret Pharaoh's dreams. Joseph then gains favour with the Pharaoh and is given an elevated position and status.

So, in the end things work out for Joseph. Similarly, in the long run, remaining in our own boat and holding on to our integrity in our marriage can have positive results. This can often be the case despite initial negative reactions.

Encountering conflict and two choice dilemmas

Dr Schnarch (2009) points out that in marriage, we often want to have it all; we want to have all of our needs met and we don't want to face any anxiety or encounter conflict. Often when couples reach a place of 'emotional gridlock' they are faced with two-choice dilemmas. Dr Schnarch says that he uses the term 'two-choice dilemma' when working with couples to explain the following four points.

1. In couple relationships we often want to stay in difficult, painful, and confusing situations in order to uphold the status quo.

2. A choice needs to be made in order for the situation to be resolved.

3. We would like to have everything our way and to have two choices, when in reality we only have one choice.

4. Concerted efforts are made to avoid having to make that choice – this may result in putting up with a painful situation so that any losses connected with giving up one option over another don't have to be faced.

If we think back to the case of Lucy and Tom, when Lucy had reached a place of emotional gridlock in her marriage, she felt really stuck. She came to a point when she realised that no matter what she did, or how much she tried to accommodate Tom and subjugate her own needs, the same problems would creep up. It was increasingly difficult for her to push aside her growing dissatisfaction. In fact, for Lucy, it felt like she was slowly dying in her marriage. The state of their relationship was deteriorating badly.

Lucy didn't know what to do, she was deeply unhappy in her marriage, but the idea of divorce was difficult, and it wasn't something Lucy felt that she could pursue. However, Lucy really didn't know how to move forward in her marriage and make it better; she didn't even think she could tell Tom how upset she was feeling.

Lucy was really stuck, she couldn't go backwards and get divorced. She also didn't know how to move forwards. She had well and truly reached a place of emotional gridlock.

Lucy also had to face her 'Two-Choice Dilemma'; Lucy wanted to be happy in her marriage, but she didn't want to face the anxiety of doing anything about it or talking to Tom. Like most people, she didn't want to have to face her dilemmas and she didn't want to have to choose what to do. She could either keep quiet, and suffer the consequences of remaining deeply unhappy, or she could confront her anxiety and talk to Tom about how she felt and try and do something about their problems. Dr Schnarch (2009) points out:

We have the fantasy that we have the choice between being anxious or not. Unfortunately, we don't. Our choice is between one anxiety or another. Do something scary – or face problems from not doing it.

— p.297

As we know, the problems built up to such an extent that they reached a point of 'critical mass' which provided Lucy with the momentum for her to talk about her problems with Tom. Lucy had to confront her anxiety that Tom would react negatively, that he may get angry with her and that he could become even more rejecting of her. Ideally, Lucy wanted to open up and tell Tom how she felt and for him to listen to her properly and take her concerns seriously. However, as we know, we're not in control of our partner's reactions, we don't get to choose how our partner responds, we can only take responsibility for ourselves and what we want to say. Dr Schnarch (2009) tells us:

*When relationships hit gridlock, everyone wants **two** choices. The problem is that you only get one at a time. You make a choice and then your partner gets to make his (or vice versa). That's when you encourage your partner to be 'reasonable' – so you don't really have to choose.*

— p.298

There was no way that Lucy wanted to bully or pressure Tom into being reasonable and listen to her. So she had to 'take the hit' and confront her anxiety and confront Tom. She had to hold on to herself and what she knew she needed to say. It was a difficult conversation. Lucy was destabilising Tom's reflected sense of self. For Tom, it was like a bucket of cold water being splashed over him, a real wake-up call, whether he wanted it or not.

If we think back to Andy and Rose, when Rose walked out, Andy was faced with his own two-choice dilemma. Really, Andy didn't want to have to choose, which was why he had tried to make Rose feel guilty and 'be reasonable'. But since that tactic failed he was forced to confront himself and the reality of their situation. Now, Andy could choose to confront himself and the anxiety he felt about opening up to Rose, and the possibility of moving back to the UK, or he could try to continue with life as normal and hope that Rose would calm down and change her mind. However, Rose seemed serious and determined; she had started down the path of differentiation and she wasn't going to stop. Andy either had to try and keep up with Rose as she was pushing for growth and change, or he could hold back and remain stuck. If our spouse isn't willing to differentiate and grow with us then we can't force them to, but it is likely to cause problems and it has the potential to place a significant strain on the relationship.

Patterns of conflict and emotional fusion

There is another important area for us to think about together, which is repeating patterns of conflict and how conflict can be used (often unconsciously) as a substitute for intimacy. David Shaddock (1998) in his book *From Impasse to Intimacy* explains this in terms of patterns of pursuit and avoidance. You may be asking yourself, well, how does this type of conflict end up being a substitute for intimacy? In Chapters 1 to 3, we looked at the difficulties that all couples face in mediating a sense of closeness and a sense of separateness. The image of two porcupines trying to come together and then pricking each other and moving back, is a good analogy for the patterns of pursuit and avoidance that we often see in couple relationships and in conflict. Conflict can keep us engaged and connected with someone else, even though it may be an unhealthy connection. For individuals who may unconsciously fear being overwhelmed or taken over by their partner, conflict may be used as a way to create distance whilst still having a very charged, emotional connection with their spouse.

David Shaddock (1998) describes two types of personality that engage in pursuit and avoidance patterns, 'mergers' and 'distancers'. Mergers tend to seek out togetherness and connection, which is paramount for them; if that connection disappears and they are not seen or recognised by their partner, it can feel like a threat to their existence (Shaddock, 1998). Distancers, on the other hand, do not want anyone to see inside of them, in fact they fear it, because they believe that the other person will try to take over and control them (Shaddock, 1998). Therefore, avoiding connection where one's emotions can be seen, feels vital to their survival (Shaddock, 1998).

Mergers have often experienced a strong sense of abandonment growing up, which would have resulted in an array of disappointments and unmet needs (Shaddock, 1998). What tends to happen for this type of person is that fighting, and conflict may become a substitute for intimacy, or the individual may use romantic fantasy to flee from the unmet needs in their relationship (Shaddock, 1998). Whilst a merger is pursuing their spouse and arguing, it may help to cover up their fear of abandonment and it helps them to have a strong, if unhealthy connection with their partner (Shaddock, 1998).

Distancers tend to fear getting close to someone because they are wary of being humiliated or taken advantage of (Shaddock, 1998). However, it is not that distancers don't want contact, in fact, underneath, they often feel very needy, but fear being emotionally intruded upon, which is most probably what their parents did whilst they were growing up (Shaddock, 1998). During their childhood, they may have been asked to mirror their parents and meet their parents' needs, instead of their parents trying to be in tune with them and meet their needs (Shaddock, 1998). They may also have been expected to live up to high expectations and experienced a great deal of pressure to 'perform' and be perfect in their parents' eyes. In essence, they would have felt very controlled as a child and in their adult couple relationship they become a distancer in order to try and avoid a repetition of that experience.

Distancers also fear having any of their vulnerabilities exposed and being criticised; however, if a distancer marries a merger, they will most likely be criticised for their emotional avoidance because the merger will feel abandoned by them (Shaddock, 1998). Then what tends to happen is that the distancer becomes defensive, they argue their point and try to prove themselves right –they don't want to admit any vulnerability (Shaddock, 1998). For the merger this can be very frustrating because they are seeking to re-establish a connection with their spouse and not argue (Shaddock, 1998). Here we see how patterns of pursuit and avoidance result in conflict and can become a substitute for intimacy. David Shaddock (1998) points out that:

Both mergers and distancers actually create the response they fear in their partner. By refusing to commit to any plan or sabotaging the agreements that they do make, the distancer heightens his partner's anxiety, making her more relentless in her pursuit, while the merger's shrillness drives her partner away.

— p.95

So we see that the couple relationship helps to keep the defensive patterns of relating going in a vicious cycle for both the merger and the distancer. It can feel too risky for them to expose themselves and their vulnerability by asking for what they truly want from each other.

It is a real 'push-me-pull-you' situation. We have seen this in the case example of Tom and Lucy. Tom was the distancer in the relationship and Lucy could be labelled the merger. Tom's mother had pushed him heavily to succeed and raise himself up by getting a good education. In some ways she was using Tom to try and meet her own unmet needs for success and recognition. There was a lot of pressure placed on Tom because of this and Tom soon learnt to put a lot of pressure on himself. As a child Tom didn't really need or want the type of attention and pressure he received from his mother, what he really wanted was to be nurtured. But that wasn't going to happen in Tom's family, so he had to push that desire to one side.

Lucy on the other hand was constantly striving for affection and could not stand it when Tom silently withdrew from her. Lucy's attempt to resolve the situation and speak about their conflict was often received as a personal criticism by Tom. This resulted in Tom defending his corner, arguing, and criticising Lucy; the defence mechanisms from his childhood kicked in and took over. So we can see how Lucy was pursuing Tom and he was busy avoiding Lucy and avoiding having to show any emotional vulnerability. Of course, Tom did not want to be abandoned by Lucy either, but he knew that if he withdrew to his study, she would still be thinking about him and their argument. Their pursuit/avoidance pattern kept them together in an emotionally fused state.

These pursuit/avoidance dialogues that we have with our partners are easy to fall into and it is easy for the cycle to keep going in various guises. So how can we can to try to alter these defensive patterns of relating and establish a truer form of intimacy with our partner? David Shaddock (1998) suggests three things, which I will summarise in turn. Firstly, a helpful aim would be to try to accept these defensive patterns of behaviour. For change to take place it is important to try and cultivate an accepting non-judgemental, non-blaming atmosphere. This can be applied to yourself as well as your spouse: you may benefit from being curious about why you're getting angry and accepting of the fact that you may be worried about feeling abandoned or intruded upon. Exploring why you may be feeling like you need to protect yourself and create some distance between yourself and your spouse, and accepting this, may help to reduce the intensity of the pursuit/avoidance behaviours.

Secondly, David Shaddock highlights that it is good to ask for contact in ways that can be heard by your partner. Lucy learnt to approach Tom and ask for contact in ways that felt less critical. For example, instead of saying to Tom, *'We never go out on dates anymore,'* she would suggest something like, *'Why don't we go out for dinner one night this week, I'll book our favourite restaurant?'* For Lucy, being more open and direct was quite daunting for her because she felt worried and almost expected her efforts for contact to be turned down. However, slowly Tom and Lucy were able to build up a new script and way of interacting and when they did engage in the pursuit/avoidance dialogue, they were slowly able to recognise what they were doing. This helped to reduce the level of distress and intensity around the argument as they realised they had initiated their porcupine dance of trying to be close, but separate.

Thirdly David Shaddock states that it is important to ask for privacy. What happens particularly for distancers is that the conflict is used to help them withdraw and avoid too much closeness or fear of intrusion. What would be healthier is to clearly ask for time alone when you need it or negotiate and agree to have some time away from your partner to socialise with friends or to enjoy your favourite pastime.

Tom found it really hard to ask for time to himself, he'd grown up in a large family and with a fairly intrusive mother, so he'd learnt that he wasn't entitled to ask for time to himself. Something Tom loved doing was going fishing because he found being outside, surrounded by nature, a deeply satisfying experience. It gave him a chance to be still and have some solitude. Lucy didn't mind Tom going fishing, but she wasn't aware that this was something that Tom wanted to do.

Tom hadn't asked Lucy before, because he thought he'd be criticised for being selfish, wanting to go off on his own, similar to how he'd been criticised as a child when he spoke up and said what he wanted. When Tom started to communicate with Lucy and negotiated when it would be convenient for him to go fishing, he found it such a relief. It gave Tom the confidence to ask for the space that he needed at times, which meant that he didn't need to have an argument to get the space that he sometimes desired. This didn't mean that Tom spent most weekends fishing, taking advantage of Lucy's openness to his request, rather they negotiated together as a couple about when time apart would work best for them both.

Let's return to thinking about the quotation at the beginning of the chapter:

> *To know what you prefer instead of humbly saying Amen to what the world tells you you ought to prefer, is to have kept your soul alive.*

Holding on to ourselves when we encounter conflict, and understanding our needs in our couple relationship, is important. When we know what we want and what we prefer, we then have the chance to communicate this instead of giving into the pressure to keep silent or humbly going along and saying 'Amen' to our spouse's wishes. It is when we are able to encounter conflict, yet still communicate our needs and preferences that we can help to keep our soul alive. Understanding how we feel about conflict and our relationship with conflict is also helpful and the 'Joint Reflection Points' below provide a good starting point for you to explore this together as a couple.

Joint Reflection Points

1. Take a look at your genograms and explore your family history in terms of the models and patterns of what has happened when family members have encountered conflict *(See 'Joint Reflection Points' in Chapter 1 for the genogram exercise if you haven't drawn your genograms yet.)* What messages have you consciously or unconsciously picked up from your family about encountering conflict? How has this impacted your couple relationship? Is there a more helpful approach to encountering conflict for your couple relationship?

2. What were some of the 'no-go' topics in your family of origin as you were growing up – areas that you may have silently agreed not to speak up about? How has this influenced your couple relationship? As a couple, what are some of the 'no-go' topics or areas that you may have silently agreed not to speak about (or you know your partner doesn't want to talk about)? How can you jointly break the silence and start to speak up? What holds you both back?

3. Take turns discussing the following:

    ♥   How does it feel for you when you encounter conflict?

    ♥   What holds you back from discussing important matters that have the potential to generate conflict?

    ♥   How could encountering conflict feel better/safer for you both?

4. What types of situations act as potential triggers and make you want to force your partner to get in the same boat and agree with you? Over the next four weeks try to practise being in your own boats. Remember to self-soothe and self-validate when you encounter conflict and review at the end of the month how this has been for you both.

5. Do you sometimes have a high toleration for pain in your couple relationship and a low toleration for anxiety? Try to identify together

situations that make you unhappy, but you have been putting up with because you're anxious about trying to make a change or 'rocking the boat'. It's helpful to adopt a non-blaming, compassionate stance when discussing this. Naming these situations and starting to talk about them together is a positive starting point and will help you to move forward in your couple relationship. Try using the Nonviolent Communication (NVC) technique outlined at the end of Chapter 4, to help structure this conversation if you would like to.

6.   How can you break free from pursuit/avoidance scripts? If you'd like to have some contact with your partner or connect with them in a certain way, but are afraid of asking directly, this is a good time to practise. Conversely, if you'd like to ask for some privacy and negotiate some time being separate from your partner to do a hobby or relax, this is also a good time to practise. David Shaddock (1998) suggests saying to your partner, *'I have something I really need you to hear and I'm wondering what is the best way I can say it to you?'* (p.106). Try this out and explore with your partner what would be the best way to discuss your needs and make a request.

7.   If you find yourselves caught up in unhelpful patterns of conflict, with the same unhelpful scripts and dialogues cropping up time and time again, then I would recommend Sue Johnson's (2011) book, *Hold Me Tight: Your Guide to the Most Successful Approach to Building Loving Relationships* (also available in audio format if you would prefer to listen to her guidance as a couple and try out the exercises together).

Spiritual Reflection Points

1. Pray to God and thank Him for the opportunities to grow through your couple relationship when you encounter conflict. Ask Him to give you wisdom and understanding of how best to respond to each other when you encounter conflict.

    > *Dear brothers and sisters, when troubles come your way, consider it an opportunity for great joy. For you know that when your faith is tested, your endurance has a chance to grow. So let it grow, for when your endurance is fully developed, you will be perfect and complete, needing nothing. If you need wisdom, ask our generous God, and he will give it to you …*
    > — James 1:2–5

2. Pray to God and ask Him to give you both the courage to speak up in your marriage when you need to, instead of being fearful and keeping silent:

    > *Fearing people is a dangerous trap, but trusting the LORD means safety.*
    > — Proverbs 29:25

3. Pray to God to give you a sense of hope and encouragement in your marriage, especially if you feel like you're going through a 'Saturday' phase after Friday's crucifixion and you're awaiting Sunday's resurrection.

    > *Three things will last forever – faith, hope, and love…*
    > — 1 Corinthians 13:13

Chapter 9

Kitchen sink dilemmas and the soulful care of the household

The ordinary acts we practice every day
at home are of more importance to the soul than
their simplicity might suggest.

Care of the Soul, *Thomas Moore*

Kitchen sink dilemmas

There are lots of 'kitchen sink dilemmas' that can crop up in couple relationships and take up a huge amount of emotional energy; you may be asking yourself, what do I mean by kitchen sink dilemmas? Well, I'm referring to the kind of dilemmas that often come up time and time again around household tasks and other practical things that need to get done. Sometimes the arrangements regarding who does what don't seem fair, or one person in the couple relationship may agree to do a task, but they don't follow through. Often these 'kitchen sink dilemmas' trigger disagreements and the resentment that flares up can absorb a lot of time and emotional energy.

In fact, having repetitive arguments about kitchen sink dilemmas can wear down levels of intimacy between ourselves and our partner. That is why I've dedicated this chapter to thinking about how to resolve them and to consider a more soulful approach to caring for the home. I will be drawing on Thomas Moore's (1992) work *Care of the Soul*, to look at how we can bring the sacred into the everyday rituals of our home life.

Kitchen sink dilemmas are often formed from the basics of domestic life, such as, *'Who's going to wash the dishes tonight?'* They also relate to being able to agree upon practical systems that are needed, such as how to file your bills, or who is going to drop the children off at school this week. However, kitchen sink dilemmas can be easily resolved if an agreement is made between both partners and you hold each other accountable to the agreement. If the agreement falls down somehow, then spending some time together figuring out what went wrong, what got in the way, and reinstating a new, improved plan is important.

It may be that it fell down because the last element of the task wasn't followed through properly. Conversely, it may have been the first part of the task that was difficult to initiate and start. The detail is important: you may need to think about the time of day, or when in the evening is best to complete the household task. You may even need to buy some equipment for the home, or other practical solutions, like additional storage to resolve the dilemma.

In Tom and Lucy's case, the weekly food shop was an issue. Lucy did the food shopping and Tom made excuses why he couldn't. He said the fact that Lucy had the car for work, and he travelled by train made it easier for her to stop at the supermarket on the way home from work. Also Tom wasn't overly concerned if they ran out of the essentials. He was happy to make a last-minute dash to the shops, whereas Lucy preferred to have a good supply of essentials in stock at home. During couples therapy this dilemma was discussed, and a solution found. Tom agreed to go to the supermarket on a Saturday morning when Lucy was studying for her higher qualification in nursing. As Tom was an accountant he enjoyed looking for bargains and he was somewhat surprised to discover that he enjoyed the weekly ritual of food shopping.

Thinking about a specific day and time to complete the household task was helpful for Tom and Lucy. Lucy felt nurtured and supported by Tom. It was only because they had sat down and explored the details of what would work that the negotiation over doing the weekly food shop was successful. Lucy had asked Tom many times to do some of the food shopping and she'd voiced her frustrations that the task typically fell to her. But they'd never sat down and made a concrete plan about how this task would become more shared.

If you're deliberating over how to share domestic tasks, don't give up on making it work, be persistent. If you are having regular couples therapy, then making such an agreement with your couples therapist present can add another layer of accountability and you have an objective third party who can help each person recall the promise that they have made.

We've talked in previous chapters about how one person may passively resist carrying out a request to do something. Outwardly they may agree to do it, but underneath they have no real intention of following through with their promise. It is really important that when any agreement is reached it is done from an adult-to-adult position of relating, rather than from a parental nagging position to the partner who then becomes like the child. If one partner is placed in or adopts this immature child-like position, it is likely that they are not going to take on the responsibility properly. They may even secretly rebel against the parental demand that has been placed on them and not do the task. Subtle power struggles can get played out in the arena of kitchen sink dilemmas and somehow we lose our focus and the importance of soulfully caring for each other and our home.

Stewardship and kitchen sink dilemmas

Exploring the idea of stewardship may provide a helpful context in which to think about kitchen sink dilemmas. In the book of Genesis, we see how God made Adam and Eve stewards of all of the earth and he gave them the power and authority to take care of their surroundings:

> *Then God said, 'Let us make human beings in our image, to be like us. They will reign over the fish in the sea, the birds in the sky, the livestock, all the wild animals on the earth…'*
>
> — Genesis 1:26

The role of being a good steward was assigned to Adam and Eve, the original couple, and for us in modern-day couple relationships I believe that both husband and wife, like Adam and Eve, are asked to be good stewards of their surroundings and take care of their home.

If we think about it, the idea of a power struggle over household chores is not what God intended. He gave man and woman equal responsibility over looking after the earth and this was a gift and a privilege. How often do we view taking care of our homes as a gift and a privilege? And how often do we view caring for our homes as a spiritual act?

I think all too often amidst the busyness of modern-day life this gets lost and we are more and more disconnected from the rituals of home life. We need to get on, achieve, be successful, meet work demands, connect with friends and family, attend church events… You may think, *'I don't have time to clean the kitchen floor!'*

Something like this happened with Andy and Rose; Andy for a long time prioritised his work over family life. Early on in couples therapy they described an incident that had upset Rose. Rose was struggling to get the children to go to bed and Andy had promised to help her before he went out to an event at church.

However, Andy started to dash for the door and leave just as one of the children had started to cry – their nappy needed changing. Rose was just finishing bathing another child and called out to Andy to help. Andy was anxious about getting to the event at church on time and said he couldn't stay and help and so he left. This was upsetting for Rose. For Andy, changing a nappy seemed like a little thing, whereas being on time for church seemed a more important godly priority.

As I've already said, kitchen sink dilemmas often revolve around the small, everyday details of domestic life and for many of us these small details can seem irksome, like having to wash the dishes or empty the bins. However, thinking about Biblical principles of good stewardship, time and time again we are reminded that it is important to be faithful in small matters and this could include the details involved in caring for the home. The Bible says:

If you are faithful in little things, you will be faithful in large ones. But if you are dishonest in little things, you won't be honest with greater responsibilities.
— Luke 16:10

This is something for us to think about; if we're not prepared to be honest with ourselves and our spouse about following through with the responsibilities and chores that we've agreed to do at home, then it doesn't set a good foundation for being trusted with more significant concerns and responsibilities in our couple relationship.

Andy viewed changing the nappy as a small, irksome thing and he was focused on the evening event he was going to. However, he had said that he would help and share the responsibility of getting the children ready for bed. During couples therapy Andy reflected on this incident and realised that he had promised to help get the children ready for bed, and he had reneged on his commitment. Andy had not been faithful with this 'little thing', which he realised was just as important to God, if not more important, than attending a church event.

Afterwards Andy was able to activate what Robert Moore and Douglas Gillette (1990) would call the 'King' archetype, and utilise some of this energy in helping to provide order with regards to household chores. For men, the 'King' archetype is a masculine role that has certain functions, one being ordering and sorting your kingdom, which for Andy in this instance was his home life.

Moore and Gillette (1990) warn us, '... *we see in modern dysfunctional families that when there is an immature, weak, or an absent father and the King energy is not sufficiently present, the family is very often given over to disorder and chaos.'* (p.58). Andy had previously been quite absent from the family and had focused a lot of his energies on work, which had certainly resulted in a wearing away of togetherness and order in his family life. When Andy was able to be more present again (both emotionally and physically) and confidently take up his responsibilities as 'King' and give some of his energy to his family and his domestic kingdom, this helped to restore a sense of order and calm.

I am reminded of the saying, which highlights the value of home: *'an Englishman's home is his castle,'* (of course, this phrase can apply to all nationalities and to women as well as men). So making sure that you are both present and jointly involved in sorting out your domestic kingdom is important. A wife may also feel compelled to spend a lot of time and energy at work. If this is the case she may also need to ensure that she doesn't overlook her responsibilities as 'Queen' of the domestic kingdom and neglect her ability to sort and order her home life alongside her spouse.

Power and feelings of superiority: a stumbling block to the soulful care of the home

You may be aware of the powerful story in the Gospels of Jesus washing the disciples' feet. Jesus is sometimes referred to as our *'Servant King'* and we can understand why this unusual phrase is used when Jesus undertakes this very domestic act. The story of the washing of the disciples' feet will help us to reflect on our attitude to menial tasks like washing, cleaning and getting rid of the dirt – both physical and spiritual. First of all, the Bible sets the scene for what is about to take place.

> *Before the Passover celebration, Jesus knew that his hour had come to leave this world and return to his Father. He had loved his disciples during his ministry on earth, and now he loved them to the very end. It was time for supper... So he got up from the table, took off his robe, wrapped a towel around his waist, and poured water into a basin...*
>
> — John 13:1–5

Jesus seems to be preparing to say goodbye to the disciples he loves and so he disrobes and takes the position of a servant. Jesus does this just before the famous 'last supper' that he shares with his disciples and so we can see what a significant moment this is. It's interesting to note that Jesus takes his robe off in order to wash the disciples' feet; it may have been possible to perform the task with his robe on. It makes me think about how what we wear can often be related to status and identity. When Jesus prepares to wash the disciples' feet, it is as if he is demonstrating that he is prepared to put who he is to one side and immerse himself in this domestic act.

In my gap year when I was 18, I went to Zimbabwe for six months and worked and lived with African families in townships, and from this experience I understand how necessary it would have been in Biblical times to have one's feet washed. The roads that we walked along were often filled with red dust. At the end of one day a pastor, who had dropped me off in the morning and was picking my team mates and I up in the afternoon, looked down at my feet, which were caked in bright red dust, and said, *'I know how hard you have worked today – I can tell by your feet!'* How I would have loved to have had my feet washed.

What happens next in the Gospel account is written so simply but, to my mind, seems like such a gentle, generous act – a real gift that Jesus wants to give. We are told,

> *Then he began to wash the disciples' feet, drying them with the towel he had around him.*
>
> — John 13:5

So what do the disciples make of this? Peter boldly speaks up and perhaps expresses some of the discomfort and embarrassment that the other disciples may have been feeling about Jesus performing this act.

> *When Jesus came to Simon Peter, Peter said to him, 'Lord, are you going to wash my feet?' Jesus replied, 'You don't understand now what I am doing, but someday you will.' 'No,' Peter protested, 'you will never ever wash my feet!'*
>
> — John 13:6–8

Now, why did Peter feel so uncomfortable about this? He wouldn't have minded if an actual servant washed his feet. It was perhaps because Jesus' position and status made Peter think that this wasn't a fitting chore for him to perform. I think this potentially gives us some insight into our own reactions about performing chores. We may see chores as being lowly in status and issues around pride may prevent us from wanting to soulfully care for our home. Feelings of superiority may make it feel difficult to disrobe and set aside our identity of a 'high-earning professional', so that we can wholeheartedly become a 'dishwasher' and enter the ritual of performing a household task.

Jesus of course explains why it is necessary for him to wash the disciples' feet and highlights the importance of this act:

> *Jesus replied, 'Unless I wash you, you won't belong to me.' Simon Peter exclaimed, 'Then wash my hands and head as well, Lord, not just my feet!' Jesus replied, 'A person who has bathed all over does not need to wash, except for the feet…' After washing their feet, he put on his robe again and sat down and asked, 'Do you understand what I was doing? You call me "Teacher" and "Lord," and you are right,*

because that's what I am. And since I, your Lord and Teacher, have washed your feet, you ought to wash each other's feet. I have given you an example to follow. Do as I have done to you.'

— John 13:8–15

Jesus is symbolically showing us that it is good to disrobe and metaphorically wash one another's feet. When we are thinking about soulfully caring for the home, preparing to 'disrobe' and fully enter into the act of performing household tasks is something for us to aim for.

The writer Thomas Moore has had a very interesting life, first as a monk for a number of years before leaving to enter the secular world where he later got married and had children. He also, amongst many other things, trained as a Jungian therapist. In his book, *Care of the Soul*, he talks about his experiences of being asked to perform tasks and chores as a novice monk. He writes:

> *... I was given the job of pruning apple trees. It was a cold day in Wisconsin, and I was out on a limb sawing away at shoots sticking up on limbs all around me like minarets. I took a minute to rest, hoping the limb wouldn't suddenly break, and I asked myself, 'Why am I doing this? I am supposed to be learning prayer, meditation, Latin and Gregorian chant. But here I am, my hands frostbitten, feeling not terribly secure in the top of a tree, my fingers bloody from an erratic saw blade, doing something I knew nothing about.*

— Moore, 1992, p.181

I love his very human response to being placed in that situation, and I think we also can question the purpose of doing household tasks while feeling that we should really be getting on with something more meaningful. Just as Thomas Moore was thinking that what he really needed to be doing was learning to meditate, we too may end up thinking to ourselves that we should be getting on with some proper work, not housework. However, Thomas Moore (1992) goes on to tell us,

> *The answer, I already knew, was that work is an important component of the spiritual life.*

— p.181

In monasteries and convents, taking part in chores is seen as a way of taking part in the spiritual life of the place: practical tasks are not seen as separate from spiritual tasks. In fact, attending to household tasks as a form of spiritual work can build up our character and deepen a sense of spirituality in our everyday life. Moore (1992) helps to make this link, stating,

> *We all know that at some level daily work affects character and the overall quality of life, but we usually overlook the way soulfulness can adhere to ordinary housework and the gifts that it can bring to the soul.*
>
> — p.180

We will return to thinking about the soulfulness that we can find in the everyday rituals of home life; but before we do, I think it is important to explore the influence of power dynamics a bit further as we consider what happens when one partner offers to 'help out' the other.

The dangers of the 'helping out syndrome'

I was really struck when I read about what Kristina LaCelle-Peterson calls: the 'helping out syndrome'. It can be dangerous when couples get into this pattern of sharing household tasks where they believe they are 'helping out' the other person. Of course it is good to want to help one another, but what I think may be underlying this particular attitude is feelings of superiority and thoughts like, *'Well, I'll help you out, but it's not really my job, so I expect you to be grateful.'* It's a kind of *'I'm doing you a favour'* mentality, and because of this you may expect a certain level of recognition or praise for the tasks that you have performed. Once again, it's linking back to a sense of superiority. However, when Jesus was washing the disciples' feet, you don't get a sense that he was trying to say, *'Okay guys, I'm helping you out here, I hope you appreciate this!'* It was a gift that he was giving out of love; a domestic act that he immersed himself in fully.

In her book, *Liberating Tradition* (2008), Kristina LaCelle-Peterson points out that when spouses fully enter into a task, then each partner often finds it a much more rewarding experience. She talks eloquently about the concept of co-parenting and how superficially we may believe in this principle;

however, books are often targeted at women regarding how they can balance having children and going to work. She argues that as a society, if we truly believed in co-parenting then these books and dilemmas would be geared towards men as well and how they can balance work with parenting.

Kristina LaCelle-Peterson notes that there are subtle ideas in our society about women being more competent when it comes to parenting and looking after children. For example, the fact that it's the woman who carries the baby for nine months may make women feel on some level that they are more of the expert. Consequently, a woman may then give subtle directions to her husband about what to do with the child, or imply that he isn't doing it quite right or should do it her way (Kristina LaCelle-Peterson, 2008).

When a woman responds to a man in this way, it may undermine his efforts and interfere with the possibility of true co-parenting. This in turn feeds into the helping-out syndrome, where the husband 'helps out' his wife, who is seen as the expert. LaCelle-Peterson points out that young children are very resilient and can thrive despite a task not being done 'just so'. Therefore, if this is an issue in a couple relationship, it may be important for the woman to take a step back and provide the space that their husband needs so that he can fully take part in co-parenting.

Of course, women are also guilty of adopting a 'helping out' attitude with their husbands, which can lead to feelings of resentment. The 'helping out syndrome' doesn't just apply to men. There may be household tasks that a wife performs, where she feels that she is 'helping out' her husband and he should be grateful. It is important to try to move away from this 'helping out' attitude, beneath which resentment can simmer under the surface.

However, if you feel that there isn't enough balance and equal sharing of household chores, you may rightly feel overwhelmed or stressed by the situation. If this is the case, sitting down and negotiating the 'kitchen sink dilemmas' around who does what, is a mature, adult, practical thing that you can do together. This is not about asking your partner to 'help you out', but trying to move towards jointly sharing the responsibility of soulfully caring for the home.

In Chapter 2, I talked about how the couple relationship can be viewed as an entity in itself, and introduced the idea of the marital triangle. The marital triangle helps to highlight that there are two equal claimants not only to the benefits of the relationship, but to the role of 'guardian' and 'protector' of the relationship's needs (Ruszczynski, 2004). See Figure 7 below.

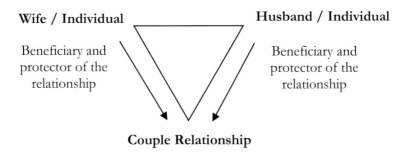

Wife / Individual   **Husband / Individual**

Beneficiary and   Beneficiary and
protector of the   protector of the
relationship   relationship

Couple Relationship

Figure 7: the marital triangle

The marital triangle was a helpful concept for Tom, who realised that he'd been making lots of withdrawals and reaping the benefits of the couple relationship; namely leaving Lucy to do most of the housework. He acknowledged that he had failed to protect the couple relationship and in some ways been greedy and just taken what he wanted. Tom had leaned into Lucy, and seeing Lucy as an extension of himself he thought it was fine for her to live up to his expectations of being a 'domestic goddess'. Taking a step back, Tom realised there needed to be more balance and saw how his previous attitude had been weakening their couple relationship and depleting the reserves that they jointly needed.

Reconnecting with the home and reconnecting with each other

I think that it can be easy to disconnect from the soulfulness that we can find in home life, just as it can be easy to disconnect from the spiritual in everyday life as we get caught up in being busy. In Western culture we value doing and achieving, so pausing and stopping to soulfully care for the home as a couple can present a challenge.

In the case of Jenny and Mike, Jenny had somewhat disconnected herself from the home, instead she focused a lot of her energy on being a lawyer. This was tricky for Mike and Jenny and they ended up having quite a few 'kitchen sink dilemmas' as a result. One of Mike's bug bears was that Jenny would randomly move his pupils' papers that needed marking and then forget where she had put them. Whilst doing this she would often be thinking about her own work and upcoming court cases. Jenny's mind was in the world of work and not resting in the home or thinking about Mike.

The way this was resolved was that Mike took over a dedicated shelf in the home for his papers. The agreement was that if Jenny found some of Mike's teaching work lying around and she wanted to clear it away, then she would put it on Mike's shelf where he could easily find it. Interestingly this meant that Jenny had to clear one of the shelves of her books because she had taken up the majority of the shelf space. Jenny wasn't too pleased about having to do this to begin with, but gradually her mind was drawn back to thinking about the home and soulfully caring for it with Mike.

For Tom, caring for the home presented a big challenge. He had grown up in a poor environment, where the furniture was often second-hand, and he hadn't been shown by his parents how to soulfully care for the home. As previously mentioned, he leaned on Lucy and expected her to be the 'domestic goddess' in their home. For Lucy, this was a lot of pressure, and because she also worked full-time she needed Tom to stop leaning on her and share the task of caring for the home.

The other factor that was having an impact on Lucy and Tom's relationship was that in Tom's family of origin there had been a fairly traditional model of marriage, where his mum did the housework and chores. At some level, this reinforced the idea in Tom's mind that he shouldn't really have to focus much energy on the tasks at home. This is an important point, because the families of origin that we grow up in can heavily influence not only how we view housework, but how domestic tasks may end up being divided because of gender.

In fact, our parents' relationship and our grandparents' relationship may have unconsciously formed in our minds a 'couple ideal', something that was explored in Chapter 4. So from the role models of our parents/grandparents, there may unconsciously be an ideal in your mind about what tasks a husband, or a wife should perform around the home. Therefore, if your spouse cannot live up to this image of what your ideal couple relationship should look like, then (like Tom) you may start to resent your spouse; and (like Lucy) you may feel overwhelmed by the pressure of having to live up to this ideal.

Gradually, through the process of therapy, Tom talked about domestic tasks that he found pleasure in and came to realise that he enjoyed cooking, and in fact was pretty good at it. Previously, he had expected Lucy to do all the cooking, as he had looked after all of their finances. However, Lucy overcame her fears about money, and she started to take care of their household finances with Tom. At the same time Tom was beginning to integrate his *Anima* side (see Chapter 7) and was learning how to nurture himself and others, so cooking took on a new meaning for him.

Over time, cooking meals for himself and Lucy became a ritual of home life that Tom found deeply satisfying. It's important to note that as with any change, it can take time for doing a new domestic task to feel normal or feel that it doesn't require such a massive push of effort to complete. It is only natural for it to take time and practise – similar to a Christian trying to get into a routine of prayer and meditation – it can take time for us to adjust, tune in to what we are doing and find meaning in the process.

Finding sacredness in the everyday

It is easy to overlook the sacredness that can be found in everyday life, in particular when performing chores. Thomas Moore (1992) points out that:

> *Care of the soul requires ongoing attention to every aspect of life. Essentially it is a cultivation of ordinary things in such a way that the soul is nurtured and fostered. Therapy tends to focus on crises or chronic problems. I've never heard anyone come to therapy and say that they want to discuss gardening or to examine the soul issues in a house they're building…Yet all these things have a great deal to do with the condition of the soul.*
>
> — p.177

Tending to the garden and tending to our house carefully is good for our soul. Therefore, it may be interesting to think about the products that you use to clean your home, the plants that you have in your garden, whether they help to feed your soul in the way that they look, bloom and smell. In addition to this, things like the materials or fabrics that you choose to buy for your home, or the pictures and art on the walls, or the quality of the plates that you eat your food from may all help to connect you with your soul.

Once again, I am reminded of the importance of being good stewards and caring for our surroundings in Thomas Moore's reference to a therapist called Jean Lall, he tells us:

> *She calls housework a 'path of contemplation' and says that if we denigrate the work that is to be done around the house every day, from cooking to doing laundry, we lose our attachment to our immediate world. There is also a close relationship, she says, between daily work around the house and responsibility to our natural environment.*
> — Moore, 1992, p.178

It is easy to denigrate housework and view it as unimportant, which is why I think the idea of soulfully caring for the home brings a helpful perspective on domestic life. Thomas Moore states that tending to household tasks attentively and with an eye for detail can be of great value to the soul. Furthermore, he states that disconnecting ourselves from the home and daily housework may induce a sense of isolation, loneliness or homelessness. This may be helpful to consider, particularly if you are not feeling 'at home' where you live. If this is the case, then it may be helpful to evaluate whether there is scope for you to dedicate more care and attention towards the domestic rituals and chores of home life. Soulfully caring for our homes is likely to help us to feel more 'at home' and at peace with our surroundings.

Spiritually examining your home: what would your house say?

After Thomas Moore had given a lecture at a conference one day, a housewife approached him and asked him if he would come and spiritually examine her house to see what it said about herself and her soul (Moore, 1992). This wasn't something that he had done before, but as a therapist he was used to thinking with clients about images in dreams and what they may symbolically mean, so he agreed to this new venture. He describes his aims and hopes for this exercise as he walked around the lady's home:

> *My idea was to see the house's poetry and alphabet, to understand the gestures it was making in its architecture, colours, furnishings, decorations, and the condition it was*

in at that particular time. The woman was truly devoted to her home and wanted to give housework a place of dignity in her life.

— Moore, 1992, p.178

Thomas Moore didn't make any particular interpretations about this woman's house, rather personal stories came up about the home and he noted that the bathroom was particularly immaculate and thought about this image with her (Moore, 1992). However, his purpose was just to try to

…glimpse signs of the soul that lies hidden in the everyday and commonplace.

— Moore, 1992, p.179

I found this concept interesting and immediately began to think about how the condition of my home may reflect aspects of my soul and the state that it is in. Thomas Moore (1992) tells us:

The home is a place of daily work, whether or not one has an 'outside' job. If you were to read your own house, you would find yourself standing before the tools of housework: vacuum cleaner, broom, dust mop, soaps, sponges, dishpan, hammer, screwdriver. These things are very simple, yet they are fundamental to the feeling we have of being at home.

— p.179

As a couple, both partners may feel more 'at home' if time, care and attention is dedicated to soulfully caring for domestic life together; purposefully not denigrating these tasks, but rather giving them a special place in your lives. I wonder if it is possible for couples to reach a place of completing household rituals and tasks feeling like domestic priests and domestic priestesses jointly caring for the sacred space of home together. At the start of the chapter the quotation tells us that:

The ordinary acts we practice every day at home are of more importance to the soul than their simplicity might suggest.

I hope that as you go through the 'Joint Reflection Points' below you are able to delve more into the truths of this statement for your marriage.

Joint Reflection Points

1. Discuss together the kitchen sink dilemmas that you may need to resolve at this moment in time. Are there any aspects of domestic life that you feel resentful about or outstanding household issues that have not been fully resolved? Sit down together and write a plan for assigning tasks and working this out in a way that seems fair and equal for you both.

    Next, try to think about the details that will make your plans successful. And if there is a simple practical solution to the dilemma, like buying a new piece of household equipment that will help with the task. Agree a time frame in which things will be done and hold each other accountable to this in a loving way. Finally, make a time to review your plan together and re-set your goals if needed. If the agreed plans have not worked out, discuss the details of what you each need to do in order to improve the outcome for you both.

2. Do you ever fall into the trap of the 'helping out' syndrome? In what particular areas of your life does this tend to happen? How could you move away from this attitude to a deeper sense of shared engagement?

3. How have your parents' relationship and your family of origin influenced the way you view the home, parenting, finances, or housework? How has your family background influenced the way you view a husband's/wife's role in caring for the home? Do you think you have formed a 'couple ideal' of what a husband or wife should do? Use your genograms if you would like to, to think about male/female role models from your respective families *(See Chapter 1 'Joint Reflection Points' for the genogram exercise if you haven't already completed this).*

4. Do either of you tend to denigrate housework and caring for the home, perhaps viewing it as an irksome or unimportant task? How could you move towards an attitude of soulfully caring for the home more? Are there particular aspects of domestic life that you could dedicate more care and attention to?

5. For some people the materials, fabrics, windows, decorations and objects in an old church building often appear beautiful and help their soul connect with God – from the stained glass windows, to beautiful carvings, candles, aromatic smells of incense, and ornate cups and plates used for Holy Communion. What objects do you have in your home, or plants in your garden, that help to provide a sense of beauty and connection for your soul? Take some time to explore together whether you would like to buy one or two things for your home or garden that would give you pleasure and lift your souls. This could be something small and inexpensive, like an aromatic candle made out of a scent that you both enjoy, a plant, or some other type of furnishings.

6. If someone like Thomas Moore was to walk around the rooms of your home and make some helpful observations, what do you think the rooms would reveal about the state of your soul and the state of your souls as a couple?

Spiritual Reflection Points

1.   Thank God for your home. Pray together for forgiveness for any times when feelings of pride, superiority or resentment may have got in the way of soulfully caring for the home together.

2.   Meditate on the verse below and ask God if there are any small things around the home that you could dedicate your time and attention to more. Share with each other any thoughts or ideas that you have.

> *If you are faithful in little things, you will be faithful in large ones. But if you are dishonest in little things, you won't be honest with greater responsibilities.*
> — Luke 16:10

3.   Pray for each other and ask God to help you both to enter into household tasks with a spirit of love and generosity, following the example of Jesus:

> *And since I, your Lord and Teacher, have washed your feet, you ought to wash each other's feet. I have given you an example to follow. Do as I have done to you.*
> — John 13:14–15

Part Four

Marriage: a sexual and soulful experience

Chapter 10

Soulful sex

The whole sphere of sex – emotion, body, fantasy, and
relationship – falls within the domain of soul.

Souls Mates, *Thomas Moore*

How do we enter the labyrinth of soulful sex? Finding our own erotic sexual path that connects with our soul is an exciting journey; it requires us to trust our instincts as we feel and sense our way forward. There is no magical answer for creating spellbinding sex, but perhaps the hidden magic and intimacy of sex, and ways to create this are not so far out of our reach as we may think. In this chapter I will highlight different ways and exercises that you could try in order to deepen the level of sexual intimacy in your marriage. You have probably heard the classic saying that 'the eyes are the window to your soul', so I will also explore how gazing into our partner's eyes relates to sexual attunement and soulful connection, and the related exercises will provide some erotic food for thought.

I decided to start what I informally refer to as the 'sex chapters' of this book with 'Soulful sex' because it starts us off on a high note, and provides the opportunity to wholeheartedly immerse ourselves in the delights that sex has to offer us; a gift God has given us to enjoy. There are plenty of complex areas surrounding sex and intimacy, that will be explored in Chapters 11 and 12. But for now, I want to pause, and give you space to explore the possibilities of a deeper, erotic connection with your spouse.

It's worth bearing in mind that the ideas presented in this chapter are laid out simply to inspire you, not to provide an ideal for you to try to live up to. So please do not place any pressure on yourselves to be having regular, mind-blowing sex. My hope is that this chapter will provide you with ideas that will excite you and that you can experiment with them in order to connect with your spouse in new, meaningful ways.

I will be introducing some new concepts from Dr Schnarch (2009), such as 'touching with feeling', and how 'doing' and 'being done' can help a couple to erotically find one another. The spiritual and erotic aspects in this chapter are amplified by the imagery and hidden meaning in the young lovers' conversations depicted in a book in the Bible called the *Song of Songs*. This book is filled with poetry and focuses on the young lovers' erotic adventures. The lovers' story from centuries ago has inspired me to think about how we can be more erotic and soulful in our sexual encounters. Hopefully, this will help to take you deeper into the labyrinth and deeper into finding the soul of sex in your relationship.

Before we get underway, I think it's important to briefly explore possible barriers to exploring soulful sex, such as family upbringing and family attitudes towards sex, which may at some level have permeated our consciousness. This may influence us deeply and have an impact on the permission we then give ourselves to embrace an erotic, soulful sex life. As much as we like to think we're our own person, it's surprising how the views of significant others can rub off on us. For Christians, church culture and the way that sex has been talked about (or not talked about) by important authority figures, such as ministers or priests, may also have a bearing on our attitude towards sex. Over time multiple factors can culminate and may either present barriers to soulful sex or may help us have a soulful, erotic sex life with our partner.

Another important factor to consider is whether we believe that sex and the soul can co-exist together and what our culture and society has to say about this. Culturally and historically a division has often been made between the body and the soul and things have been categorised as either spiritual or physical; heavenly or earthly. Historically, in the Christian culture there has been this divide; and in many other religious traditions the idea of denying earthly desires in order to focus on the spiritual side of life has been promoted and seen as the way to truly live out one's faith. However, this attitude is unbalanced and if followed to the extreme, would result in us living a very lopsided existence.

There is another aspect of Christian culture to consider. Christian couples prior to marriage are often encouraged to abstain from sex and remain virgins until the wedding night. I think this may potentially set up an unhelpful idea early on in marriage, that being sensual and sexual with one another should be moderated. The pressure not to have sex and to suppress sexual desire until marriage may generate not only elicit excitement, but also a wariness and anxiety around sex. Prior to marriage, not having sex is seen as a way of living a godly, spiritual life as a couple. However, once married, Christian couples experience what Jung refers to as 'enantiodromia', which means a complete turnaround or 'flipflop' in attitude, where sex suddenly becomes an act which is spiritually good to participate in.

Erotic intelligence

So how do we start to find our own way towards soulful sex, trusting our instincts to guide us? In his book, *The Soul of Sex* (1998), Thomas Moore points out that people often encounter sexual confusion because they feel timid in the face of their desires and sexual fantasies. However, he advocates trying to develop 'erotic intelligence': non-judgementally weighing up whether it would be good to follow these feelings if they make sense in terms of the values and commitments that we hold, instead of dismissing them out of hand.

This feeling of timidity and potential dismissal of an erotic sex life may also be influenced by our family upbringing. It is useful to think about what subtle messages you may have picked up about sex from your family and parents, and what some of your early exposure to sexual things may have been. For Tom, he had strong sexual feelings for Lucy, but was often reticent about exploring ways to cultivate and deepen their intimacy through sex. One of Tom's earliest and most embarrassing memories was accidentally walking into his parents' bedroom whilst they were having sex, when he 'should' have been playing outdoors with his brothers. However, this incident wasn't even spoken about, Tom wasn't criticised or told off as he would have been for other things. In fact, the topic of sex wasn't spoken about at all in his family.

His father hadn't taken him aside to explain sexual matters, instead it had been left to the school to provide Tom with the sex education that he needed. There was a repressed silence around sexual matters, which left Tom feeling embarrassed, uncertain, and a little lost at times when it came to talking about sex or feeling able to share his sexual fantasies with Lucy.

Consequently, although Tom loved having sex with Lucy, there was an underlying embarrassment and Tom definitely felt timid about attempting anything that was too sexually adventurous. Consciously, this attitude was covered up and Tom reassured himself that he didn't need to talk about sex, it was manlier just to get on with it and 'do it'. Also, during his teenage years Tom heard a lot of Christian talks at youth camps, which reinforced the importance of having 'sexually pure' thoughts, which on some level confirmed for Tom that there was something almost shameful about his sexual desires. Recognising where some of his feelings and unhelpful thoughts about sex came from was useful for Tom and freed him to cultivate his own 'erotic intelligence'.

For some people the divide between body and soul still exists and it can be hard for some to fully embrace the soulfulness that sex can offer. Yet, Thomas Moore in his book, *The Soul of Sex* (1998) reminds us how important this is:

> *One of the first achievements to be made in the reconciliation of body and spirit, which is a prerequisite for a deepened, soul-filled sexuality, is a rediscovery of the virtue and value of the body's eroticism.*

> — p.23

Enjoying the sensuousness of our bodies and the mysteries and delights that they have to offer us in sex is one way of reconciling body and soul. We will be able to explore this later in more depth when we examine the subtle and hidden sensual nuances that are revealed in the poetry of the *Song of Songs*.

Sexual desire, touch and the eyes to the soul

Sexual desire and a sense of erotic connection are important for partners and this takes place within the context of the couple relationship. Attachment theory and related research has helped to show us that when we look into our lover's eyes, connect, and touch or caress one another, 'mirror neurons' are being stimulated in our brains. It's the sensory input we receive from our partner, as we gaze at them, and absorb what they are doing. We notice the loving intentions in their movements, and this results in 'mirror neurons' firing and sending signals to our brain.

Something very similar happens in the parent–infant relationship – when a parent is attuned to their baby, they may hold them in a certain way or rock them and gaze into their eyes. This too, triggers 'mirror neurons' to start firing; it aids brain development in the child, and helps bonding to develop. A secure sense of attachment is then formed.

Researchers have found that the processes involved in adult attachment in couple relationships are very similar to those in the parent–child relationship. Touch, gaze, and attunement all help to create a secure base for an adult sexual relationship. Attunement means being emotionally and physically present so that you are available and can respond to your partner's emotional/physical cues and the signals that they send you – whether that be directly, or indirectly through movement and body language.

In his book, *Passionate Marriage*, Dr Schnarch expands upon the idea of attunement and highlights the necessity of being fully present whilst trying to connect with your partner through touch. Otherwise we end up with what he refers to as, *'touching without feeling'* (Schnarch, 2009, p.218).

Dr Schnarch helps us to think about really slowing down when we touch our partner in order for us to be able to touch our spouse so that we truly feel them, which allows sexual vibes to be sparked. He points out that all too often in our society we touch without feeling. Perhaps as a defence or way to avoid connection, or perhaps due to our busyness and goal-focused behaviour, we move so quickly that we do not feel the other person. This, of course translates to sex, which may end up being slotted into a busy day, or we may end up so focused on reaching the goal of orgasm, that we fail to really touch and connect with our spouse.

Dr Schnarch describes an interesting experiment that he used to do when he taught human sexuality to medical students. He called it a demonstration on touching and would typically ask for two male volunteers to come forward. One person was asked to be the receiver and the other the giver of touch. The giver was then asked to caress the other person's hand. Dr Schnarch reveals that he deliberately picked two men because he hypothesised that they would have most difficulty touching the other person and allowing themselves to actually feel them. This was indeed usually the case and Dr Schnarch recalls how often medical students would briskly rub and even scour the other person's hand, finding it difficult to respond to his instructions to slow down. If the student actually reached a point when they really felt the other person, the change in atmosphere was dramatic: in fact, Dr Schnarch relayed that students often suddenly stopped touching if they reached this place of connection.

A more mature male student took part in this experiment one day and he allowed himself to really try and touch the other student, who appeared highly embarrassed by his efforts (Schnarch, 2009). Sometime afterwards he spoke to Dr Schnarch and told him that the experiment had made him realise that he often touched his son without feeling. In fact, it made him aware that he engaged in a lot of rough and tumble play as a way of touching without feeling. He realised that this was because he was fearful of turning his son into a 'sissy'. He told Dr Schnarch that his son had been diagnosed with hyperactivity disorder, but had been unusually calm and settled since he had been able to touch him with feeling and he had connected with him emotionally through touch. I think that this story highlights the power and importance of touching with feeling in our relationships.

For Andy, sex was often slotted into his busy schedule, although he of course wanted to leave Rose feeling satisfied from sex, he applied his workaholic attitude towards maintaining a regular sex life and trying to ensure as much as he could that Rose climaxed. When he was a child touch, hugs, and embraces reduced following his father's accident and interactions with his parents gradually became brusquer over time. Similarly, Andy and Rose's sex life was pretty brusque, it was something that Andy tried to do before having to go to work or see to the children.

Rose, too, had grown up with little physical affection, touch or cuddles, so it was difficult for her to initiate connecting with Andy through touch. In lots of ways Andy and Rose were like 'babes in the wood', wandering around lost together in the woods, with no idea of how they were going to get to the place where they could really connect with each other through touch. Andy worked hard at making Rose feel aroused, but the pace of their lovemaking left very little time and space for Andy to really feel Rose or vice-versa. In lots of ways Andy and Rose were 'touching without feeling'.

Being emotionally and physically present during sex is important. Dr Schnarch (2009) talks about this further:

> *When couples stop sending and receiving sexual vibes, they are touching without feeling. This pattern surfaces in the myriad repetitive patterns of touch that wear out your skin (and your patience). Being on the giving end isn't much better. Touching your partner while he or she is mentally 'absent' is living proof that sex isn't inherently intimate (or erotic).*
>
> — p.218

Often Andy would be emotionally absent whilst having sex and his mind would drift off to other things. Dr Schnarch (2009) refers to this as blocking your emotional connection to your spouse whilst having sex and says, *'It's how you withhold yourself from someone even while you're bringing him or her to orgasm.'* (p.218). When Andy started to realise what had been taking place emotionally in his relationship he began to acknowledge how unsure he was, at times, of really connecting with Rose.

He realised that if he was more emotionally open and connected with Rose during sex he was at risk of exposing himself and having to acknowledge that he wanted her, which would leave him feeling vulnerable. For a number of years Andy had suppressed his desire to be connected through touch. After all, he had grown accustomed to receiving little physical affection from his parents. Gradually, Andy started to withhold less of himself from Rose during sex and was able to withdraw some of the erotic, passionate energy that he ploughed into work, which enabled him to be more present with Rose as they made love.

The other main problem that Dr Schnarch highlights is our approach to sex and our focus on our own sensations instead of trying to emotionally connect with and tune into our partner during sex. He describes it well:

> *Lots of people withdraw into their sensations when they're having sex and break contact with their partner, who becomes a travel agent sending them on a trip. They*

give instructions like they are sending back travel postcards saying 'Everything's wonderful. Rub just a little to the left. Glad you're not here.'
— Schnarch, 2009, p.220

One way to counteract this problem is to stop trying to tune out your partner during sex, but rather to open yourself up to them; try to touch them with feeling, and emotionally tune into them. Dr Schnarch advocates having 'Eyes-Open Sex' and 'Eyes-Open Orgasm' as a way of connecting with your partner during sex. Looking at our partner during sex can help to bring about a deeper emotional connection, which is not surprising since the eyes have often been recognised as windows to the soul. In his book, *The Soul of Sex*, Thomas Moore (1998) tells us:

Sexual attraction is not at all a purely physical event. The soul is always in search of whatever will complete its desire, and our physical eyes are never separate from the eyes of the soul.

— p.9

Looking and gazing at our partner during sex and even at the point of orgasm is one way for us to bridge the body and soul divide as we simultaneously experience our bodily sexual pleasure whilst connecting to the spirit and emotion of our partner. Gazing at our partner during sex and point of climax is one way of entering into the sacred space of soulful sex.

However, Dr Schnarch points out that this may be difficult for some people who may tune out their partner and focus on their sensations during sex as a way of not having to confront problematic relationship issues. He says:

To feel comfortable looking each other in the eye, you'll probably have to confront conflicts that you've swept under the carpet, which is why some couples continue to have sex with their eyes closed. You aren't likely to let your partner look deep inside you until you've done that yourself. If you're avoiding your partner (or yourself) when you're out of bed, you're not likely to act differently between the sheets.
— Schnarch, 2009, p.227

Really seeing your partner during sex and letting yourself be seen is a potentially vulnerable and exposing situation. However, it is also a place where a deeper connection can occur. Dr Schnarch points out that it is a sign of differentiation when we feel able to invite our partner to really take a look inside of us and at our souls and to really let them know that we want them there.

Earlier on I referred to the importance of looking at our partner, gazing and touching and how this sensory input triggers 'mirror neurons' in our brain, which promotes bonding and attachment between ourselves and our spouse. Gazing at one another during sex, initially during foreplay and at different points during intercourse is one way to develop your erotic attunement with each another. Looking up and gazing at your partner as they caress, or sensually touch, lick or suck a part of your body is a way of soulfully connecting with each other during sex, instead of focusing on sensations and tuning each other out. 'Eyes-Open Sex' and 'Eyes-Open Orgasm' can be highly erotic for couples.

Some couples may like to gaze at each other intermittently during sex, taking a peep to look into the eyes of the other person and gaze at the sensual acts that you are engaged in. There may be ways in which you already connect deeply during foreplay or sex or times when you really touch with feeling. Trying out, 'Eyes-Open Sex' and 'Eyes-Open Orgasm' maybe something that you could add to your repertoire if you haven't already tried this.

Song of Songs and soulful sex

For those of you who may not know, *Song of Songs* is a book in the Bible depicting the awakening and fulfilment of erotic love between two young lovers. According to Hebrew scholars, Bloch and Bloch (2006) the author of this piece of poetry is unknown, although it was once thought to be King Solomon: however, this is not the case and the references to King Solomon in the poem are thought to highlight a sense of majesty and splendour in the fantasy world of the two lovers. I believe that this piece of Biblical poetry will help to highlight and confirm that erotic sex can be a soulful experience.

Bloch and Bloch have written a brilliant commentary and translation of *Song of Songs* into English, and they also provide the original Hebrew text. I will be quoting from their in-depth translation.

At the start of the poem, the young woman (referred to as the Shulamite) begins the dialogue and she declares:

> *Kiss me, make me drunk with your kisses!*
> *Your sweet loving*
> *Is better than wine*

— Song of Songs 1:2

For centuries the relationship between the two lovers was thought to be chaste and full of lustful longing, scholars had assumed that the lovers were not sexually active or intimate with one another (Bloch & Bloch, 2006). However, the original Hebrew informs us that this isn't the case; the word *dodim*, occurs six times in *Song of Songs* and is translated as 'love', but actually refers specifically to sexual love (Bloch & Bloch, 2006). In fact, the plural of *dodim* refers to the entirety of what comprises sexual lovemaking – caresses, foreplay, and intercourse (Bloch & Bloch, 2006). So at the beginning of the Song, in the verse quoted above, we hear the young woman declare: 'Your *dodim* (sexual loving) is better than wine.' And what a risqué statement. Not one that I necessarily expected to come across in the Bible.

Slightly later we hear about the lovers embracing each other, and once again the Hebrew clearly highlights this as a sexual embrace:

> *His left hand beneath my head*
> *his right arm*
> *holding me close.*

— Song of Songs 2:6

Bloch and Bloch point out that the original Hebrew word *habbeq* means 'a sexual embrace' and is used elsewhere in the Bible to denote this (for example, Proverbs 5:20). So the scene of the lovers embracing is part of the sensual, erotic activity that is taking place between them. The whole of the poem is filled with sexual imagery and metaphors, using nature, landscape and flowers to depict their blossoming erotic love. There is a complete lack of anxiety between the lovers or fear or hesitancy, instead there is a joyful exuberance and delight in one another's body. Their interactions and the wording of the poem provides us with hints and ideas about how we too, could live a more exuberant, erotic sex life with our partner.

Early on in this chapter I talked about the need to be emotionally and physically present in order to be sexually intimate and attuned to your partner during sex. The two lovers show how important it is to withdraw from the world and create time and space to be alone together sexually.

And he calls to me:
Hurry, my love, my friend,
and come away!

— Song of Songs 2:10

There is an urgency and excitement around the two lovers getting away from it all, withdrawing from the world in order to be with each other sexually. We hear similar cries of 'come away with me' throughout the poem and the need to be alone together in a sacred sexual space is a strong pull for both lovers.

If we think back to Andy and Rose, before they entered couples therapy Andy would religiously make time for sex with Rose, but this was a rushed affair, slotted in before work demands took over. Also, Andy wasn't really fully emotionally and physically present, so in some respects part of him hadn't really 'come away' with Rose to the marriage bed to joyfully revel in erotic sex with her. Rose also hadn't really 'come away' with Andy, because sex had become so rushed Rose often took herself off into her own fantasy world, when they had sex. On some level Rose had sensed Andy's disconnection from her, so feeling overlooked once again, she sought comfort in her own fantasy world.

For all couples, withdrawing some of your energy from the world and daily hassles and routines and truly coming away with your partner is important. Thomas Moore (1998) who used to be a monk, before entering the secular world and marrying, points out how engaging in sex can take us out of 'clock time' and give the soul some needed rest from the pressures and demands of life:

Something deep in the human makeup needs and longs for a taste of eternity – at least a momentary release from the relentless pace of time … [The Soul] needs regular excursions out of a busy life, demanding relationships, and incessant productivity. For

the monk, contemplation is one kind of deliverance from clock time and busyness,
while for the average person sex can serve the same purpose.

— p.8

Entering a deeper sense of intimacy through sex can take our couple relationship to another level – it can almost feel like we have transcended earthly time and commitments as we enjoy a deeper level of sexual and soulful connection through the joining of our bodies.

Song of Songs – seeking and erotically finding one another

There is so much beautiful imagery in *Song of Songs*. In this next verse we can almost imagine the couple playing a game of hide and seek, with the young Shulamite woman playfully hiding from her lover. They are perhaps teasing one another in this game, and the anticipation builds as they both want to erotically find and be found by the other person.

My dove in the clefts of the rock,
in the shadow of the cliff,
let me see you, all of you!
Let me hear your voice,
your delicious song.
I love to look at you.

— Song of Songs 2:14

He compares her to a dove and tries to coax her out of her hiding place, and once again he is exuberant in his desire – it doesn't sound like he half-heartedly wants to see her and find her, rather he is wholehearted in his pursuit. He is pursuing her, but the young Shulamite woman isn't running away, part of her remains temptingly in view and you can imagine that she wants to be found (sexually) by him. Again, we are reminded of the deep soulful and sexual connection that can come from the eyes, and the lover's gaze when he says, *'let me see you, all of you!'*. There is a sense that he doesn't just want to look at her lustfully, but that he wants to look deeply at her, her body and soul.

Another interesting observation is that throughout the poem we hear how the lovers take turns seeking one another and calling out to one another to *'come away'*. There is a deep sense of mutuality and reciprocity in the lovers' interactions. We hear him cry out, *'Hurry, my love, my friend come away.'* (Song of Songs 2:13). Here, the young Shulamite woman is not only referred to as a lover, but as a friend, which underlines the reciprocity and equality in their sexual encounters (Bloch & Bloch, 2006).

The level of reciprocity and shared eagerness to connect with one another as lovers that is conveyed in *Song of Songs* provides a helpful example for us to try and follow. Of course, one partner may not feel 'in the mood' to connect sexually with their partner – they may be hiding, and, unlike the Shulamite woman, they don't want to be found (sexually).

Thomas Moore notes that an individual's desire to connect sexually may ebb and flow and it's good not to judge this, but rather be open to what your soul may be trying to tell you as a couple. The soul may be helping to highlight something that requires your attention; or this lack of sexual desire may help you to start considering other issues in your couple relationship, or for you as an individual that would be helpful to look at.

Dr Schnarch also acknowledges that there is often a *low desire* and a *high desire* partner when it comes to sex, and he points out the fact that it's the low desire partner who tends to control the level of sexual intimacy in the couple relationship. This type of dynamic may influence the extent to which there is a reciprocal seeking and sexual finding of one another in your marriage. How sex tends to influence, shape, and control levels of intimacy will be explored further in Chapter 11.

As we are thinking about seeking and finding our lover, it is interesting to see that at one point in *Song of Songs*, the Shulamite wants to see her lover, but when she wakes up he is not there. She responds by desperately searching for him, putting herself in danger as she leaves the safety of her home during the night.

I sought him everywhere
But could not find him.
I called his name
but he did not answer.

— Song of Songs 5:6

I find this a very poignant and moving scene as she tells us that when she awoke, her lover was gone, *'he had slipped away'* (Song of Songs 5:6) and she feels bereft and desperate without him. As a lone woman wandering around the streets at night looking for her lover, she is in a very vulnerable position and we find out that:

Then the watchmen found me
as they went about the city.
They beat me, they bruised me,
they tore the shawl from my shoulders
those watchmen of the walls.

— Song of Songs 5:7

I think that we too can lose our 'lover', whether that's losing our sense of sexual connection with our spouse or noticing that our partner's sexual desire for us has 'slipped away'. It's also possible that we may lose contact and connection with the adult, sexual 'lover' that is within ourselves and find that for some reason our own sexual desire has 'slipped away'.

This part of the poem may be trying to tell us that at times in our life we may need to go searching for our lost 'lover'. It can feel like a dangerous venture to seek out erotic desire and find it again. If you've awoken one morning to realise that the sexual spark has left your marriage, it may feel painful to broach this topic with your partner, or it may feel too difficult to venture out and make sexual moves towards rediscovering each other as lovers.

However, the rewards of rediscovering our lost 'lover' can be immense. It's perhaps the promise of finding the deep sexual intimacy and connection again with her lover that drives the young Shulamite woman through the streets at night. It is good to know that she recovers from this incident with the watchmen and finds her lover again and enjoys many more erotic adventures with him.

There is perhaps scope for all of us to take on some of the erotic energy of the young Shulamite woman in searching for our inner and outer lover, cultivating and rediscovering deeper intimacy through our sexual encounters with our spouse. One way of reciprocally taking turns to seek out and sexually find our partner is to consider what Dr Schnarch has to say about 'doing' and 'being done'. Of course, there are many other ways to reciprocally give and receive, or sexually seek and find our partner, but these ideas may provide you with some erotic food for thought.

There is a significant amount of turn-taking throughout *Song of Songs*: the different lines that the man and the young woman speak to each other; the hints at different sexual positions they would like to take in the imagery and metaphors that they describe; and the seeking and finding one another. 'Doing' and 'being done' presents us with another type of sexual turn-taking, giving to and receiving from your partner.

During one of your sexual encounters you may set out with the erotic intention of giving to your partner sexually and there may be many things you could do that you know would arouse and turn them on. This is not merely about having intercourse or bringing your partner to orgasm, but it's rather a passionate intention to really *do* your partner (Schnarch, 2009). Dr Schnarch (2009) describes 'doing' as involving the following five principles:

1. M*oving **into** your partner*

2. *Tasting his or her essence*

3. *Ravishing him/her with fervour and generosity*

4. *Sending him or her to the edge, and*

5. *Experiencing your own eroticism in the process.*

Doing *someone is pleasurable in itself, but your partner reciprocates by receiving.*

— p.264

In *Song of Songs*, each of these five principles is reflected in the verses. We certainly get a sense of each of the lovers ravishing the other with fervour and generosity. When you read the steamy, erotic verses it is also easy to imagine them sending each other to the edge sexually. In addition, the whole of the poem is filled with ideas of tasting one another. We hear the young

Shulamite woman say:

> *Let my lover come into his garden*
> *And taste its delicious fruit.*

— Song of Songs 4:16

Now this is a highly erotic metaphor, the garden is thought to represent the young woman's sexuality, and she is asking him to enter and taste its fruit or, in other words, taste her sexuality. So she is inviting him to move in and take possession of his garden, which reflects point *a) moving* **into** *your partner.* Also, in terms of 'tasting' the essence of your lover, there are a myriad of other examples in *Song of Songs,* such as:

> *His cheeks a bed of spices,*
> *a treasure of precious scents, his lips*
> *red lilies wet with myrrh.*

— Song of Songs 5:13

It's easy to imagine the two lovers from *Song of Songs* taking turns at either 'doing' or 'being done', particularly because they appear so uninhibited and free from sexual anxiety or worries about being vulnerable during sex. However, allowing oneself to 'be done' can be difficult and exposing as you open yourself up to receive and fully experience the emotions (and possible vulnerability) of what this feels like, without any attempt to actively give back in that moment. The way that you are giving back to your spouse is by receiving their sexual touch and the pleasure that they wish to give you.

'Being done' *'involves surrender, union, and the power of receiving.'* (Schnarch, 2009, p.266). It also requires a certain degree of letting go and allowing your partner to set the pace as they attempt to attune to you, explore your body, discover what gives you pleasure; and it's also about allowing them to find ways that they can truly touch you with feeling and fully and completely and passionately *do* you sexually. Allowing your partner to *do* you is a gift that you can give them, and it is usually a very erotic experience for the giver. For some people 'being done' may present more of an emotional challenge as they allow themselves to open up and be in the position of receiving from their spouse.

However, taking turns at 'doing' and 'being done' may be one way to erotically seek and find each other in your relationship.

Song of Songs – sacred spaces and the marriage bed

Throughout *Song of Songs*, we read about the lovers running away together to their secret hiding places. In fact, they use their imagination and turn the landscape around them into a beautiful, majestic setting for their lovemaking. We hear the young Shulamite woman say:

> *... My lover, my king, has brought me into his chambers...*
>
> — Song of Songs 4:1

Bloch and Bloch (2006) point out that in this verse the lovers are taking us into their world of fantasy and make believe as they provide for us an image of them entering the king's chambers. Because most of the lovers' sexual encounters seem to take place outdoors, Bloch and Bloch hypothesise that 'into his chambers' may be referring to a hidden, sheltered space perhaps in the vineyards or woods where they meet.

As modern-day lovers, we too may benefit from creating a sacred space for sex and using the surroundings in our bedrooms to facilitate this. Thomas Moore (1998) highlights the importance of the marriage bed, stating:

> *The sleeping, dreaming, talking and lovemaking that take place in the marriage bed weave the couple together.*
>
> — p.213

Personally, I love the story described in Homer's epic poem the *Odyssey* where we hear of Odysseus spotting an olive tree and deciding to build his marriage bed around this tree. He uses the tree trunk to create a beautiful bedpost and builds a bed chamber with a wall and door around the tree. In this telling of Odysseus and Penelope's marriage we glimpse at the importance of the marriage bed. Odysseus's efforts to create a unique space for their bed chamber and a beautiful, living, breathing marriage bed, provides an example of how we too can create a special place for our own marriage bed (Moore, 1998).

There is something sacred about the marriage bed. We can tell how important it is if we think about an affair happening in this space. This act tends to be universally condemned as there can be almost nothing worse than to find out that your partner has been unfaithful and has used the marriage bed to conduct the affair. This act seems sacrilegious as it defiles the sacred space – the Bible also reminds us of the importance of the marriage bed:

> *Marriage should be honoured by all, and the marriage bed kept pure…*
>
> — Hebrews 13:4

In *Song of Songs*, we often hear the lovers talk about their bed, and they also provide us with a glimpse of how the beauty of their imaginary bedchamber forms the perfect setting for their sexual encounters.

> *You are beautiful, my king,*
> *and gentle. Wherever we lie*
> *our bed is green.*
> *Our roof beams are cedar,*
> *our rafters fir.*
>
> — Song of Songs 1:16–17

Lying down together to embrace one another sexually in a beautiful space can help sex to feel soulful as our senses and imagination are stimulated. By doing this, we can end up creating a sacred space for sex. Thomas Moore (1998) has something very interesting and challenging to say about this matter:

> *Sex can become routine in marriage, especially if all the accoutrements remain plain and familiar; but if sex is seen as an art rather than mere self-expression or duty, then the whole of one's life can prepare for it and at the same time be carried on in the afterglow of sex. My ideal would be a couple making love in a bedroom, lovingly prepared for sex, in a house pulsing with the sexual sensations of color, aroma, and touch, in a world rich in sensuality that appropriately holds and sustains the couple's sexuality.*
>
> — p.216

Now you may be thinking, 'hold on, that's a lot to ask!' but I was thinking that it's interesting how we often plough a lot of energy into creating spaces for hospitality in our homes; or a playroom for children; or a music room, yet we perhaps don't put in the same amount of energy into cultivating a space for lovemaking in our bedrooms. However, when we dedicate a room for music, for instance, or for children to play in it can feel liberating and creates a different sort of space where music flows more freely, or children delight in playing. Perhaps we too, can find ways to dedicate our bedroom and marriage bed to the act of lovemaking, and create a space where being sensual with one another is promoted. Designing and putting energy into creating such a room can be one way to erotically prioritise your marriage.

Song of Songs – sexual fantasy and role play

Within the sacred, hidden space where the lovers meet we are often introduced to their fantasy world and the role play that they engage in during their lovemaking. Their lovemaking comes across as very sexy and raunchy and they obviously delight in each other's bodies, and use their imagination to fulfil and convey their sexual desires to one another.

The verse that we read earlier shows the imagination and fantasy of the lovers as they imagine the woods to be part of their bedchamber,

> *Our roof beams are cedar, our rafters fir.*
>
> — Song of Songs 1:16–17

It's also possible that the lovers are imagining themselves to be in the luxurious rooms owned by King Solomon, which were known for their lavish cedar beams (Bloch & Bloch, 2006). Some couples when having sex may imagine themselves to be in certain beautiful locations or will whisper their fantasy to their spouse, and their imaginations will take them to that place during their lovemaking. You may well have your own version of being whisked off into the king's chambers when you make love together.

Sexual fantasy is important in a marriage, in all its forms: whether that be erotic ideas of sexual positions; ideas of where you would like to make love with your partner; what you may like you partner to wear; or whether role play forms part of your erotic sex life. The two lovers were not reticent about using sexual fantasy and role play during their sexual encounters. Thomas Moore (1998) also highlights how sexual fantasies can be a helpful form of self-expression:

> *Our sexual fantasies, too, have a great deal to do with our search for meaning, direction, and individuality…In a stable and generally happy relationship, sexual fantasies may help keep desire itself alive and at work.*

— p.95

The two lovers in *Song of Songs* eagerly seem to share their sexual fantasies and convey their desires to one another in the sexual imagery that they use.

> *My love, I dreamed of you*
> *as a mare, my very own,*
> *among Pharaoh's chariots.*

— Song of Songs 1:9

It was apparently common for a beautiful woman to be compared to a horse and in this verse we get a sense of the erotic image and fantasy of a sexual position, because '… *it is the young man who is the potential rider*' of the young female lover, who is his mare (Bloch & Bloch, 2006, p.144). Later on in *Song of Songs* there is another erotic reference to horses and chariots:

> *And oh! I was aware,*
> *She sat me in the most lavish of chariots.*

— Song of Songs 6:12

Bloch and Bloch unpack the meaning in this verse and help us to see that the young woman places her lover in a chariot, as a sexual position of elevation to potentially ride her again; she is also giving him a position of honour through sex. Being placed in a chariot was an honour that was given to other people in the Bible, such as Joseph, the viceroy of Egypt in Genesis 41:43 (Bloch & Bloch, 2006).

If you read *Song of Songs*, you can be left in no doubt that the young lovers have no problems sharing their sexual fantasies with each other – they delight in it. However, for a lot of couples this is not so easy. We really have to be differentiated and take the risk of *wanting* our spouse and wanting them to know us and our sexual desires, and risking the possibility of rejection.

You may be aware that your partner feels uncomfortable about trying something new, so you may hold back and choose not to reveal some of your erotic, sexual desires. You may want to be in the same boat as your partner and you certainly don't want to rock the boat (see Chapter 8: 'Encountering conflict'). Of course, they may reject your suggestions and on some level that's okay, because they're in their own boat and get to make their choice too. However, really considering and entertaining your partner's sexual fantasies is one way of honouring them and their desires, just as the young Shulamite woman honours her lover by metaphorically placing him in a lavish chariot during their lovemaking.

Sharing your fantasies with your partner is one step forward, regardless of whether you act upon them. If we return to thinking about Andy and Rose, their sex life didn't involve discussing and sharing fantasies. Andy was unsure about whether he could or should ask anything of Rose beyond the sexual repertoire that they had developed. Rose also struggled with the idea of sharing sexual fantasies with Andy. Since Rose had become so practised at subjugating her needs, one of her main problems was being able to identify what she wanted during their lovemaking.

Rose just usually went with the flow; she certainly didn't direct any of the action and let Andy lead the way. In a sense Rose leaned into Andy and there was a lack of reciprocal turn-taking in their sex life. Because subjugation (as discussed in Chapter 3) was such a huge problem for Rose, what she needed to start doing was to communicate what she wanted, and to voice some of her preferences during their lovemaking, even if she wasn't completely sure. It was helpful for Rose to make some tentative decisions and take turns with Andy in directing some of their erotic foreplay.

Rose changed from an 'I don't mind, whatever you want' attitude and slowly found her voice. She then began to tune in to what she wanted and discovered what aroused her sexually. This was a surprise and exciting for Andy: over time they started to open up to each other and were brave enough to share some of their sexual fantasies. Andy realised that he wanted Rose to really know him and his sexual desires and he was spurred on by Rose's new sexually adventurous attitude.

Song of Songs – sexual affirmation and erotic self-esteem

Song of Songs reminds us how important it is to praise and affirm our partner sexually – all of the chapters are saturated with erotically affirming words that the lovers speak to one another. They are almost constantly vocalising their sexual love and admiration for each other. We hear them proclaim things like:

> *How wonderful you are, O Love,*
> *how much sweeter*
> *than all other pleasures!*
>
> — Song of Songs 7:7

It can be easy to forget to sexually affirm our partner. If we were like the young lovers in *Song of Songs* we would be almost constantly affirming our partner sexually, declaring how wonderful their breasts, arms, necks, or buttocks are. Throughout *Song of Songs*, the lovers compare their bodies to different aspects of nature, for example, the male lover's sexuality is often paired with apricots. We hear the young Shulamite woman say:

> *And my beloved among the young men*
> *is a branching apricot tree in the wood*
> *In that shade I have often lingered,*
> *tasting the fruit.*
>
> — Song of Songs 2:3

Once again, we are given a strong, erotic impression of the young woman tasting and enjoying her lover's sexuality, the apricots. Later we hear her declare:

> *Let me lie among the vine blossoms,*
> *in a bed of apricots!*
> *I am in the fever of love!*
>
> — Song of Songs 2:5

Thomas Moore (1998) tells us that '*the body is an erotic landscape with regions of special interest …*' (p.19); and it's true that we may also find regions of special interest in our spouse's body. Perhaps take a moment to think about this now

– are there special regions of erotic interest in the landscape of your partner's body that you enjoy and could affirm? Thomas Moore (1998) helps us to try and connect with the depth of our own sexuality by comparing it to nature, he writes:

> *...if you want to know what sex is, think long and hard about a flower, especially its beauty and its appeal to the senses. Then think about all of nature and your own place in it. Whatever makes a flower glow with enchantment is the essence of your own sexuality.*

— p.8

If you were to think of your favourite flower and the shape, and the smell, and the feel, and the colour, and bloom; and then allow yourself to connect with these images as a way of tapping into the essence of your sexuality – what feelings, sensations, or thoughts come up for you?

The young Shulamite woman proudly compares her blossoming sexuality to flowers. She tells us,

> *I am the rose of Sharon, the wild lily of the valleys.*

— Song of Songs 2:1

And what a statement this is, as these flowers are not common everyday flowers, but are beautiful, symbolic flowers mentioned elsewhere in the Bible. In the Hebrew language, the rose of Sharon is *habasselet* and in Isaiah we read:

> *The arid desert shall be glad, the wilderness shall rejoice and blossom like the habasselet.*

— Isaiah 35:1–2

By selecting this beautiful flower to compare herself with, she underlines the extent to which she is rejoicing in her sexual beauty, she isn't hesitant or shy and she certainly doesn't convey a sense of low self-esteem about her body (Bloch & Bloch, 2006). I think that this is something for men and women to aim for – a delighting in our bodies and the curves, shapes, angles and folds that we have. There is space, I believe, for more people to give themselves permission to enjoy their body and the way it looks sexually, instead of focusing on imperfections, and parts of our body that we have somehow convinced ourselves are unappealing.

In their commentary, Bloch and Bloch reveal some of the erotic nuances in the Hebrew words that were chosen to describe the body. For example, in the original Hebrew, the phrase: 'the gold of your thigh,' (Song of Songs 7:2) hints at the shapes and curves of the thighs; in fact, the root of the word in Hebrew relates to ideas of slippery smoothness (Bloch & Bloch, 2006, p. 99). Once again, I'm reminded of Dr Schnarch's idea of touching with feeling and really slowing down to notice the slippery smoothness of different areas of the body, and slowing down enough to enjoy and notice the interesting curves and turns that belong to the landscape of our partner's body.

God has given us a lot to enjoy sexually, and perhaps sometimes we don't take the time to enjoy it enough. Some of you may also feel hesitant about doing this and you may not always allow your partner to gaze openly and enjoy the erotic landscape of your body. However, we have talked about how the eyes help us to connect with our souls and allowing your partner to lovingly gaze at your body is one way that you can try to connect more deeply on a sexual and spiritual level.

Song of Songs – 'showing off' your sexual love

One of the most well-known lines from *Song of Songs* is: *'his banner over me is love'*. As part of my wedding ceremony, one of the songs we sang was based on this famous verse and the chorus goes, 'He brought me to his banqueting table, and his banner over me is love.' Now I have come to understand the erotic meaning behind these words, I'm looking back on this song in a new light; and I'm glad that we chose it for our wedding day. In Bloch and Bloch's translation this phrase reads:

> *Now he has brought me to the house of wine and his flag over me is love.*
> — Song of Songs 2:4

Wine and vineyards are strongly paired with the couple's lovemaking in *Song of Songs* (Bloch & Bloch, 2006), so her lover has brought her to the house of wine and his flag over her is love (sexual love).

The words used in the original Hebrew struck me and made me think more deeply about what the young Shulamite woman may have been trying to say. The Hebrew word, *nidgol* that is used here, means to 'raise high, make conspicuous' in reference to the banner or flag (Bloch & Bloch, 2006). Of course, in the past banners were used so that when soldiers or noblemen were approaching your castle or home, you knew who they were or whom they were fighting for. The banners were conspicuous designed to be easily identified from a distance and to be raised high. It's thought-provoking that the metaphor of a banner is being used in relation to the lovers' erotic love.

This challenged me to consider ways in which we can raise high and make conspicuous our erotic, sexual love for our partner. Or to put it more plainly, how we can 'show off' our sexual love and make our desire for our spouse clearly visible. I think it's an interesting challenge to think about ways in which we can 'show off' and display our erotic love, like raising a banner/flag. This may involve gazing at your partner in a certain way, touching them with feeling, wearing a piece of clothing or underwear that you know arouses your partner, or sexually affirming and recognising the beauty of your partner's body.

Song of Songs – being available for your partner

I have talked a lot about being present and available to your partner during lovemaking and the importance of this. In *Song of Songs*, a sense of readiness and availability between the two lovers is revealed:

The air is filled with the scent of mandrakes
and at our doors rare fruit of every kind, my love,
I have stored away for you.

— Song of Songs 7:14

According to Bloch and Bloch the 'doors' that are referred to belong to the places outdoors where the two lovers meet and the word 'our' is used to relay a sense of loving intimacy, rather than ownership. There is special symbolism in this specific Hebrew phrase, which can be translated literally as 'at the door', because this suggests immediate availability, closeness at hand,

and within easy reach (Bloch & Bloch, 2006).

It made me think about how we can make ourselves 'at the door' for our partner, making ourselves immediately available for them sexually, more so in our attitude, rather than just physically being available for sex. Perhaps sometimes we shut the door, rather than being within easy reach, emotionally and physically. Yet these two young lovers often seem to be 'at the door' and available for each other. This presents an interesting challenge for us to consider.

Song of Songs – come away!

The amount of erotic intimacy and soulful sex in *Song of Songs* may take most people by surprise. I knew this book was filled with sexual nuances, but when I started to unpack it and understand the poem in more depth, it provided me with a deeper appreciation of soulful sex; and I hope that this has been the case for you. As I finish writing this chapter now, the lines from *Song of Songs* that come to my mind are:

> *And he calls to me:*
> *Hurry, my love, my friend,*
> *and come away!*
>
> — Song of Songs 2:10

When we're thinking about trying to cultivate soulful sex with our spouse, I think there are no better words to hold in mind – the obvious desire, urgency and drive to 'come away' is hopefully inspiring. Of course, there's always challenges to finding the time and energy to cultivate one's erotic sex life. However, despite this, we can still find time to do small, but meaningful things such as: sexually affirming our partner; noticing the slippery smoothness of their arm or shoulder for example; gazing at our partner in the eyes and kissing them briefly; and touching our partner's hand or cheek with feeling.

All of these things don't take much time and can increase your sense of erotic connection with one another. The 'Joint Reflection Points' below will also provide a way for you to take some time out to consider ways of developing a soulful sex life. I hope they inspire you to find the time to hurry and erotically 'come away' with your partner as you practise the exercises together.

Joint Reflection Points

1. What do you think was helpful and what do you think was unhelpful about the messages that you received about sex during your upbringing? How has this had an impact on your couple relationship? You could look at your genograms here as a helpful prompt and consider the atmosphere around sex in your family. For example, was it closed, celebratory, hidden, anxious, embarrassed, open, repressed, happy, relaxed, private, avoidant, tentative, or exuberant? *(See Chapter 1 'Joint Reflection Points' for the genogram exercise if you haven't already completed this and would like to.)*

2. Discuss any thoughts that you had when reading about Dr Schnarch's idea of 'touching with feeling'. In what ways do you touch your partner with feeling? How could you introduce more 'touching with feeling' during or prior to your lovemaking, or even outside of the bedroom?

    Follow up exercise:

    ♥   Schedule some time over the next couple of weeks to practise 'touching with feeling'. Mutually agree on an area of your partner's body to touch with feeling – this could be your partner's shoulder, cheek, chest, foot, stomach, bottom, arm or upper thigh. Gaze into your partner's eyes and once you sense that you have got to a place where you are 'touching with feeling' continue for a few minutes, alternating your strokes and caresses in ways that you sense your partner finds pleasurable. Take turns being the giver and receiver of touch and discuss what this was like for you both before swapping over.

3. Gaze into each other's eyes[2]: This exercise provides a way to stimulate each other's 'mirror neurons' and is a helpful way of attuning to one another through physical touch. It's also an opportunity to slow down

---

[2] This exercise has been adapted slightly from an exercise that I came across in Val Sampson's (2002) book.

and 'touch with feeling'. It's a simple exercise, although it may feel a bit uncomfortable or unusual if you haven't practised anything like this before as a couple. As you relax into the process it should feel easier. All you need to do is follow the six steps below in turn.

♥ Place your right hand on each other's heart, whilst gazing into each other's eyes.

♥ With your out-breath, imagine letting the loving energy that you have for your partner pass from your heart into their heart. It can be helpful to picture this as a gold or white light being transferred from your heart to your partner's heart.

♥ With your in-breath, imagine inhaling the loving energy from your partner's heart into your heart.

♥ Once you've practised this a bit and feel comfortable with this exercise, try breathing alternately. So as you breathe out, your partner breathes in. In this way, the loving energy you feel for each other is being circulated between you both, still gazing into each other's eyes whilst you're doing this.

♥ At the end of this exercise share with each other how it made you feel. If it made you feel good, great. If it was hard for you, or made you feel uncomfortable, or perhaps you got the giggles trying to do this, don't worry. Just notice that that's how you felt in a loving, non-judging way. Don't give up on this exercise, come back to it another time and try practising it again. Hopefully after a few times you may feel more comfortable and enjoy the sense of connection.

♥ You can try doing this exercise before having sex as a way to try and emotionally attune to one another. Alternatively, you may like to practise this exercise as you set aside some quality 'couple time' together and use it as a way of connecting with each other.

4. If you've never tried 'Eyes-Open Sex' make some time to experiment with this, looking at each other during foreplay or peeking at each other during sex as a way to soulfully and emotionally connect to one another. 'Eyes-Open Orgasm' is also something you could consider trying if you haven't already. After trying 'Eyes-Open Sex' or 'Eyes-Open Orgasm', talk to each other and share what this experience was like for you.

5. Over the next few weeks, find some time to surprise your partner and have a go at 'doing' them. Like the two young lovers from *Song of Songs*, prepare to ravish your partner with fervour and generosity, sending them to the edge sexually as you attune to their body and what arouses them. After having a go at 'doing and being done', share with your partner what this experience was like for you.

6. What is the sacred space of your 'marriage bed' like? Are there ways that you could prioritise this space and make it more of an open, sensual space for sex, giving it a place of priority and respect in your home? What small steps could you take to help you move towards this?

7. How regularly do you sexually affirm and praise your partner? Take some time over the coming weeks to notice the shapes, curves and planes of your partner's body and affirm them sexually as you gaze at them. This could be one way of 'raising your banner' and making your erotic love and desire for your partner known.

Spiritual Reflection Points

1. Thank God for the gift of sex and that He delights in our erotic sex life, just as we read about the two young lovers from *Song of Songs* delighting in their lovemaking.

2. If you feel that you have lost 'your lover' either within yourself or in your marriage and maybe you feel that some of the erotic, sexual energy has 'slipped away', pray to God and ask him to restore this. Even if you feel that your sex life is okay, why not pray to God and ask him to deepen the emotional and soulful connection between you and your spouse during sex.

3. Pray to God and ask Him to give you a positive image of how to view yourself sexually and how to view sex in your marriage. Try to visualise your erotic sex life being like the *habasselet*, the rose of Sharon, a beautiful symbolic flower, bringing new growth to your couple relationship:

    > *The arid desert shall be glad, the wilderness shall rejoice and blossom like the habasselet*

    > — Isaiah 35:1–2

Chapter 11

Control of couple intimacy: what's sex got to do with it?

I want you to want me.
I need you to need me.
I'd love you to love me.
I'm beggin' you to beg me.

Song lyrics by the band 'Cheap Trick'

Issues related to sex are inextricably linked with the emotional well-being of a couple's relationship. Often sex is treated as a separate issue, set apart from the rest of the couple relationship. You may have heard couples say things like, *'Oh, we have a great relationship, we just don't have sex very often,'* or conversely, you may hear someone say, *'Oh we have real chemistry in the bedroom, we just can't communicate and talk about our emotions.'* It's interesting how we often accept these comments at face value, buying into the idea that sex is different and almost disconnected from all other aspects of the relationship. However, emotional problems and ways of relating are often played out in the arena of sex. It can be difficult to see how problems to do with emotional intimacy and sexual intimacy are interlinked, but if we look under the surface we begin to see how sex is central, and may be used to mediate and control levels of couple intimacy in our marriage.

This chapter is going to look at what lies beneath the surface of sexual intimacy; firstly, exploring issues about who is the low desire or high desire partner when it comes to sex. We'll also be re-visiting some of Dr Schnarch's concepts, such as how couples can end up needing their partner to provide them with a *reflected sense of self*, thinking specifically about how this affects sexual intimacy and desire. Daring to *want to want* our partner when we have sex, as opposed to needing them, and needing them to validate us will also be explored. We'll then transition to looking at attachment theory, what our adult attachment style may be and how this influences sexual intimacy. Afterwards, ways of forming a safe base to explore sexual intimacy as a couple will be discussed.

In *Passionate Marriage,* Dr Schnarch quite rightly tells us that when it comes to sex, the low desire partner is almost always considered the one who has the problem. He also points out another troublesome assumption, which is that good sex just happens, especially if partners love each other. When couples come to therapy one person in the relationship is often identified as 'the problem', particularly when it comes to sex and it is them on their own who needs to be 'sorted out' and fixed. When this happens there is a moving away from what may really be going on and a defence against really looking at what's happening in the relationship. We could hypothesise that one person in the relationship has been given a 'double dose' of low desire and is holding the sense of sexual inadequacy for both parties.

Another problematic assumption that Dr Schnarch highlights is that sex is often viewed solely as a biological drive, instead of a desire for one's partner. This means that the question becomes, *'Do you want sex?'* as opposed to, *'Do you want ME during sex?'* The overarching thought is then, that you're not supposed to want anything during sex, instead you're supposed to be satisfied (Schnarch, 2009). So sex becomes purely biological, not an emotional act and the one aspect is divorced from the other. However, it is important to realise that desire is not just about tension building up, being satisfied, and reaching your climax (Schnarch, 2009).

Dr Schnarch highlights the following six overlooked aspects of sexual desire:

1. *Sex forms an essential part of the way that we communicate on an interpersonal level; we often give off 'sexual vibes' and sense each other's sexual interest.*

2. *Sexual desire highlights our yearning to bond together as a couple as we seek out physical touch and contact.*

3. *A range of meanings and emotional expressions are exchanged through sex, which relate to our capacity for intimacy.*

4. *Sexual desire is linked to the intensity and depth of our engagement in the process of sex, or the degree of our active passion for intimacy.*

5. *Eroticism takes place in action, as individually we have our own ways of engaging with our partner sexually and exploring what our preferred sexual styles may be.*

6. *Our culture influences what arouses us and defines our ideals around sexual satisfaction.*

In our couple relationships there are patterns of desire that we experience, which may help to provide some useful insight into what sexual intimacy means for you and your partner. If we think about Rose, her pattern of desire was shaped by her belief that she was never going to be fully satisfied in life. She believed that good things would get taken away and simply don't last, which in turn meant that she tried to suppress feelings of desire. When it came to sex, this became a self-fulfilling prophecy, because what Rose needed to do was tune into her desire, and discover her preferred way of being erotic with Andy. However, because Rose suppressed her sexual desire, she couldn't communicate what she wanted to Andy. This left her feeling disconnected emotionally and dissatisfied during sex. Of course this became a vicious circle, which confirmed to Rose that she was right to suppress her feelings of sexual desire for Andy. So Rose was the low desire partner, the one who seemingly wasn't that interested in sex. However, Rose's problem wasn't that she didn't want sex, what she was actually afraid of was 'wanting to want' Andy.

Rose avoided 'wanting to want' Andy by escaping into her own fantasy world during sex, which brought her some relief and was one way that Rose soothed herself sexually. The problem wasn't really that Rose was the low desire partner and there wasn't anything biologically wrong with her when it came to sex. The issue was deeper than that. Rose approached sex the same way that she approached the rest of her life, with the view that she was never going to be satisfied and significant others in her life were likely to abandon her and not meet her needs.

Superficially Rose happily went along with their established sexual protocol because it provided her with a reflected sense of self – during sex it felt like Andy needed her and he was the one who always initiated sexual contact with Rose. This reassured her that he wasn't going to leave her and must be happy in their relationship if he wanted to have sex regularly. However, neither of them wanted to face the issue of actually daring to want one another and really connect on a deeper level through sex. It was feelings of anxiety and a reliance on other-validation that drove the sexual contact between them, not a desire to want to know the other person more deeply and connect through sex. Rose was fearful that Andy would stop wanting to touch her and have sex, which in her mind would signal that their relationship was in trouble. Because of this overriding fear, Rose never stopped to think about what she wanted in terms of sexual intimacy with Andy.

When I was reading *Passionate Marriage*, I was really struck by Dr Schnarch's assertion that the person with the least desire for sex always controls the level of sexual intimacy. And we have to remember that the couple relationship is a sensitive system, so one person's lack of desire can have a powerful effect on the other. For example, a man who underneath may be fearful of sexual intimacy and scared of his partner's desire can condition his spouse so that over time her desire for sex disappears. How could a husband have such a strong influence over his wife's desire? Well, when a man continually ejaculates prematurely he ends up conditioning his partner to be *'sexually inert and unenthusiastic'* (Schnarch, 2009, p.141). As the wife begins to experience feelings of desire and arousal, her husband ejaculates prematurely, which means that over a period of time the wife learns that there's no point in getting sexually aroused (Schnarch, 2009).

In addition, the person with least desire for sex always controls the frequency of sexual contact (Schnarch, 2009). It's strange, but true that a partner can have a greater degree of control over the couples' sex life by doing nothing and looking helpless. It's the high desire partner's dependence on a reflected sense of self, which places the low desire partner in control. When the low desire partner doesn't want to have sex, their partner may start to berate them, with the underlining thought that, '*They should want me sexually!*' As Dr Schnarch points out, this type of behaviour isn't very appealing sexually and is unlikely to increase their desire.

Of course, it's always possible that the reptilian part of the brain may take over (see Chapter 8 on encountering conflict) and we can end up lashing out at our partner if we feel sexually frustrated (Schnarch, 2009). Trying to coerce our partner to engage in sexual intercourse in the way we want them to, isn't likely to increase their desire; we cannot order our partner to want us. The first line of the song lyrics at the beginning of this chapter is, '*I want you to want me*', and whilst this is natural, we cannot force our partner to want us. Couples can sometimes reach a place of sexual gridlock, and here, it is important to remember to hold on to your sense of self – you have the opportunity to say what you want, and then your partner gets to make their choice (Schnarch, 2009). Then it may be important to self-soothe and self-validate if the outcome wasn't what you had hoped for.

If we think about Andy, he tried to control sex because he had a timetable in his mind of when it should happen. Rose often went along with the timetable, but she was the low desire partner and was actually in control of the frequency of sexual contact. She would sometimes decline Andy's request for sex, often giving the excuse of feeling tired from looking after the children or feeling low in mood. Rose tended to withhold sexually from Andy when she felt he had been particularly absent. The low desire partner holds a lot of power through their very passive position. Rose didn't have to do anything sexually to get Andy's attention, she just had to passively resist having sex and she knew this would have a big impact on him.

Another interesting phrase from the song lyrics at the start of the chapter is: '*I'm beggin' you to beg me*'. The low desire partner can sometimes induce their partner to hassle and beg them for sex. However, Rose's withholding didn't continue for long because she was too concerned that Andy would get fed up and lose his desire for sex, which was the one couple activity that Andy seemed particularly keen to maintain. Rose obtained her reflected sense of self from Andy asking her for sex, and Andy got his reflected sense of self from believing that he was able to regularly satisfy his wife sexually. Sex for Andy and Rose was all about, '*I need you to need me*', rather than allowing themselves to *want* each other, which was far more exposing and would put them in touch with their fears of losing the person they desired.

During the process of couples therapy Rose started believing that she deserved good things in her life generally, as well as in her marriage and in their sex life. She realised that what she wanted was important and this changed her position from the low desire partner to the high desire partner during sex; and what a shock that was for Andy. Rose helped to slow down the pace of lovemaking; she was no longer afraid that she wouldn't reach orgasm; and Andy was no longer afraid that if he didn't leave Rose satisfied, she would walk out or start an affair. Both of them gradually became less dependent on a reflected sense of self during sex.

When Rose started to think about her needs and what she wanted whilst having sex with Andy, it was scary at first for Andy. He was used to being the one in control, so when Rose started to want him during sex, and slowed down the pace of their lovemaking, he was thrown initially. For a short time, he became the low desire partner and something unusual happened: the regular timetable for sex stopped. Sexual contact took on a new meaning and level of intimacy, which felt potentially threatening. Andy wasn't sure he could take part in sex under these new conditions; for the first time he struggled to stay aroused during their lovemaking.

Rose adopted a more differentiated stance: she no longer wanted to engage in sex in order to obtain a sense of validation from Andy. Consequently, she managed to self-soothe and self-validate when Andy became disinterested in sex. Rose's growth and desire for intimacy meant that Andy had to confront himself and what he wanted out of sexual intimacy. He also had to face the fact that he often felt scared of real contact. His timetable for sex had in fact been a way of distancing himself from Rose, so although superficially he looked like the 'normal' partner with a regular, healthy level of sexual desire, that wasn't the whole picture. Andy in fact leaned into Rose and demanded that she be satisfied and reach orgasm quickly, which killed off any true desire and resulted in Rose escaping into a fantasy world during sex. Rose gave Andy the reflected sense of self that he wanted from her during sex as she appeared to be a satisfied partner in their sex life. However, as Dr Schnarch makes clear, leaning into our partner and relying on other-validation; and obtaining a reflected sense of self from your partner during sex, is one sure fire way to create problems with genuine desire and sexual intimacy with our spouse.

Andy needed Rose to affirm him sexually, but he didn't truly want Rose during sex, and he didn't want to know her and what her sexual desires were. Of course, on a conscious level, Andy could convince himself that his aim was purely to please Rose, but this wasn't the case – on some level Rose knew she was there during sex to provide Andy with a significant amount of affirmation. This certainly wasn't sexy or a turn-on for Rose. Andy had learnt from his childhood to suppress his desire for affection and touch from his parents. He had to toughen up to survive and this got played out in his sexual relationship with Rose; Andy didn't *want to want* her. He needed her to need him, that way he could feel sure that she would stay close.

The importance of wanting our spouse, instead of needing them, was discussed in detail in Chapter 3. And as Dr Schnarch observes, remaining differentiated with our partner becomes more difficult as our partner increases in emotional importance to us. Consequently, it's easy for couples to become emotionally fused, which can leave partners feeling fearful that their spouse will leave them, or their marriage will deteriorate, if they speak their mind or fail to compromise (Schnarch, 2009). However, being emotionally fused tends to lead to low sexual desire and sexual boredom (Schnarch, 2009). Dr Schnarch points out that there are two main fears that contribute to this pattern:

1. *Fear of being rejected by your partner and losing their acceptance. When you fear losing your partner's validation and acceptance more than losing out on what you want and your integrity, it means that you're likely to adjust your eroticism and desires in order for them to fit in with your partner. It may mean that you suppress certain desires or ideas of erotic foreplay in order to keep the status quo. When thinking about it this way, it's easy to picture how this could create low sexual desire and boredom. In addition, it explains why some individuals have affairs or one-night-stands as they do what they want sexually without fear of rejection. As the new and fairly unknown sexual partner is not so emotionally important to them, it means that they may feel able to be more sexually adventurous because the situation may feel less risky and less exposing emotionally. Shortly, we'll take a look at some couple relationships in the Bible where we can see this dynamic in action.*

2. *Fear of separation and loss of your partner. Over time, as the importance of your partner increases, the greater the perceived risk becomes when you want something significant that your spouse doesn't want. When the importance of a partner overrides the ability to be differentiated and impairs the ability to self-soothe, then couples may end up not wanting to want. Couples may think that they want their partner; however, what's really happening is that being emotionally fused they end up needing each other and needing each other's validation in order to be reassured that their partner won't leave the relationship. If we think about needing our partner, then we are almost taken back to a parent–child way of relating: one person being reliant on the other. When couples get caught up in needing their spouse and parent–child-like interactions then, of course, this isn't very sexy. This also explains why low sexual desire and boredom can take centre stage in a relationship. The desire to stay safe and not rock the boat in order to ensure your spouse doesn't get upset means that couples don't get to fully know each other and their sexual desires.*

When I think of this interesting dynamic, I'm taken back to the song lyrics at the start of this chapter: *'I want you to want me. I need you to need me'*. This seems to highlight the dilemma that we face, *to want* or *to need* our partner in our couple relationship and particularly in relation to sex.

Dr Schnarch (2009) tells us that *'When your partner becomes more important to you than your relationship with yourself, you have four choices:*

- *withdraw emotionally*

- *engulf your partner*

- *allow your partner to engulf you*

- *raise your level of differentiation.'*

— p.152

In some ways, Andy engulfed Rose with his needs and leaned into her to get his reflected sense of self. The way that Rose coped with this was to step back emotionally and withdraw into her fantasy world during sex. However, they both made brave attempts to raise their level of differentiation as they dared to want each other sexually and slowed the pace of their lovemaking down so that they could start to 'touch with feeling' (see Chapter 10).

The story of Judah and Tamar – fear of sexual intimacy

It's not an easy thing to dare to *want* our spouse – intimacy, especially sexual intimacy, can feel very threatening because if we truly open ourselves up to our partner we may feel dangerously exposed. There is a very interesting couple relationship in the Bible which I think will help us to think more deeply about these issues: the story of Tamar and Judah. In the story, Tamar seems to embody the fear that men can sometimes feel towards women when it comes to sex and intimacy. Of course, women can also fear sexual intimacy and we'll take a look at another Biblical story later that explores this.

The story of Judah and Tamar is fascinating. As events unfold we come to realise that Judah possibly fears that being in a relationship and intimate with Tamar may mean death – yes, pretty extreme, but true. Here is some background information about Tamar's first two marriages. Originally, she was married to Judah's eldest son, called Er. However, Er was a wicked man, so in the Bible we are told that God decided to kill him. The custom in those days was for the widow to marry the closest male relative, which was Judah's second eldest son, who was called Onan. Judah says to his son,

Go and marry Tamar, as our law requires of the brother of a man who has died. You must produce an heir for your brother.
— Genesis 38:8

But because Onan didn't want to produce an heir for his brother he always made sure that he withdrew from Tamar prior to ejaculating in order to prevent her from getting pregnant. This behaviour displeased God, who punished Onan and made sure that he was killed. Judah then sends Tamar back to her father's house and promises to send his third eldest son Shelah to her when he has grown up. However, Judah doesn't really want to do this perhaps because he fears that his third son will also die if he marries Tamar.

So Tamar is pushed aside, she has no husband and no sexual intimacy with anyone; Judah is perhaps scared of her and somehow seems to pair the misfortunes of his sons dying with Tamar.

You may be left thinking: 'What an unusual story'. However, in more recent history we have the example of Jackie Kennedy, whose first very powerful husband was assassinated and killed. Then she married another powerful man, Aristotle Onassis, whose son tragically died in a plane crash. In the documentary 'Jackie: A Tale of Two Sisters' we hear that Aristotle Onassis soon became convinced by family members that Jackie was bad luck, a black widow, and it was her fault that his son had died. In his grief Jackie was viewed as the common denominator with regards to the loss of a loved one: that she had somehow brought the spectre of death into his family. Similarly, suspicions about Tamar may have started to circulate following the death of her second husband. This may explain why Judah fails to send his third eldest son to marry Tamar.

For Tamar's sake you may be glad to hear that she decides she doesn't want to put up with being abandoned and left as a vulnerable widow in her father's house, with little status and few prospects. She decides to take matters into her own hands. Tamar hears that Judah's own wife has died and that he is on his way to a sheep shearing festival in Timnah.

So she changed out of her widow's clothing and covered herself with a veil to disguise herself. Then she sat beside the road at the entrance to the village of Enaim, which is on the road to Timnah. Judah noticed her and thought she was a prostitute, since she had covered her face. So he stopped and propositioned her. 'Let me have sex with you,' he said, not realising that she was his own daughter-in-law.

— Genesis 38:14–16

Here, we can see the truth in a point that Dr Schnarch makes in *Passionate Marriage* (2009), that it can feel easier to have a one-night-stand with someone we don't know, or have an affair, because we don't have the same emotional connection with that person. So there is not the same risk of feeling rejected or exposed as one would feel with a close partner. Tamar has covered her face, which seems to signal her out as a prostitute. I think this is interesting in itself because it implies that sexual exchange with a prostitute is inherently not intimate as you don't even get to properly see the face of the person with whom you are having sex.

We then hear a discussion between Judah and Tamar about payment for sex. Judah says that he will send a young goat from one of his flocks and Tamar asks for a guarantee, she asks him to:

> *'Leave me your identification seal and its cord and the walking stick you are carrying.'*
> *So Judah gave them to her. Then he had intercourse with her, and she became pregnant.*
>
> — Genesis 38:18

Afterwards, Judah sends his friend to give the prostitute (Tamar) the young goat, but he cannot find her. Subsequently, Judah is informed that his daughter-in-law is pregnant, and he responds harshly, announcing that she should be burned. However, cunning Tamar sends a message to Judah:

> *'The man who owns these things made me pregnant. Look closely. Whose seal and cord and walking stick are these?' Judah recognised them immediately and said, 'She is more righteous than I am, because I didn't arrange for her to marry my son Shelah.'*
>
> — Genesis 38:25–26

Judah sees that it's him who is at fault and perhaps feels shamed by his own actions.

Of course, he marries Tamar, and the couple are listed in the Gospel of Matthew as ancestors of Jesus, which marks them out as having significant importance. Sadly though, after Judah acknowledges the truth of Tamar's message and her right to be married to him and have his children, we are told,

> *...And Judah never slept with Tamar again.*
>
> — Genesis 38:26

So although Judah appeared keen to have sex with Tamar whilst she posed as a prostitute, he didn't want to have sex with her again as his wife. It's interesting that we are even given this detail about their sexual relationship as we don't often get to know about the frequency or lack of frequency of sexual intercourse between couples in the Bible. Marriage and sexual intimacy, or the lack of it, seems to be one of the significant themes in Tamar's life.

Here, Judah is clearly the low desire partner and the issue of sexual intimacy with Tamar seems to have held fast and remained a problem even in her third marriage. Of course, on some level Judah may have felt tricked and betrayed by Tamar even though he declares *'She is more righteous than I am...'* (Genesis 38:25–26). It's possible that Judah may have wanted to withdraw and punish her for her actions. Chapter 4, *'The ideal couple and feelings of betrayal'* looks more closely at this dynamic and the dangerous territory of punishing our spouse.

What can we learn from Tamar and Judah's interesting, yet sad story? Well, perhaps we don't fear literal death when we have sex with our spouse, but we may fear the death of our relationship and the loss of our partner's acceptance of us if we don't go along with validating our partner all, or most of the time. It's this fear that perhaps holds us back from trying to show more of our true selves during sex and expressing what we want.

Tamar, of course, attempts to be differentiated and steps outside of the cultural expectations that are placed on her. She wants to be known sexually and wants a husband, so she makes her choice and approaches Judah as a veiled prostitute. Judah eventually realises that he has wronged Tamar and does the right thing by marrying her, but he is not prepared to take the sexual side of their couple relationship forward. He gets to make his choice too, which is to withdraw from Tamar sexually, perhaps in order to feel in control, and keep his fears at bay. Or as a way to distance himself and punish her.

It would have been nice to see Tamar's courage and pluckiness inspire Judah to 'up his game' and resolve the sexual problems in their marriage. For it to have been third time lucky for Tamar, but that didn't happen. I imagine there wasn't a 'happily ever after' for Tamar, although she may well have found great comfort in the birth of her twin boys.

In other couple relationships, when one partner makes a break for it, and does the unexpected – like Rose asking for the sex to be slowed down – it provides an opportunity for the other partner to grow and raise their level of differentiation also. Usually, we get unsettled when our partner is prompting us to step out of our comfort zone, or is disturbing our reflected sense of self. The reptilian part of our brain may come out and we may berate our partner, attempting to get them back into a position of emotional fusion and agreement with us, or we may want them to stop pushing for growth and change. Maybe thinking, 'Why can't you be happy with the way things are?'

In Tamar's day, as a woman she probably had limited influence and ways to try and improve her marriage. If Tamar was living in today's world and had a husband who refused to grow and didn't want to put any effort into the couple relationship, she perhaps would have had more options and help. Sadly, when one partner doesn't want to change, and the relationship feels stuck, this is when we often see couples separate or have an affair (see Chapter 12: Disillusionment and adultery). Judah clearly did not *want to want* Tamar, so he distanced himself from her.

For our own couple relationships, the good news is that our partner's growth often pushes or inspires us to grow too and we are forced to confront ourselves. Being in a couple relationship often brings us into a head-on collision with ourselves and our hidden personal issues and fears. I think that this is a good thing, and perhaps one of the reasons why 'in the beginning' God told Adam that it was not good for him to be alone: a husband and wife not only provide each other with company, we help each other to grow.

The woman at the well – avoiding sexual intimacy

The account of the 'woman at the well' in the Gospel of John perhaps shows a woman, as opposed to a man being wary of sexual intimacy. Later on in this chapter I want to explore how our attachment styles have an impact on the sexual dimension of our couple relationship. And one could hypothesise that the woman at the well had a *dismissive-avoidant* attachment style. The dismissive-avoidant type is similar to what I referred to as the *distancer* in Chapter 8. *Distancers,* or people with a dismissive-avoidant attachment type, quite literally interact in ways that avoid or dismiss emotional connection. They don't want anyone to see inside them, in fact they fear it, because they believe that the person will either try to take over and control them, or abandon them (Shaddock, 1998). The fear of being humiliated, emotionally intruded upon, or abandoned may mean that they arrange their lives and sexual lives, so they feel in control, and the potential for a deeper emotional connection is avoided.

People with a dismissive-avoidant personality type may have also experienced a complete absence of care whilst growing up, and as adults they often position themselves in relationships so that they don't get too attached.

They can be afraid of feeling needy and dependent on someone else, because as a child they were let down and so learnt that it's best to be as self-reliant as possible. Nevertheless, they still want to be in some form of relationship with someone else.

I think the story of the woman at the well is interesting because the scene opens with her approaching the well at noon-time, the hottest part of the day, when she knows that no-one else from the village will be around. So already we see her avoiding contact and connection with people in her community. In fact, she is so used to people ignoring her that she is surprised that someone like Jesus not only talks to her, but seems interested in her life.

> *Soon a Samaritan woman came to draw water, and Jesus said to her, 'Please give me a drink.' He was alone at the time because his disciples had gone into the village to buy some food. The woman was surprised, for Jews refuse to have anything to do with Samaritans. She said to Jesus, 'You are a Jew, and I am a Samaritan woman. Why are you asking me for a drink?'*
>
> — John 4:7–9

Jesus disregards the cultural norms and expectations that he shouldn't talk to a Samaritan woman, and he disturbs the woman's normal routine of collecting water at a time when no-one else would have been around to interact with her. Jesus, of course, offers her some 'living water' rather than the plain old water from the well. When her interest is sparked, he commands her to do something which reveals to us the state of her sex life:

> *Jesus replied, 'Anyone who drinks this water will soon become thirsty again. But those who drink the water I give will never be thirsty again. It becomes a fresh, bubbling spring within them, giving them eternal life.' 'Please, sir,' the woman said, 'give me this water! Then I'll never be thirsty again, and I won't have to come here to get water.' 'Go and get your husband,' Jesus told her. 'I don't have a husband,' the woman replied. Jesus said, 'You're right! You don't have a husband — for you have had five husbands, and you aren't even married to the man you're living with now. You certainly spoke the truth!'*
>
> — John 4:13–18

The woman at the well is revealed to be sexually promiscuous and there is also speculation that she may have been a prostitute. This may explain why she completes her chore of collecting water from the well during the hottest part of the day in order to avoid contact with the villagers. Jesus points out that this woman has had five husbands, inferring that she has slept with multiple men, and that although she is living with another man now, he isn't her husband.

The woman at the well may have been divorced or abandoned by the men who she was seeing, and, in this way, she may not have had much control over her situation. The power to end the relationship or initiate divorce would have lain primarily in the man's hands. However, it is interesting that there is a pattern of multiple relationship break-downs. From a psychological perspective, I wonder whether she gravitated towards men who were unlikely to commit to her.

By sleeping with multiple men, this woman may be trying to avoid any deep emotional connection with any of them – she doesn't have to risk being known by them in any deep, meaningful way. For her, this may have been one way of avoiding *wanting to want*, her sexual partners. *Wanting to want* her partners could have left her in a position of feeling vulnerable – something that a person with a dismissive-avoidant attachment style doesn't want to risk.

I think it's quite poignant when Jesus says, 'Go and get your husband', because he's highlighting the absence of a man who she can have a deep and meaningful connection with. Thinking back to Rose in case example 2, she also needed to listen to this piece of advice to 'Go and get your husband', because she was avoiding having a deeper contact with Andy. She didn't *want to want* him because she had learnt from her childhood that if you want things, they usually get taken away. She also needed to respond to this advice because she often didn't try to connect with Andy during sex, she took herself off into her fantasy world. Andy also needed to be told to 'Go and get your wife', instead of taking himself off into his world of work. There are lots of ways that we can avoid emotional connection and intimacy when we have sex.

With the woman at the well Jesus shows a spiritual interest in her and at that moment he becomes a significant person who enters her life. Interestingly she opens up to him instead of trying to avoid the interaction. The mere presence of Jesus at noon time by the well seems to helpfully disrupt the woman's possible dismissive-avoidant attachment pattern. Furthermore, Jesus' command, *'Go and get your husband'* may have helped her think about her past couple relationships. Jesus, of course is primarily offering spiritual transformation, using the metaphor of life-giving water; however, his words are also pointing the Samaritan woman to transform the way that she goes about trying to have an intimate relationship.

Although Jesus challenges her about her lifestyle, he offers acceptance instead of rejection or condemnation. This presents a helpful example for us to follow – being able to challenge ourselves about our attempts at sexual intimacy with our partner, whilst accepting the position we're in, in a loving, non-judgemental way.

Jesus' advice to 'Go and get your husband/wife', is an interesting command for us to take on board in terms of our own sex lives. Sometimes our desire needs to be sparked in order to go and truly find the one person, our spouse who we can have a deeper emotional connection with through sex. This is particularly the case when we move towards a position of *wanting* our spouse and *wanting* them to know us fully through sexual intimacy.

Attachment bonds: feelings of security and insecurity

I briefly mentioned attachment bonds in relation to sex in Chapter 10 and how when we gaze at our partner and attune to them, responding sensitively to their needs, this helps a 'secure attachment' bond to form. In fact, scientific research supports attachment theory and shows us that when secure attachment behaviours are displayed, such as responding sensitively through gaze and touch, 'mirror neurons' start to fire and send signals to our brain. Neurologically, sparks start to fly.

Psychologists have done a lot of very valuable research around attachment styles that develop in childhood between the infant and parent, and how this impacts our attachment style in adulthood. For the purpose of this chapter, I'd like us to look at how our attachment style and related behaviours not only affect our couple relationship, but our sexual interactions with our partner. First, we'll need to visit the ground-breaking ideas and research which resulted in the different attachment categories. Subsequently, we will then be able to make sense of what our adult attachment style may be, before going on to think about how our attachment style influences sexual intimacy. Stay with me and brace yourself for a bit of psychological theory – it will be a great help as you recognise your attachment style and how it affects your relationship.

In their book, *Adult Attachment* (2004), Rholes and Simpson help to define what 'attachment style' means, outlining that there are individual differences in our:

1) tendencies to seek and experience comfort and emotional support from the person with whom one has an attachment bond

and

2) presumptions about the responsiveness of attachment figures to bids for comfort and support.

— p.4

If we think about Lucy and Tom, in case example 3, they both have different attachment styles. From Tom's childhood attachment bonds he learnt that significant others are unlikely to be responsive to his need for emotional comfort, which in turn means that he is less likely to seek out emotional support as an adult. In fact, Tom is likely to avoid seeking out emotional support from significant attachment figures, like Lucy, as a way of protecting himself from possibly being let down, like he was as a child. And this is an important point, because the attachment styles that we develop as children are often self-protective and necessary to our emotional survival whilst growing up.

In Tom's case, having his emotional needs continually ignored meant that it wouldn't have made sense for him to continue to seek out emotional support and comfort when none was going to be given – he learned that he had to look after himself. As adults, we do have the opportunity to try and take a step back and examine our attachment patterns and if we feel secure enough in our couple relationship, we can try out different ways of relating. For example, during couples therapy, Tom slowly began to open up and share some of his emotions, and instead of having his feelings dismissed or criticised, they were listened to. This provided Tom with a different template of what to expect and he could start to adjust his presumptions and expectations about whether his bids for emotional support would be met. However, like most people, when feeling under threat, Tom could easily slip back into his former attachment behaviour of avoiding emotional connection.

So, how did researchers discover more about attachment styles and the different categorisations? Mary Ainsworth and her colleagues developed an experiment called the Strange Situation, from which she devised three main attachment categories: 1) anxious-ambivalent; 2) avoidant; and 3) secure (Rholes & Simpson, 2004). The Strange Situation involved parents and their 12–18-month-old infants being placed initially together in a room with toys before a range of separations and reunions were staged. The researchers found that when securely attached children were reunited with their mother, they went to their mothers to seek comfort, which they received, and they were then easily calmed and would typically resume their previous activities, such as exploring the room or playing with the toys (Rholes & Simpson, 2004).

However, the anxiously-ambivalent child would display contradictory, mixed behaviours, such as approaching their mother in distress, but then resisting comfort and they would often fail to resume previous activities (Rholes & Simpson, 2004). Placed in the same 'Strange Situation', the avoidant child would tend to ignore and disregard their mother and try to distract themselves from feelings of distress by continuing with their activity and play in the room (Rholes & Simpson, 2004). Later on an additional attachment category was developed, which is often referred to as disorganised attachment. As the name suggests, the child doesn't know how to respond to the caregiver and this is often because the parent may be responsive occasionally, but more often than not would behave in a frightening or abusive way towards the child. In the Strange Situation, a child with a disorganised attachment may respond quite unusually when their parent returns, for example, by rocking or freezing. Disorganised attachments may develop when a parent behaves in extreme and often contradictory ways, for example, they may lavish unwanted attention or demand hugs from their child, only to react in the next minute in a harsh, punitive way, physically and/or verbally abusing their child.

I'll explain the three main attachment categorisations in a bit more depth before we go on to think about our adult attachment style, which is of course shaped by our upbringing. The secure attachment style develops because the parent or main caregiver tends to respond sensitively and consistently to their child's needs. In attachment theory language, the parent provides a 'secure base' to explore, so a child can go off and play in a room full of toys and with other children. They can take some risks because at the end of the day, they know that they can return to the 'secure base' if they need to be comforted or supported in any way. The parent is also thought of as a 'haven of safety' – over time the secure attachment pattern is internalised. As the child grows up they don't need the parent to be physically there to support them all the time, because they have internalised that sense of security that their needs will be met.

With an anxious-ambivalent attachment style, the parent or main caregiver may be overly anxious and clingy with their child and not let their child venture out and explore on their own. Generally, what tends to happen is that the caregiver is inconsistent with their responses, sometimes the parent will be neglectful, whilst at other times they may respond to their child's needs. Often a child may have to increase their signs of distress, and attachment-seeking behaviours in order to get a response from their parent. For example, a child may have to cry for an extended period of time before getting a response, or they may misbehave, or present as being physically unwell in order to secure the attention they require from their parent.

In her early years, Jenny had formed a fairly secure attachment bond with her parents prior to her brother dying of leukaemia. However, following her brother's death, her parents were preoccupied with their grief and often responded to her inconsistently, sometimes hugging and comforting her and sometimes unable to really pay attention to her needs because of the loss of her brother. Once Jenny's parents were over the worst of their grieving, they became somewhat clingy and anxious about Jenny's safety. They wanted her to stay close to the family because they feared separation and losing Jenny, like they'd lost their son. This 'clingy' behaviour was presented to the outside world as being a loving, close family unit. This was also how Jenny viewed her parenting before becoming more in tune with some of the difficult aspects of her childhood during therapy.

Jenny's parents also ended up doing lots for her in their attempts to keep her close. So ultimately, they didn't provide Jenny with a secure base to explore from because their anxiety levels prevented healthy degrees of separation and risk-taking. So although Jenny had originally formed a template of what a more secure attachment looked like, this got subsumed by an anxious/ambivalent attachment pattern after her brother died. Similarly, in her relationship with Mike, Jenny could swing from feeling securely attached to being anxious and clingy, fearing separation and not wanting Mike to go out and socialise with his friends.

Tom's early upbringing provides us with a good example of an avoidant attachment style – this is when there is a consistent pattern of neglect and dismissal of the child's emotional needs A parent may try to encourage their child to be overly independent and discourage crying and the need for comfort. In Tom's case, expressing emotions tended to be criticised or ridiculed. Conversely, a child may develop an avoidant attachment to a caregiver who is overly controlling and intrusive. An example of this would be a parent who wishes to live vicariously through their child's life, and forces their child to 'perform' for them and learn hobbies, like playing the piano or tennis, because they never got to do that as a child. So an intrusive/controlling style of parenting also tends to foster an avoidant attachment style. When a parent is overly controlling and intrusive, the child's actual needs are as equally neglected as the child who is ignored. In both situations, the parent shows no interest or attunement to the child's actual emotional needs.

The attachment style that forms between parent and child provides a template – or what is often referred to in psychology as an 'internal working model' – of what to expect from interactions and attachments with significant others in our lives. So, our early experiences of attachment tend to have a significant impact on our relationships later on in life. For Christians, God as a mother/father parental figure can provide us with a secure form of attachment. Research has shown that when God is viewed as always available, always reliable, and ready to listen and respond to one's emotional needs when distressed, a secure attachment forms. Viewed this way, God provides His children with a 'secure base' to explore, and confidence to go out into the world, knowing that He will always be there when needed. In this way, our attachment to the parental figure of God can sometimes help us to overcome or adjust our previous attachment style. Particularly if our own parents have been inconsistent, neglectful, controlling, or abusive in their care and were not able to provide us with the 'secure base' that was needed.

Adult attachment bonds and couple relationships

In adulthood, the attachment categories have slightly different names and descriptions to reflect adult, as opposed to child, attachment behaviours with our partners and significant others. However, the labels are fairly transferable, and you can see the correlating child attachment label in brackets. The four main categories of adult attachment are: 1) secure *(secure)*, 2) anxious-preoccupied *(ambivalent)*, 3) dismissive-avoidant *(avoidant)*, and 4) fearful-avoidant *(disorganised)*.

So let's turn our attention to adult romantic relationships and think about the four different attachment styles in this context. Adults with a secure attachment style have grown up with a positive view of themselves and so their partner is often viewed in a similarly positive light. They tend to feel happy about entering relationships and secure about intimacy, they are also able to tolerate being separate from their partner, whilst maintaining good levels of connection and intimacy.

Adults who tend to be anxious-preoccupied in their attachment style usually have less positive views about themselves and their partners; they may worry about their relationship and the strength of their attachment to the significant other in their life. They also tend to seek reassurance from their partner, typically wanting high levels of intimacy and responsiveness. Consequently, they may display a high degree of emotional expressiveness in their quest for responses from their partner. This type of attachment style fosters a sense of dependency and reliance on the partner, who may be looked to for approval and affirmation in order to ease underlying anxieties.

Adults with a dismissive-avoidant attachment style can often be quite self-critical, and this inner critical voice may spill out at times onto their partner. In relationships they often present as self-sufficient and independent, as if they don't need the attachment relationship. They often try to distance themselves and minimise opportunities for deeper intimacy and avoid connecting with their own feelings and those of their partner. Adults with a dismissive-avoidant attachment type may try to be 'in control' of the relationship in a variety of subtle ways. This also helps them to maintain a level of distance.

Adults with a fearful-avoidant attachment type tend to experience significant problems with intimacy. They often feel unworthy of being in a loving relationship and have difficulty trusting their partner or their own feelings. They are also likely to be highly ambivalent about connecting with their partner, wanting the attachment, whilst feeling fearful about opening up and trusting their partner. This may result in efforts to disconnect and suppress their feelings as well as avoiding opportunities for deeper intimacy.

Of course, you may have had different types of attachment with different caregivers. For example, Lucy experienced her father as controlling/abandoning and her mother in comparison was more responsive to her needs, although at times her mother could be unavailable because she was often overwhelmed by Lucy's father's demands. This meant that Lucy could sometimes be dismissive-avoidant in her interactions with Tom, just like her father, but because Lucy's primary attachment was with her mother, who she spent most of her time with, Lucy's predominant style of attachment was that of being anxious-preoccupied. With Tom, Lucy often sought reassurance and longed for deeper, emotionally meaningful conversations and more often than not, she needed to increase her obvious signs of distress in order to get a response from Tom, just as she had been forced to do as a child.

It's not unusual to have had different types of attachment styles form with different caregivers when growing up. For example, you may have experienced a more positive, secure attachment with a grandparent or other significant attachment figure, whilst having an ambivalent attachment to your parents, who may not have always been available. Someone like a family friend, neighbour, nurse, teacher or librarian may also have been a supportive attachment figure in your childhood. As I have already mentioned the attachment figure of God can also provide an alternative form of secure attachment. This may have provided you with a 'haven of safety' if your relationship with your parents wasn't as secure. This positive model of interacting is also internalised and can help influence your attachment style and romantic relationships.

Following this very brief overview of attachment styles you may be able to start to identify what your attachment relationship was like with your main caregivers and significant others whilst you were growing up. You may now have a sense of how that translates into your adult relationship with your partner. Next we'll take a look at how our attachment style has the potential to influence our sexual interactions.

Sex, attachment, and feelings of security/insecurity

When we feel under threat, our attachment seeking behaviours may get activated and increase. For example, if feeling stressed at work, you may seek comfort and emotional support from your partner in order to feel calmer and draw a sense of security from that significant attachment figure in your life. Similarly, for Christians, when under stress our attachment seeking behaviours may get activated and increase. We may for example, start to pray more and seek comfort and try to re-establish a sense of security and equilibrium through our attachment and belief that God, our parent is there for us.

In *A Dynamic Maturational Model of Attachment*, Crittenden (2006) points out that sexual desire induces a state of arousal and tension in our bodies. Physiologically our arousal levels also go up when we feel under threat due to stress, fear, pain, and hunger. So sexual desire as a body state can feel threatening because it typically means that we have to open up to a significant other, who may or may not respond to our attachment seeking behaviour around sex.

Adults with a secure attachment have the expectation that their needs are likely to be met by their significant attachment figure. So for securely attached adults, sexual desire may pose less of a threat. If we are feeling securely attached with our partner, we may respond like the securely attached infants in the 'Strange Situation', free to explore sexually in the bedroom in a playful way. We don't get too upset if something doesn't work out, we are able to self-soothe and resume our 'sexual play'. For securely attached adults, sex can be a satisfying experience and a way to deepen intimacy in the couple relationship.

If we think back to the couple that we got to know in *Song of Songs* in Chapter 10, they seemed to be securely attached and enthusiastically enjoyed exploring their sexual fantasies, sexual positions and reciprocal giving and receiving during moments of erotic intimacy. There was, however, (perhaps reassuringly so) a rupture in the secure attachment between the two young lovers in *Song of Songs* as they were separated, and the young Shulamite woman found that her lover had 'slipped away'. Consequently, she felt compelled to go out at night and search for him. I think that this helpfully highlights that even if we are particularly in tune with our partner, securely attached, and enthusiastically enjoying sex, we may still experience moments of difficulty in terms of connecting through lovemaking and there may be times when it has felt like we have lost that connection and our lover has 'slipped away'.

Insecure attachment and sexual intimacy

Let's think about some of the other adult attachment styles in relation to sex, because all of the insecure attachment styles have an impact on our desire to *want to want* our partner. Instead of *wanting to want* our partner, we may end up feeling dismissive or avoidant of our own sexual desire or our partner's sexual desire. Alternatively, we may feel very anxious or ambivalent about *wanting to want* our partner, and if anyone has experienced physical/sexual abuse as a child, then at certain times they may feel fearful and avoidant of sexual intimacy.

So, if one has a dismissive-avoidant, or anxious-ambivalent, or particularly if you have been abused and tend to operate from a fearful-avoidant attachment style, feelings of sexual desire may trigger a range of emotions and anxieties. The unconscious expectation may of course be that your sexual needs won't be met; there may be fears around your partner being inconsistent, neglectful, dismissive, or even potentially taking advantage of your body during sex, which could echo memories of abuse from the past. If a person has a dismissive-avoidant attachment style they may try to avoid getting in touch with sexual feelings in a deep and meaningful way, or they may orchestrate their sex life in order to minimise the impact of opening themselves up to sexual intimacy. For example, they may have affairs as a way of avoiding deeper, sexual intimacy with just one person, their spouse.

During couples therapy, Tom disclosed that he often watched a lot of pornography as he felt that this was a safe outlet for his sexual desire and feelings. He didn't have to open up to anyone, just the images on the screen, which meant that he didn't have to risk feeling exposed or rejected during sex. Tom didn't *want to want* Lucy, unconsciously he withdrew from Lucy and avoided opportunities to connect through sex with her because he didn't want to let her down or be revealed as inadequate, so he just didn't try. Pornography became the non-threatening sexual relationship for Tom as it can be for other men or women. Tom had a dismissive-avoidant attachment style, so he often dismissed his own sexual needs and Lucy's. He tried to avoid a deeper level of connection through sex.

Lucy on the other hand, had an anxious-ambivalent attachment style and was often anxiously preoccupied about sex and desperately sought reassurance from Tom through sex, which he was often reluctant to give. Lucy wanted reassurance from Tom that she was sexually desirable and that he needed her. She was seeking a reflected sense of self from Tom. So there was often a vicious circle of Lucy pushing for more sex and sexual intimacy, which would make Tom withdraw and increase his avoidance. Lucy felt very ambivalent about *wanting to want* Tom – part of her did and part of her didn't. She was certainly anxiously preoccupied about sex and wanted Tom to need her sexually.

Often when Lucy and Tom found time to have sex together, Lucy felt slightly fed up with Tom's lack of enthusiasm. This meant that Lucy felt ambivalent about relaxing into foreplay, 'touching with feeling' and giving to Tom sexually. Tom, of course, sensed Lucy's subtle resistance and holding back, which only confirmed for him that he needed to withdraw and protect himself from wanting Lucy. These behaviours and thoughts were not entirely conscious. During couples therapy, they could step back and look at their couple relationship together and see how sexual desire and sexual intimacy triggered feelings of threat and anxiety about whether their respective needs for intimacy would be met.

Andy, too, often operated from an anxious-preoccupied position when it came to sex, he often felt worried about whether he was having enough sex with Rose. He would question whether he was fulfilling his duty as a husband and underneath it all, he felt anxious about what not having enough sex would mean. For Andy it meant that he wouldn't be a 'proper man'; that it wouldn't be a real marriage, and ultimately that Rose may be dissatisfied with him.

Andy had convinced himself that if he provided a regular income for the family and had regular sex with Rose, then he was fulfilling his duty. However, the fact that Andy wasn't really emotionally and physically present during sex was the main issue. Rose sensed his absence and withdrew into her fantasy world to protect herself, thus replicating the pattern of dismissive-avoidant attachment that she was used to. The fact that Andy turned their sex life into a religious routine also meant there were few opportunities for spontaneity and creativity when it came to sex; it was one way that Andy could have sex with Rose without really having to emotionally connect with her.

As I've already mentioned, it's likely that an individual with a fearful-avoidant attachment style has been exposed to physical or sexual abuse as a child. This means that their body may have been harmed and there may be memories that are stored in the body about being hurt, as opposed to being cared for and attended to in a loving way. When such individuals are faced with sexual intimacy, instead of being able to relax their bodies may freeze or feel under threat. Even if an individual has managed to obtain a sense of healing about the past, the body state of sexual desire may on occasions cause the person to slip back into a fearful-avoidant position; they may wish to suppress feelings of sexual desire and sublimate their erotic energy into other activities. For example, a person may feel passionate about helping out in a charity, or may feel very passionate about a hobby or plough their energy into gardening and being creative in a different way. As Thomas Moore (1998) says, the question is not about what happened to the sexual desire and why it has disappeared, but rather, where is the desire? In what part of your life is there desire and passion? The answer may provide the hint about where some of your erotic energies get displaced if they are absent from the bedroom.

With individuals who have a fearful-avoidant attachment style, there is potential for the partner and their actions to be interpreted as abusive, even if this is not the case. After all, our attachment style provides the template and affects our expectations about the type of care we think we will receive from significant others. So if someone has a fearful-avoidant attachment style, one unconscious expectation may be that a partner will be abusive in some way, although the behaviour may be at the lower end of the spectrum. For example, a partner could be misinterpreted as being too sexually enthusiastic, placing too many demands and being 'greedy' sexually; or the person may at certain points feel physically hurt or uncomfortable during sex, and they may feel that their partner could have taken a bit more care with their body. It's important to be mindful of this and discuss together as a couple what you may need from one another in order to relax and enjoy sex more fully. Something that I have not talked about yet is that sex has its 'shadow side', and it is likely that we have perhaps all felt wounded in the area of sex at some point in our lives. Thomas Moore (1998) says that:

> *To find sexual intimacy we may have to acknowledge that sex is wounded.*
> — p.185

He helps to remind us that it's not always good to champion health and wholeness, and it can be healing to allow some space for our sexual wounds – to acknowledge them and accept that they are there, without feeling driven to 'fix' them. At the same time, he warns us that it's important that we don't allow ourselves to wallow in our sexual wounds and injuries. It may be important to find some time and space where we can acknowledge and accept our sexual wounds in order to open up to a greater sense of erotic freedom.

Sometimes if we are aware that certain situations, like sexual intimacy, can touch raw spots and trigger feelings of mistrust, then as a couple there is the potential to work with these feelings and move towards a place of healing together. If you have a history of abuse, and you have felt that your body has been taken advantage of when your partner has initiated sexual contact, then you have the potential to re-orient yourself and self-soothe. You can try to identify what you are feeling and where that emotion is coming from. If the emotions originate from the past and are not fully connected to your partner, then by recognising that you can reduce your sense of distress in the moment. You can know that the emotion doesn't belong to the 'here and now', identify it as a legacy from the past and carefully put it to one side. You can self-soothe and remind yourself: *'My body is mine now, it's not being hurt, my partner loves me, it's safe for me to connect with them sexually.'* You can put this sentence into your own words, personalise it, so that it resonates with you and helps you to feel soothed. As you try to calm any fears, you may become more relaxed and tolerate your partner getting some things wrong, and then gently let them know what feels good and what doesn't.

However, you may sometimes still be the low desire partner because you fear that your partner will engulf and overwhelm you sexually. Then you may feel that your only option is to withdraw sexually from your spouse. Talking about this pattern with your partner can be freeing in itself as the couple relationship can help to contain some of your anxieties. Entering couples therapy may also help you to find a containing space to explore some of the strong emotions that emerge around sexual intimacy.

Of course, if you have a fearful-avoidant attachment style, this may also be particularly true with regards to your own relationship with your body. You may not fully trust your own bodily sensations, particularly your sexual feelings. Therefore, you may benefit from active attempts to try and have a better relationship with your body. Looking after our bodies is important, and it may be helpful for you to explore ways of tuning into your body's needs. For example, mindfulness exercises, particularly body scans which incorporate breathing and relaxation techniques may help you to tune in to and trust your body more (see Williams & Penman's, 2011 guide to mindfulness or other mindfulness resources). Exercise classes, the type where there is space to tune in to your body may also be of some help.

In addition, taking the time to pamper your body by having a massage or facial, which a lot of men enjoy as well as women, may be an important way to spend your time and money. This means that you don't repeat the pattern of abusing/neglecting your body, instead, you purposefully choose to look after it, not in a punishing way – by over-exercising or pushing your body to excess – but by treating your body in a gentle and compassionate way. Even if one of you in your couple relationship tends to switch into a fearful-avoidant attachment style when it comes to sex, looking at this pattern together as a couple can provide you with a secure base to explore ways of deepening sexual intimacy and overcoming fears about sexual connection.

Now, if you have identified yourself as not having a secure attachment and you're left feeling envious and wishing that you had 'perfect' parenting and a secure attachment style, which would make life and sex with your partner easy, then let me tell you, you don't have to feel so envious. Adults with a secure attachment can also feel anxious around sex and feel insecure at times; sex is a deeply intimate act where we open ourselves up and allow ourselves to be vulnerable with our partner, so it's easy to flip from feeling secure and happy about sexual intimacy to feeling ambivalent or avoidant. How the couple relationship that we form with our partner can create a secure base to explore sexual intimacy from will be discussed in more detail next.

Attachment style and creating a secure base to explore sex

Susie Orbach (2009) has written an interesting chapter on 'Separated attachments and sexual aliveness'. By separated attachments she is referring to couples who are able to remain *differentiated* and who manage to balance being separate whilst maintaining a healthy sense of togetherness. Having a 'separated attachment' would be the opposite of being emotionally fused as a couple. I found it fascinating to read Susie Orbach's conclusion that the couple relationship itself can provide a secure attachment and base from which the couple could explore sexual intimacy, even if at times one or both partners may become anxious, avoidant, controlling, or clingy about sex. I've translated Susie Orbach's concept into pictorial form and used the framework of the marital triangle we looked at in Chapter 2 (see Figure 8 below).

According to Susie Orbach, recognising your individual attachment style – particularly in relation to sex – and looking as a couple at how your respective attachment styles fit together (or for many of us, how they don't necessarily 'fit' together, but perhaps come together in more or less unhelpful ways) can be the starting point from which a renewed sexual aliveness emerges.

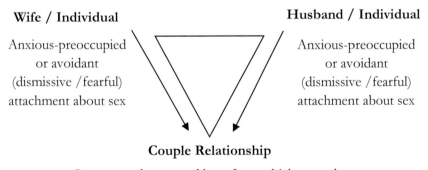

Wife / Individual

Anxious-preoccupied
or avoidant
(dismissive /fearful)
attachment about sex

Husband / Individual

Anxious-preoccupied
or avoidant
(dismissive /fearful)
attachment about sex

Couple Relationship

Secure attachment and base from which to explore sex

Figure 8: the sexual marital triangle

If we consider Jenny and Mike, they both tended to have anxious-preoccupied attachment styles. This combined with their internalised image of what a couple relationship should look like, and what form sexual intimacy should take in a marriage, was heavily influenced by their respective upbringings. Mike worried a lot about sex, wanting to be close to Jenny, but he feared being intrusive and sexually aggressive, like his father had been towards his mother. This meant that Mike often held back from making any sexual overtures. He watched and waited to see if Jenny would approach him for a hug and spent a lot of time looking to see if Jenny appeared be 'in the mood' for sex or whether she appeared tired. Jenny, on the other hand, had internalised from her mother that a wife should be sexually passive and let the husband take the lead when it came to sex. So Jenny was often desperate and longed for Mike to initiate sexual contact and show her that he wanted her without her having to ask for sexual touch. Her belief was that *'even if I want sex I shouldn't have to ask!'*

Their respective attachment styles and 'fit' created a lot of problems for them and meant that sexual contact happened infrequently. During couples therapy their pattern of sexual interaction was explored further, and the lack of sexual contact also seemed to serve another function. Both Mike and Jenny had had the experience of being emotionally overwhelmed by their respective family's demands and need for them to merge and be available for them. Jenny felt this especially when her parents became clingy following her brother's death. Mike had a significant amount of emotional pressure placed on him by his mother and sister as his family role was to protect them and deflect his father's anger.

Unconsciously, they both on some level feared being overwhelmed by an emotionally needy 'other'. So when they experienced the bodily sensation and 'threat' of sexual desire, it meant that they were faced with the possibility of opening themselves up to a significant attachment figure that may overwhelm them. Therefore, both Mike's and Jenny's anxious hesitancy around sex reduced the frequency of sexual contact, which protected them from their unconscious fears about being merged and overwhelmed. However, it also meant that there was no sexual aliveness in their relationship. In fact, it felt like they were stuck, their anxiety holding them back and limiting the creative, spontaneous, and playful potential of sex in their relationship.

When Mike and Jenny were able to come together and talk about their feelings about sex from the safe base of their couple relationship, this enabled them to recognise what had been happening and they started to emotionally open themselves up to each other during sex. They were able to explore together their strengths and their vulnerabilities when it came to sex. Looking at sexual intimacy from the position of the couple relationship helps to remove any blame or judgement of each other's shortcomings. Instead, it helps sexual intimacy to become a shared issue, which can be worked on. The importance of coming together and talking about sex from the third position, the position of the couple relationship, offers a simple, yet beautiful opportunity for healing:

> *Sexual intimacy is dependent not so much on each individual sorting themselves out as individuals as it is on creating a platform of security from which the couple can nourish itself.*
>
> — Orbach, 2009, p.74

The above quotation is how Susie Orbach ends her chapter on sexual aliveness, and I would recommend reading it several times to yourself. There is healing potential in you (the two individuals in your couple relationship) in coming together and creating a safe base to explore your relationship's needs, including that of sexual intimacy. It's heartening to know that the key to moving forward and resolving issues is closer than we often think, as the potential is all there waiting for us in our couple relationship. That is what this book is all about as it encourages you to come together and discuss relationship issues jointly – and I shall leave you to create your own platform from which you can nourish your marriage as you look at the 'Joint Reflection Points' below.

Joint Reflection Points

1. Discuss together about who is the high-desire or low-desire partner in relation to sex? Does this positioning tend to change, and if so, when does it change and why do you think it tends to change? Try to explore together why you may be the high/low desire partner in relation to sex.

2. When it comes to sexual intimacy, do you tend to approach your spouse from the position of *'Do you want sex?'* and it's about satisfying a physical desire? Or do you approach your spouse from the position of *'Do you want ME during sex?'* and it's about wanting to connect with each other through sexual intimacy? Try to have an open and honest discussion about this together. How could you as a couple move to a position of wanting to know each other more through sexual intimacy?

3. The Kissing Exercise[3]. The purpose of this exercise is to each take turns in directing and leading the type of kiss that you would like, just using your lips, so no tongues are involved. Follow the steps below:

    ♥   One of you will be the 'kisser' and the other will try to follow your partner's lead, trying to attune to what they seem to want by following and mirroring their movement. Just using your lips, no tongues involved. Allow 5 minutes for the 'kisser' to kiss you.

    ♥   Switch over, so that the other person takes the lead in directing the type of kiss that they would like, again allotting 5 minutes for the kiss.

    ♥   Talk together about what this exercise was like for you. What was it like to let someone else take the lead on kissing? What emotions or thoughts came up for you during this exercise? Did anything unusual happen that you didn't expect?

---

[3] The Kissing Exercise has been inspired by an exercise described by David Slattery (2012) during his course on 'Relational Couples Therapy'.

4. I would like you to move positions if you need to, so instead of sitting separately, sit together on a couch or on your marriage bed. From this position (symbolically representing the couple relationship) talk together from the perspective of the couple relationship and consider the following questions:

    ♥   What do you think your vulnerabilities are as a couple (not individuals) when it comes to sex? If you notice yourselves talking about individual vulnerabilities, pause and come back to thinking about your vulnerabilities as a couple when it comes to sex.

    ♥   And conversely, what do you think your strengths are as a couple (not individuals) when it comes to sex?

    ♥   Bearing these issues in mind, how would you as a couple (not individuals) like to move forward and explore deeper levels of sexual intimacy and aliveness in your relationship? Perhaps think of one or two small steps that you could make.

Spiritual Reflection Points

1. Spend some time thinking and praying silently together about Jesus' advice in John 4:16 to *'Go and get your husband'* or conversely *'Go and get your wife'*. Ask God to show you what stops you from connecting on a deeper sexual level with your spouse. Put some worship music on if you would like to, holding at the back of your mind the words: *'Go and get your husband/wife'*. At the end of the silent prayer and meditation time, share any thoughts that came up for you or words or images from God.

2. If you have had any particularly difficult experiences growing up that have had an adverse impact on your adult attachment style and relationship with sex and your body, pray together as a couple for healing. Thank God that, as a parent, He offers us a secure base and is always available for us and ready to meet our needs.

Chapter 12

Disillusionment and adultery

We need some innocence in order to enter marriage in the first place,
and then we discover that marriage is not unadulterated happiness,
but rather another of life's initiations.

Thomas Moore, Soul Mates

If you have been curious enough to start reading this chapter with an interested, open mind as opposed to bypassing it, then I would like to congratulate you. I imagine that some couples may be looking at the title and thinking, *'Well, this chapter has very little relevance to my life and marriage'.* However, I'm hoping to look at disillusionment in a broad and meaningful way, and how this in turn can have an impact on our faithfulness to our partner – not just in terms of full-blown adultery, but in many other subtle ways too.

I was talking to a close friend about the chapters in my book, and she said to me, *'So you're going to end your main set of chapters with Disillusionment and adultery?'* There was a puzzled look in her eyes and I imagined that she was thinking, *'Well that will mean that you're ending on a bit of a low.'* To her, as perhaps to you, this initially made no sense, but I hope that this chapter will be a helpful read as we look together at how to restore our sense of wonder and interest in marriage. Of course, we will need to fully examine the complex elements of what may be going on before we reach an understanding of how restoration can take place, but this too, I believe, has the potential to be an interesting journey.

Our potential to be a creative couple – the Biblical story of Sarah and Abraham

So how does disillusionment result in us disconnecting from our partner and looking elsewhere for fulfilment in our lives? I'd like to take a look at the Biblical story of Sarah and Abraham, who became disillusioned with their relationship and their inability to be fruitful and have children. For them, it seemed like they couldn't be the creative couple, it was as if they lacked the potential to come together and produce something new, in this case a child. Couples may similarly feel that they can no longer be creative together; they may experience difficulty coming together in lots of ways. Even in conversations it may feel like their respective thoughts or feelings aren't really heard or exchanged. Consequently, there's no possibility of the two people creating an interesting third position, of a combined perspective, or shared way of looking at something anew.

Sarah, in her relationship with Abraham, ended up in a position where she felt that they couldn't be a creative, fruitful couple. Sarah seemed to be holding a lot of the doubt as to whether she would be able to produce children, feeling conscious about her age. As a couple, they couldn't envisage a way forward together, so Sarah and Abraham started to look for solutions outside of their marriage. The solution that Sarah came up with was to encourage Abraham to sleep with her maid, Hagar.

> *So Sarai [Sarah] said to Abram [Abraham], 'The LORD has prevented me from having children. Go and sleep with my servant. Perhaps I can have children through her.' And Abram [Abraham] agreed with Sarai's [Sarah's] proposal.*
> — Genesis 16:2

Both Abraham and Sarah feel lost and desperate. They resort to this tactic because they are disillusioned and don't believe that their sexual union will produce anything of worth; they fear that they can no longer be the creative couple that they had hoped to be.

Abraham continues, as prompted by Sarah, to sleep with Hagar and she produces a son, called Ishmael. This, however, becomes a sad affair for all three parties. Sarah becomes envious, and Hagar gloats about her accomplishment:

> *... But when Hagar knew she was pregnant, she began to treat her mistress, Sarai [Sarah], with contempt.*
>
> — Genesis 16:4

Abraham is stuck in the middle and doesn't know what to do about this mess; however, he ends up giving Sarah permission to respond to Hagar however she sees fit. So Sarah treats Hagar harshly, causing her to run off into the desert. God, however, doesn't abandon Hagar and hears her cry for help in the wilderness.

This was a painful experience for all involved, and it provided no solution for Abraham and Sarah. It can be like this in modern-day couple relationships: when feeling stuck, instead of looking for the resources within the marriage to make things work, either or both partners may start to look for satisfaction and solutions elsewhere. Whether this results in looking for an alternative relationship, activity or an addiction to fill the gap. *(Addictions or compulsions can include many things such as food, alcohol, gambling, workaholism, exercise, sports, fashion/appearance, fantasising, pornography, hobbies, technology and gadgets.)*

An alternative activity, relationship or addiction may temporarily be used to protect the partner from feeling impotent, barren or empty inside. Even heavy involvement in church activities has the potential to become a form of compulsion and can be used to buffer one's self-esteem, keep one busy and can become a 'godly' barrier to intimacy. Andy used to escape the confines and problems in his marriage to Rose by over-committing himself to helping out with church events. This form of workaholic behaviour used to make Andy feel good about himself, whereas he sometimes felt inadequate in his relationship.

So, what happens to Sarah and Abraham in the end? There is a positive outcome for them both – God is faithful to the promise He made them and against all odds Sarah conceives a child in her old age and they call their son Isaac. Abraham and Sarah had to hold in there and wait for something fruitful to happen. Sometimes it can be equally difficult for modern-day couples to 'hold in there' when feeling disillusioned, and like Sarah and Abraham it can be tempting to look for solutions outside of marriage, such as having an affair.

What strikes me most about this story is that it feels like Abraham and Sarah really felt that they couldn't be a creative and fruitful couple and produce anything of worth on their own. The potential for something good to happen seemed to get projected outside of their marriage relationship. Like Abraham and Sarah, there may be the thought that all you need to do is have sex with someone younger and more virile, who can help to rekindle a sense of desire and fruitfulness in your life. This is how disillusionment can lead us towards adultery as we start to fantasise that the solution and only hope of moving forward lies outside of the marriage relationship.

It's interesting, isn't it, to see that when we start to think that we are missing out on good things the only possible way we can imagine finding them is to step outside of the confines of our relationship. It's almost as if we deceive ourselves that the goodness lies outside of our marriage. It reminds me of when I spent 18 months working with adults with mental health issues in the USA. During this time, I remember a friend of mine saying to me in their strong Bostonian accent:

Well, you know, the grass is always greener on the other side – until you have to go mow it!

That phrase has always stuck in my mind, and it's almost as if we like to delude ourselves that with someone else, the grass really wouldn't need mowing and life would be easier, if only we had a different partner, or we could escape into the easiness and excitement of an affair.

Unfortunately, this idealised hope that someone else, like Hagar, may be able to finally satisfy your needs and desires is often false and can result in a lot of pain and unhappiness. As with Abraham and Sarah, there is always hope that within the marriage something good and fulfilling can come out of the relationship. I think that the problem can be that like Sarah, we start to lose faith in a solution and perhaps modern-day couples have a lower level of tolerance when it comes to waiting patiently for things to change and working on issues together.

In today's culture, when something goes wrong, finding the time and energy to fix it can feel like hard work. Often people may feel like just buying something new to replace the broken object. Similarly, in couple relationships, our culture, media and movies all seem to promote the idea that if you become dissatisfied in your marriage, the natural thing is to let your erotic gaze drift and find satisfaction and excitement elsewhere.

Of course, working on a relationship requires the efforts of both parties, so if one person is unwilling to do this, and doesn't want to grow, then sadly the difficulties may continue, no matter how eager and willing the other person is. Nevertheless, there is often a high desire and low desire partner when it comes to seeking growth and change. A bit like Lucy and Tom; Tom was the low desire partner and he certainly didn't want to go to couples therapy at first, but Lucy didn't give up and she persisted in her desire to make their relationship work. In Lucy's case her persistence paid off and Tom eventually agreed to go to couples therapy. So, whilst it may be important to persist with our partner, and we may naturally encounter some resistance, eventually there needs to be some willingness to engage in the process of change to make the relationship work.

For me, the story of Sarah and Abraham is not just about how disillusionment can result in having sexual intercourse with someone else. This story is about a sense of 'stuckness' and a shared couple belief that they can no longer be creative and fruitful together in the way that they had hoped. When couples feel that they have lost this creative, energising connection, then they may start to seek fulfilment elsewhere, whether that be in their work, in their relationship with their children, or in a special interest or hobby. And remember, if you're ploughing your emotional energies into your children as a way of making up for the lack of emotional connection with your partner, you may be inadvertently creating an *'emotionally incestuous'* relationship with your child, which as the name suggests is unhealthy (see Chapter 2).

When a partner's passion and creative energy isn't ploughed into their relationship, another outlet is sometimes found, which they believe will be more fruitful and rewarding. As the outlet may not necessarily involve having an affair, this type of unfaithfulness may be subtler, so it's important to be aware of this and look out for it. The heartening thing is, that it is possible to become unstuck and move to a position where we can be a creative couple again. The connection is not lost forever, it may just take some patience and hard work to realise the full potential of your relationship. Like Sarah and Abraham, all is not lost, we too can 'hold in there' and over time surprise ourselves that the potential for growth and change can come from within our own couple relationship.

Passivity as a form of unfaithfulness

Thomas Moore (1994) reminds us that imagination is important in marriage as it helps us to feed the fantasies of our partner's soul and helps fulfil what they want from marriage and of course from sexual intimacy. However, there is a problem that can get in the way of this. Robert Bly (2001) highlights a phenomenon that he refers to as 'the passive man' in marriage. Of course, there can also be a problematic 'passive woman', particularly as women in modern-day couple relationships are faced with competing demands and also desire to excel in other areas of their lives, such as their careers. Women can also end up having less of an active presence in their marriage, but Robert Bly (2001) in his writings focuses primarily on men.

He points out that:

> *Women, until recent times, have not been praised for their activity. They have been asked for centuries to live in enforced passivity… Women are coming out into activity just as the men are passing them the other way, into passivity.*

— p.62

The problem is further complicated and possibly subtly encouraged by women, as Bly tells us that these days: '*Some women want a passive man, if they want a man at all*' (p.62). If we think about couple relationship theory and the idea of one person in the couple relationship having a 'double dose' of a certain emotional disposition (see Chapter 1), we could hypothesise that the woman in the relationship may end up giving her passivity to her partner, leaving him with a 'double dose'. Perhaps the wife may unconsciously be searching for a passive man, so that she can find the metaphorical hook to hang her own passivity on; not wanting to feel trapped in a traditional subservient role, she may feel safer being the active one in the relationship.

Another problem with the growing phenomenon of the 'the passive man' in marriage is that he doesn't apply his efforts to his marriage, let alone use his imagination to try and feed the fantasies of his partner. *'The passive man, for example, may ask the woman to do his loving for him.'* (Bly, 2001 p.63). Thomas Moore (1994) points out that some men have no vision for their marriage, no sense of clear goals of where they would like to be in their relationship in five years' time. The lack of direction and a pervading sense of passiveness for such a man in his marriage is concerning, but actually, what is probably more concerning is our acceptance that this is normal. We do not necessarily expect men and women to have an active vision or goals for their marriage relationship.

For both men and women, it's helpful to take more of an active role in the relationship and make an active effort to get to know what touches the soul of your partner. Rose, for example, wanted to get to know Andy more, so she asked him what she does that helps to feed his soul and what makes him feel connected in their relationship. Things that stood out for Andy included: the way that Rose strokes his hair in a certain way; the times that she makes special cookies just for him; when they get the time to play their musical instruments together in the evenings; when Rose has written him a loving note; and when they go on walks together on the afternoons when the children are with their grandparents. There is a sense of joy, pleasure, playfulness and connection that Andy receives from Rose during these moments.

Previously, Rose had been very passive and depressed in her marriage, which meant that there were fewer opportunities for connecting with Andy in these ways. As we know from the case of Andy and Rose, there was a reason why passivity and depression had come to the fore in their relationship. It's important to bear in mind that excessive passivity may be a symptom of a deeper-rooted problem and couple relationship dynamic.

One way couples can become disillusioned by the marriage and feel disconnected, is if there's a lot of passivity and lack of focus, or effort, or few attempts to continue to get to know one's spouse. Being overly passive in your relationship, not putting in the effort, not attuning to your partner's desires and not bothering to continually get to know them is, I would suggest, another way of being unfaithful in marriage. It is not surprising, under such circumstances, that some people's relationships falter, and the wife or husband, when asked for a divorce, may be left feeling puzzled thinking: 'But I didn't do anything'. And this may have been precisely the problem: passivity, apathy and neglect can erode a relationship. We know that in the Bible, the same issue is raised, and Christians are aware that it's not good to be apathetic. God would prefer us to have a strong reaction in our relationship with Him one way or the other:

> *But since you are like lukewarm water, neither hot nor cold, I will spit you out of my mouth!*
>
> — Revelation 3:16

Being lukewarm in our couple relationship is problematic because, in a passive way we are rejecting the other person and creating distance.

In *Soul Mates* (1994), Thomas Moore writes about people who have been shocked or surprised by the breakdown of their marriage and had no idea that divorce was on the cards. You too, may well know people for whom divorce, or separation seemed to come as a complete surprise. But how could a relationship get to such a point without both partners realising the state that their relationship was in? Sometimes people delude themselves and the outside world into thinking that everything is okay. Thomas Moore (1994) talks about such a man:

> *The distraught man who told me that he had no idea that his wife was planning to divorce him mentioned offhandedly that he and his wife had not had sex in five years because they were angry at each other.*
>
> — p.37

This can also be a common occurrence in churches, where others in the congregation feel shock at the apparently very sudden and dramatic breakdown of a marriage. One person in the relationship who appears to be the 'victim' may end up protesting, 'I didn't even know my partner was unhappy.' Consequently, fellow church-goers who are not privy to the ins and outs of the relationship may superficially accept this as the truth and agree that it's unfair that the other person didn't give the relationship a chance. However, something is amiss if the person is saying that they weren't in tune with their partner's unhappiness and distress. Again, passivity may have a role to play:

> *There seems to be a widespread tendency in modern life to observe events as they happen passively, with a gauze in front of one's eyes … Nothing is shocking, there are no problems, things happen, there is nothing to be done, said, or thought. Yet certain situations cry out for reflection, such as five angry years without sex in a marriage that from both inside and outside appeared placid.*
>
> — Moore, 1994, p.37–38

For some couples there may well be a numbing acceptance of the problems, which contributes to the sense of passivity and disconnection.

Being active and present (emotionally, physically and spiritually) in our marriages is a healthy position to adopt. When facing couple relationship issues, one way of promoting an active focus on your couple relationship is to enter couples therapy. I think it's interesting that, in the UK at least, there often seems to be a stigma around couples going to therapy together. It's almost as if it feels like a negative, embarrassing thing to do, which signals some degree of failure in the relationship. However, I would urge you to see it as a positive, active stance to take and a way of investing and caring for the couple relationship. Sometimes in marriages individuals unintentionally, passively accept problems perhaps believing 'this must be as good as it gets', and they are fearful of striving for deeper levels of intimacy and connection.

In the realm of the physical I think we've got better at taking care of ourselves and paying attention to warning signs, like high blood pressure, which may prompt us to change our diet, and do regular exercise. But in the area of emotions, I wonder if we still feel a little lost and unsure about how to respond when we start spotting the warning signs that our relationship is not as healthy as it could be and there are problems that need addressing. If you're taking the time and energy to read this book and do the joint reflection exercises together, then you are already doing something very positive, nurturing, and active for your couple relationship. But you may want to think and pray together about whether couples therapy would be an additional, helpful, step forward for your marriage.

Also, if you're the only one in the relationship who is reading this book, then you may need something more active, like couples therapy, which can galvanise you as a couple into action. Sitting down to talk about your relationship can be hard and easy to put off. There is nothing like having a regular appointment time with a couples therapist, where you are expected to turn up together and focus on your relationship, to help you reconnect. Couples therapy helps to ensure that important conversations happen. Spending your money on couples therapy is also another helpful, active commitment and investment, for as we all know:

> *Wherever your treasure is, there the desires of your heart will also be.*
> — Matthew 6:21

The role of *Anima* and *Animus* in affairs

If you have read Chapter 7 of this book you will remember that we explored the Jungian terms of *Anima* and *Animus*. I will provide a brief recap of these complex concepts and how they impact on our relationships, before thinking about the influence of *Anima/Animus* projections on affairs.

As I've mentioned previously, it is important for men to develop what Jung would refer to as the corresponding contra sexual element in their unconscious, their *Anima* and women to develop their corresponding contra sexual element and this is called the *Animus*. The *Anima* is not feminine, and the *Animus* is not masculine in the sense of how we define that in everyday life, but rather they form a natural, inherent complementary opposite aspect of ourselves. When a woman integrates her *Animus,* or a man integrates his *Anima*, this can help to bring balance and a sense of wholeness.

However, both men and women can be wary of their *Anima/Animus,* because it is not their primary way of functioning, so it often feels foreign and hard to relate to. One of the ways that individuals may try to deal with this 'problem' is that a husband may project his *Anima* onto his wife and a wife may project her *Animus* onto her husband. Of course, we don't always project our feminine or masculine ideals onto our partner, if tempted, we can project them onto other men and women outside of our marriage and this can lead to affairs. I believe that this is another important reason to try and get to grips with *Anima/Animus* and the idealised feminine/masculine images that we hold.

Of course, men may have an idealised image of an *Anima* woman – what the perfect wife should look like – which may be influenced by their family upbringing and wider culture. So, when a wife cannot live up to this idealised image, the husband may be left feeling disappointed and disillusioned. He may then in fact start to wonder whether this *ideal* woman exists somewhere outside of his marriage. In our society we often tend to polarise the roles of women and there are very different *Anima* projections that exist. For example, there is the *Anima* image of the pure virginal wife, like Mary, the mother of Jesus and there is the *Anima* image of the sexy temptress, which we could liken to the image of Eve in the Garden of Eden.

What can happen in marriages is that men may project the idea of a pure womanly *Anima* image onto their wife and then believe that they need to look for the sexy temptress outside of their marriage. There may be the false belief that once married, your wife can longer be the sexy, tempting woman; instead she should be the stable, homely figure in your life. Tom, in particular, had an image of Lucy as his pure wife, who he didn't want to sully with what he believed to be his dirty, sexual thoughts and fantasies. So, Tom looked for images of sexy, tempting women in the pornography that he viewed. This made it difficult for Tom to integrate his erotic life into his marriage, which deprived Lucy and Tom of opportunities for deeper sexual intimacy.

Women too, may have an idealised image of an *Animus* man, a hero figure, like Clark Kent who transforms into Superman, ready to sweep them off their feet and take them to a place of ecstasy. When this doesn't happen in a woman's marriage, then the wife may be left thinking, where has my hero gone? They may also start fantasising, like Rose did, about what Toni Grant (1988) refers to as a 'Ghostly Lover', who becomes the male figure of your dreams who will meet all of your sexual needs. A woman's 'Ghostly Lover', may represent a real, fantasised-about man outside of marriage, a man that a woman has loved and lost, a love that can never be; or the 'Ghostly Lover' may simply represent an ideal (Grant, 1998). If this is the case, he simply remains a figment of the imagination (Grant, 1998).

We know that for a woman,

Her Ghostly Lover is a demon master, jealous of her attempts at intimacy with real men, he holds the woman fiercely in his grip. He serves as a barrier between her and

real life, thereby reinforcing her self-sufficiency and keeping her trapped…
— Grant, 1998, p.89

Rose's 'Ghostly Lover' certainly helped to reinforce her self-sufficiency and lack of connection with Andy, which made sense in terms of her dismissive-avoidant attachment style (see Chapter 11 for attachment styles). For some women their 'Ghostly Lover' may be sought after in pornographic images or erotic literature.

A woman too, may have very polarised *Animus* images, viewing her husband as the stable, familiar, and sexually unexciting, dependable man in her life. She may also hold the idea that there is an exciting, mysterious and unknown man waiting to be discovered outside of her marriage. A wife, like her husband, may be intrigued and tempted by this unknown person of the opposite sex.

Of course, it's likely that we're projecting the unknown, unexplored and unfamiliar sexual side of ourselves onto this person; a side that we perhaps have not dared to explore in our marriage. As Dr Schnarch (2009) reminds us, it's far less exposing to be sexually adventurous and have an affair with a stranger because we have little emotional investment in a person we don't know. We're not afraid of losing them, because we barely know them. The trick is to recognise these projections and try to explore the exciting and sexually unfamiliar sides of ourselves within our marriage. We may need to take the risk of opening up to our partner in new, erotic ways.

Jung is clear that for our own growth and development we need to take back these unrealistic *Anima* and *Animus* projections that we may place on our partners. For men, it may be important for them to try and access more of their own sensual, relational *(Anima)* side, as opposed to projecting this onto other women and possibly having an affair. A husband may also benefit from integrating and recognising different aspects of his wife, acknowledging her role as a nurturing wife, mother, or grandmother, but also recognising her as his adult sexual partner, who can be desirable, erotic and tempting.

And for women, they may need to find their inner hero (*Animus* figure) and assert their sexual desires and needs in their relationship, instead of fantasising about their 'Ghostly Lover', who is not real and who is not going to satisfy their every need. Rose managed to let go of her 'Ghostly Lover' and instead of fantasising, she took charge of articulating what she wanted during sex with Andy, which led to a deeper sense of intimacy for them as a couple.

When we become disillusioned with our husband or wife, who isn't living up to the role of being the sensual lover of our dreams, then we have two choices. We can search for them in our fantasies, through pornographic images, or by having an affair, or we can search for our lost lover in our own couple relationship, daring ourselves to *want to want* our partner again.

The 'shadow side' of marriage

The quotation from Thomas Moore at the start of this chapter helps us to think about the innocence that we need in order to step into the realm of marriage. The 'temporary insanity' (as Freud called it) of falling in love definitely helps to lead us down this path, and happily down the wedding aisle. Yet, at some point in marriage, the rose-tinted spectacles come off, we lift the painted veil to see that marriage is not made up of *'unadulterated happiness'* (Moore, 1994, p.55) all of the time. For some couples this realisation can come as quite a shock, and disillusionment can set in.

Thomas Moore (1994) warns us against idealising marriage and how holding an overly sentimentalised view of marriage and 'wedded bliss' can place a strain on a couple as the expectations are too much to live up to. In fact:

> *Excessive innocence about marriage can breed trouble. We might see the sentimental view of marriage that is often presented in movies and in advertising as a defence against the dark challenges that marriage offers, or at least a compensation...*
>
> — p.55

There are other ways that our society helps to bring a bit of relief and acknowledge the darker, more troubled side of marriage: humour in movies, sitcoms, and greeting cards highlights some of the difficult dynamics by poking fun at marriage (Moore, 1994). We often laugh in relief and recognition at the jokes that resonate with our life experiences and the awareness that marriage is not always smooth and easy. Humour allows us to acknowledge that there is a 'Shadow' side to marriage (Moore, 1994).

It is important for our view of marriage to be broad enough to encompass and recognise the strengths and intimacies of marriage as well as the 'Shadow', or darker elements. For that to happen, our initial ideals about marriage, our partner and ourselves may need to be relinquished (Moore, 1994). I suppose what we're talking about here is being able to find a healthy, middle ground, where marriage is not viewed as all good, yet not viewed as all bad either. Thomas Moore (1994) likens marriage to one of life's initiations, and we know that when we undergo an initiation into something, it requires effort and may be painful as we transition into a new role, identity or way of being.

I've talked about archetypal roles or images that we have of men and women in our culture in Chapter 7, such as the idea of the 'princess' or the 'hero', and it's interesting to note that there are strong archetypal images and roles that are associated with marriage. When we enter marriage, we are not simply entering a relationship with our partner, we are entering an archetypal realm, full of cultural expectations and unconscious associations that are stored in our collective unconscious.

During the wedding ceremony we are joined together and like a king and queen, the beauty, weight and responsibility of marriage descends upon us, like crowns upon our heads. With the 'Shadow' elements present, we all have the potential to turn into a tyrannical king or queen, shouting demands at our spouse, wanting our way to prevail in the domestic kingdom of married life. Yet, we also hold the power to raise up our partner through love, we don't have to force them to 'bow down' to us, even though we may be able to wield the emotional weapons and power to accomplish this. Thomas Moore (1994) helps us to recognise that we enter a whole new world when we cross over the threshold into the archetypal realm of married life.

> *… so marriage rearranges the emotions and one's view of life itself, often with painful stretching of the heart and the imagination. Often people who expect to find bliss in the arrangement discover bitter confusion in the re-sorting of feelings and thoughts occasioned by marriage. They may blame each other for being outrageously inappropriate, not realising that they have evoked the maelstrom of the soul through the 'simple' decision to live as a couple rather than as a single person.*
>
> — p.59

Recognising marriage as an initiation and a journey of the soul into one of life's mysteries can help us to step away from individual blame when we encounter problems. We can then begin to recognise that we are jointly responsible for entering the realm of marriage, an archetypal realm, which for centuries has stirred up strong emotions.

Erotic repression and sexual compulsions

If you've read the other chapters of this book, you may have already picked up on the idea that if we try to repress unwanted feelings and bury them in our unconscious, then at some point these feelings are likely to re-emerge in another form. The same thing can happen with erotic feelings and fantasies: the more we try to push these down, the more they are likely to pop up unexpectedly like a 'jack-in-the-box' and take us by surprise. As an adult sexual partner, it's natural to want to live an erotic life with your spouse; however, sometimes we don't trust our feelings and desires, and this can prevent us from enjoying sexual intimacy with one another. As Thomas Moore (1994) highlights:

> *We live in a world that trusts logic, and from this commitment we distrust desire, but if we lived in a world that validated desire, we would know how to trust it.*
> — p.158

It's when we start mistrusting our desires that they end up being repressed and often turn into compulsions. For example, Tom mistrusted his sense of desire and sexual fantasies and because of this he didn't want to share them with Lucy. This resulted in Tom compulsively viewing pornography instead of fully enjoying an erotic sex life with Lucy and sharing his fantasies with her. Of course, compulsions around viewing pornography can also be experienced by women in marriage.

If one person in the marriage is gripped by sexual compulsions, then this symptom may be one way of the soul trying to communicate that action needs to be taken – not by giving in to the compulsion, but by thinking about what may be lacking in your relationship or life that is driving this need (Moore, 1994). Tom was living his life in a stingy way, not giving to himself or Lucy in an open, loving way. He didn't really know how to enjoy his erotic side and part of him didn't really believe that he deserved to enjoy a deeper level of sexual intimacy.

Often, women or men who repress their desires are the type of people who live their lives with a strong sense of obligation, and therefore they may compensate for this by spending their evenings indulging in sexual fantasies or, like Tom, viewing pornography (Moore, 1994). Thomas Moore (1994) suggests that when people become gripped by sexual compulsions, they would benefit from living their lives more erotically in a broad sense and taking the time to enjoy the sensual aspects of their daily lives. This could include many things, such as taking pleasure in different forms of touch, taste, smell and what we look at. Food, too, can also be sensual as are the fabrics and clothes that we wear and the smells that we surround ourselves with. Enjoying our bodies in general as opposed to being focused overly on the mind and spirit may also help to bring a sense of balance and reduce the tendency to disconnect and repress our bodily desires.

If we don't live out our desires actively and consciously, they are likely to go underground and seek out expression elsewhere. Both men and women in marriages may focus their erotic gaze elsewhere, whether that's in their secret fantasy life, reading erotica or steamy romantic fiction, gazing at and fantasising about 'heart throbs' in the movies, viewing pornography or enjoying someone else's body during an affair.

Pornography, as previously mentioned, can end up becoming another sexual compulsion. Thomas Moore (1994) comments:

> *It sometimes happens that one person in a relationship shows an interest in pornography, while the other is offended or at least disturbed by it.*
>
> — p.180

When this happens, it is important not to dismiss what is going on, or judge it, but to be curious and ask why pornography is making an appearance in the person's life (Moore, 1994). What function is it serving? When we think about the function that pornography is serving, we may then be able to understand it as a symptom. A symptom that may indicate that something needs to shift in the individual's life or that some change needs to come to the fore in the couple relationship.

In Chapter 10: 'Soulful sex', there was a focus on our human need for an erotic gaze and ability to look at each other sensually. And perhaps this is what is missing in the person's life and could come to the fore more during moments of sexual intimacy. Looking at and enjoying each other's bodies and enjoying sharing fantasies are all part of the erotic activity that takes place between the two lovers in *Song of Songs* (see Chapter 10). The two lovers are good role models for us when we think about our erotic gaze, enjoying each other's bodies and using all of our senses to enjoy an erotic sex life.

Sometimes when sex is talked about in sermons at church, the focus may be on problematic areas. This was Tom's experience, he had grown up with lots of messages about the importance of having sexually pure thoughts when he was a teenager and had attended Christian summer camps. This contributed to his sense that he couldn't share his sexual thoughts and fantasies with Lucy – at some level Tom believed that these thoughts weren't right or godly. Tom used to attend a church where his minister regularly preached on the dangers of men having affairs, or looking at other women lustfully. Tom felt embarrassed and often wouldn't be able to make eye contact with the female church members during the coffee time at the end of the church service.

Like Tom, some Christians may have heard similar messages, which may indirectly encourage a repression of sexual desire and fantasies. This in turn can lead to unhelpful compulsions. Thomas Moore (1994) highlights how we can become fearful of the power of sex and use our moralism to try to protect ourselves:

We may try to keep the power of sex at bay through many clever manoeuvres. Our moralism, for example, helps keep us clean of the mess sex can make of an otherwise ordered life … Yet despite all of our efforts, sexual compulsion interferes with marriages, draws people into strange liaisons, and continues to offend propriety, morality, and religion. Its dynamic is too big to fit into the cages we make for it.
— p.158

We want to have a healthy sex life in our marriage, and we want sex to be robust, and yet ironically we don't want it to be too robust, perhaps because of a fear that it will dominate and spread into unhelpful areas (Moore, 1994). It's this fear and our moralism that drives the repression of desire and waters down the possibility of a satisfying and healthy, erotic sex life.

Here we have thought about the two extreme poles of either being 'moralistic about sex' or 'driven by sexual compulsions', like when women or men are addicted to pornography. It's also important to be aware that when we are overly moralistic about sex or try to suppress our sexual desires, sexual compulsions are more likely to emerge as a form of compensation. What we are aiming for is the healthy middle ground where our values and morals unite sensitively with our sexual desire: then we can live our lives from a position of 'erotic morality' (Moore, 1994). We will revisit the concept of 'erotic morality' shortly. The spectrum of positions that have been discussed can be viewed below in Figure 9: 'influences on sexual expression'.

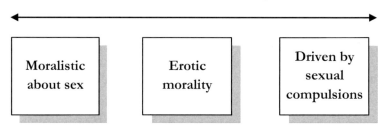

Figure 9: influences on sexual expression

Affairs, denial and feelings of betrayal

There are not many steps from feeling dissatisfied in our marriage, to fantasising about the more 'ideal' man or woman, to acting on these fantasies and starting an affair. As soon as disillusionment sets in, a woman may start to search for her Ghostly Lover in earnest and a man may search for the sexy, tempting woman of his dreams. There is a shadow side of sex that can draw us into having affairs and having sex with people who are unsuitable for us.

> *The magical power of sex to link hearts has a shadow side which we overlook at our own peril. We may be drawn sexually to people who in every other respect do not make good partners.*
>
> — Moore, 1994, p.163

When we are tempted to have an affair, Thomas Moore (1994) suggests once again, that we could listen to this desire and not act on it literally, by giving way to the compulsion, but honour the desire by living life more erotically:

A person can live more erotically every minute of the day by valuing deep pleasures, beauty, body, adornment, decoration, texture, and color – all things we too often consider secondary or even frivolous.

— p.164

However, often in marriages individuals do step over the threshold and enter into an affair. When this happens the individual can be left feeling torn between two dilemmas. They may not really want their marriage to end, but feel deeply unhappy and dissatisfied in their relationship. Conversely, whilst they may enjoy the satisfaction that the affair brings, they may also feel ashamed or unhappy in some way with the predicament and complications involved in having an affair.

Sometimes couples believe that there are only two options open to them, to stay or to go; whereas there is always a third possibility. It can be important to explore and intensify the feelings and underlying meanings related to staying in the marriage, and the feelings connected to pursuing the affair (Moore, 1994).

At one point in her marriage, Jenny considered having an affair with one of the senior law partners in her firm. This man, unlike Mike, was sexually aggressive; he pursued her and flirted with her, making her completely aware that he found her sexually attractive. When Jenny explored her feelings about having an affair, part of her was extremely turned on by the idea, whilst another part of her felt repelled.

When she thought about staying in the marriage Jenny realised that, at some level, she felt trapped by her relationship with Mike. Her thoughts and fantasies about having an affair were ways to feel more emotionally free and less merged and dependent on Mike for validation. Jenny was used to seeking and getting approval and validation whilst growing up and she realised that this pattern was driving her to seek sexual approval outside of her marriage.

However, when Jenny intensified her feelings around acting on her thoughts and having an affair, she realised that she wouldn't really feel approved and validated: part of her would feel disgusted by the betrayal. Also, she wouldn't have felt able to approve of herself, which deep down, was important.

During couples therapy, Jenny came to realise that her longing for sexual affirmation and clinginess with Mike was responsible for killing off some of the sexual desire between them; it meant that she leaned into Mike, *needing* him to affirm her, rather than *wanting* him sexually. Mike too, was able to acknowledge how his fear of being sexually assertive made him appear sexually disinterested and was driving Jenny away. In a passive way, Mike realised he was encouraging Jenny to look for sexual affirmation outside of their marriage.

Underneath it all for Jenny, was the hidden fantasy that an affair would make her feel desirable and free her from the merged state of her marriage. However, it was really a way of Jenny trying to escape and find an easy way out of having to address separation issues in her marriage. It was also a way of Jenny feeling in control because Mike didn't know what was going on at the office with the flirtations and he didn't know what was going on in her fantasy life. Jenny's Ghostly Lover helped her to feel self-sufficient, like she didn't really need Mike, which eased her fears about being too reliant on him.

It's helpful to remember that there are always two sides to sex, anxiety versus pleasure, and vitality versus impotence (Moore, 1994). When people start having affairs, they may be trying to defend one side from the other, so if they are feeling impotent and sexually frustrated in their marriage, they may try and seek a sense of vitality and sexual satisfaction elsewhere (Moore, 1994).

Once again, we can see the tendency for polarised positions to crop up when it comes to sex. Trying to find the middle ground and a helpful third position, where it's possible to allow for both feelings to occur in the relationship, may be important. When we feel disillusioned and think we have failed, it's perhaps natural to want to escape from those feelings and recapture a sense of sexual success and desire. Sadly, in marriages individuals may jump to having an affair as a way of achieving this, as opposed to trying to transition from a sense of impotence to vitality with the same person in the relationship.

Of course, when adultery does occur betrayal moves in to take centre stage. Sometimes men and women try to disown their sense of betrayal through simplistic repentance, telling their partner that 'It didn't mean anything' (Moore, 1998). However, if you are the person who has been betrayed, it can feel like your whole world has been torn apart.

In *The Soul of Sex* (1998), Thomas Moore tells us that the person who has been betrayed may have more of an opportunity to go deeper into the suffering and learn from the experience compared to the betrayer. The betrayer may be too defended against the loss of control that they experienced; having done something wrong, it may be hard for them to come to terms with the fact that they were taken over by the dark powers of passion and the shadow side of sex (Moore, 1998).

If you are having an affair, or thinking about having an affair, or recovering from the aftermath of adultery in your marriage, then you may well be caught up in the painful shadowy elements that sex can draw us into. If you would like to explore the emotions surrounding these events together as a couple, then I would recommend seeking out a couples therapist who can be your guide.

When couples have therapy after an affair it doesn't remove the guilt or the wrong, but it does help couples look at feelings of remorse and ways to move forward again (Moore, 1998). Sex can lead us deep into painful shadowy areas, but we can survive this and come out on the other side. We still have the potential to be a creative couple.

It's important to remember that betrayal shouldn't be indulged and given a position of prominence in marriage, and neither should its significance be denied (Moore, 1998). Again, it is a tricky balancing act, finding the middle ground from which there is potential for healing to take place.

Rediscovering erotic morality

Our morals can be a helpful compass for us in our relationships; they help us to uphold and value fidelity and our commitments to our spouse. However, morality can be unhelpful if it inadvertently becomes the enemy of desire and pleasure (Moore, 1994). When it comes to sex, we are perhaps looking for the healthy, middle ground. Thomas Moore (1994) tells us:

When moral sensitivity and respect for sexual love merge, the two are so close the result might be called 'erotic morality.' For the soul, morality should be life affirming, rather than prohibiting and respectful of sexual love rather than suspicious.

— p.179

If like Tom, we end up mistrusting our sexual desires and fantasies, trying to disallow them from entering our couple relationship, these desires often go underground and can get acted out in other ways. During couples therapy Tom developed a greater sense of respect for sexual love and intimacy with Lucy and this brought a new sense of sexual aliveness to their relationship. He was gradually able to shake off the messages that he had grown up with from his church, that had presented sexual desire as something to be wary of and to keep in check.

Some individuals may try to distance themselves from their sexual desires. Christians may think that it's better not to be overly concerned by the sexual realm. Rather, it would be better to concentrate their thoughts on more 'spiritual' things, discounting sex as something that is not particularly soulful.

In fact, some people may take great pride in not focusing on the sexual side of their life, stating that they prefer to live their lives on a higher, spiritual plane, thus giving the impression that concentrating on things of a sexual nature is almost beneath them. Or at least, something they don't see as important to think about. Thomas Moore (1994) points out:

Those who live by morality, as opposed to soulful morality believe they know all the answers. They can make quick judgements about the affairs of others. Even intelligent, sophisticated people who don't consider themselves moralistic often become drawn into moralism in areas where they are emotionally vulnerable.

— p.179

However, if we close ourselves off to our sexual desires and try to focus solely on the spiritual, we can become vulnerable; the sexual side of our nature still wants to have its space and if this is not given freely, it may pop up in strange and unusual ways. There is a story that Thomas Moore tells in *Soul Mates* (1994) of a dedicated priest and a group of nuns who used to meet together for spiritual matters. Such was their reverence for this man, the priest, and such was the priest's appreciation of their devotion to him, that at a certain time each day the nuns agreed that they would stop what they were doing, kneel down, pray, and focus their thoughts on this man.

Thomas Moore (1994) cites this as a strange compulsive ritual with strong sexual overtones; that the behaviour was semi-disguised by a veneer of religiosity. It's another example and a warning against living too much of a one-sided life.

As previously mentioned, if we don't attempt to fully live out our sexual desires in a healthy, conscious way, then we may end up falling into the trap of either becoming moralistic about sex, or, at the other extreme, driven by sexual compulsions. We are searching for the balance of 'erotic morality', where we feel free to explore our sexual desires in a respectful and healthy way with our partner.

At the wedding in Cana, Jesus famously turned water into wine, and this provides us with an interesting metaphor for marriage. In our relationships we of course have the everyday, mundane things: the water, but there is the potential and a great need, to bring a sparkling, intoxicating, element into our relationship: the wine (Moore, 1994). Jesus did this for the couple on their wedding day in Cana: his first miracle. This perhaps highlights the importance for us as couples to welcome an intoxicating and sparkling element into our marriages.

Playfulness versus disillusionment

One way to bring a sparkling, fun element back into our relationship is to rediscover our sense of playfulness. Thomas Moore (1994) tells us that the word *illusion* comes from the Latin *'in ludere'*, which means *'in play'*. So maybe when we start to feel disillusioned in our marriage or by the way that our partner has let us down, what we may need to do is to recapture the playfulness and joy that we once felt. For:

> *To be in love, is to be in play, to be taken by illusions. We **are** deceived so that the soul can create something out of the stuff of our emotions and fantasies.*
> — Moore, 1994, p. 144

It may be interesting to think about whether there are elements of playfulness in your relationship and if so, when do these moments seem to arise? For Mike and Jenny there had been limited amounts of playfulness in their respective childhoods. Jenny became quite a serious, hardworking child after her brother died and in Mike's family home, it was difficult to fully relax because of the changeable and volatile moods of his father. So often, life could feel somewhat serious for Jenny and Mike.

At times, when they felt let down, resentful or disillusioned in their marriage, it was difficult for them to move away from these feelings in order to recapture a sense of loving playfulness. What tended to happen was that Mike would withdraw and bury himself in work, marking his students' assignments and Jenny would similarly prepare the papers that she needed for upcoming court cases.

During couples therapy, it was interesting for Jenny and Mike to think back to earlier times in their relationship, when a sense of playfulness was more present and the ways that they used to connect through this 'playful' mode. This started to give them ideas about how they could once again recapture a sense of playfulness in their marriage, which was a useful antidote to feelings of dissatisfaction and disillusionment.

However, prior to being able to reconnect with their playful sides, Mike and Jenny had to go through the process of recognising what their 'couple fit' was (Chapter 1) and they had to work on being more differentiated (Chapter 3). Not only that, as a couple they had to process the feelings of betrayal that they had experienced (Chapter 4) and explore their feelings of resentment fully so they could forgive each other (Chapter 5).

Being playful with our spouse requires us to open up and to be vulnerable with them. If you haven't worked on some of your core issues, this will feel difficult, and if feelings of resentment continue to linger then this will also present a block to being playful and letting go.

If disillusionment and adultery are significant issues in your relationship and you have started by reading this chapter first, I would recommend that you go back and work through this couple guide sequentially. Each chapter will lead you step-by-step through some of the core issues and dynamics that you may need to address.

Conclusion

Having reached the end of this chapter, I would like to pause and once again congratulate you. If it feels natural to do so, why don't you pause and congratulate yourself. It's not an easy task to explore the topic of disillusionment and look at ways that we may have been unfaithful in our couple relationship. Naturally, I think that we may want to shy away from this topic. As with lifting the painted veil or removing the rose-tinted spectacles, we tend to experience fear and hope about what we may see, and what we may come to understand about ourselves and our partner. There are no easy answers when it comes to disillusionment and adultery, but if we are able to look for the solutions we need within our marriage instead of outside of the marriage relationship, and if we are able to combat passivity, recognise the shadow side of marriage, and release ourselves from moralism/sexual compulsions to live a life of erotic morality, then we are starting to head in the right direction.

Joint Reflection Points

1. Take a few minutes to think on your own about the times when you may
    have felt dissatisfied or disillusioned with your marriage and ask yourself,
    have you withdrawn some of your energy from your partner and
    ploughed it into something else, such as an activity, hobby, compulsion,
    fantasy, work, or your children? Follow up exercise:

    ♥   What things do you tend to focus on outside of your marriage when
        dissatisfaction or disillusionment creeps in? After thinking about
        this on your own for a few minutes or more (make some notes if
        you would like to), share what tends to happen with each other. Try
        listening to each other in a kind, non-judgemental, and
        compassionate way. The aim here is just to try to understand what
        happens for each of you before you go on to the next reflection
        point.

2. Now discuss ways in which you feel that you could draw on the
    resources in your couple relationship when dissatisfaction and
    disillusionment start to creep in. Perhaps ask the following questions:

    ♥   What could you do as a couple to focus on finding the solutions
        within your relationship, as opposed to focusing on things outside
        of the relationship? How can you support one another to do this?

3. As a way of combating any passivity and taking a more active stance in
    your relationship ask each other: *'What do I do, or can I do, that would stir
    your heart and help keep your soul alive?'* You want to discover the unique
    things that you alone can give to your partner; things that really uplift
    their soul and make them feel special. Write down your partner's
    responses and make a plan to do some of these things over the next
    month. For example, some of the things that stirred Andy's soul
    included: Rose stroking his hair; when Rose made special cookies just
    for him; playing their musical instruments together in the evenings;
    loving notes being left for him; and going on walks together.

4. Discuss together about where you individually fall on the continuum below in Figure 9: 'influences on sexual expression'. You may tend to swing from one end to the other, like Tom, who felt very moralistic about sexual desires, then compulsively viewed pornography, or like Rose, you may end up fantasising about your Ghostly Lover. Pornography or literary erotica may also form part of a woman's hidden fantasy life. Alternatively, you may feel that you manage to sit for most of the time in the healthy middle ground, achieving a balance of erotic morality. Or you may feel that your upbringing and life experiences draw you towards being moralistic about sex and you would like to experience a greater sense of erotic morality and freedom.

♥ Try and be supportive of one another as you open up and discuss your respective positions. If there are sexual compulsions present, try being curious about this, asking yourselves: *'Why are they making an appearance in my life now? What is this symptom trying to say to us as a couple? What action needs to be taken to bring the right balance?'*

♥ How can you support one another to move to the position you would ideally like to be on the continuum? What could help you to get to that position? Make a list of your ideas.

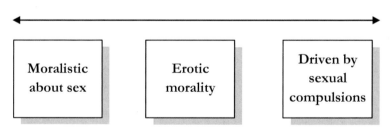

| Moralistic about sex | Erotic morality | Driven by sexual compulsions |

Figure 9: influences on sexual expression

5. How can you embrace and affirm the sense of being erotic in your couple relationship and in your day-to-day lives? Discuss together ways of broadening the erotic that you experience in your lives, trusting it and welcoming it, as opposed to being suspicious of it. Remember:

A person can live more erotically every minute of the day by valuing deep pleasures, beauty, body, adornment, decoration, texture, and color – all things we too often consider secondary or even frivolous.

— Moore, 1994, p.164

List some of the very practical ways you could try out being more erotic together and make a plan of action to incorporate some of these ideas in your lives and couple relationship. For example: taking pleasure in different forms of touch; taste; smell; and what you look at: like art; as well as fabrics; clothes; nightwear; furnishings in the home and bedroom; plants and flowers; food; massage and enjoying your body.

6. Playfulness can be a valuable antidote to disillusionment. Talk together about the times in your relationship when playfulness has come to the fore, what kind of activities, environment, and emotional atmosphere helps you as a couple to connect with your playful side? If you need to, think back to the early days of your relationship and the type of things that helped to create a spark and fun. Follow up exercise:

♥   Now use your imaginations to think about how you could create opportunities to be playful together. You can also be very practical here, planning what time, money, or energy may need to be set aside. Remember, play is a serious thing, as any child will tell you, it requires a great deal of concentration. Children may forgo food, toilet breaks, or even be prepared to get told off by their parents for continuing with their play beyond the allotted time. We too, as adults could do with remembering how to take play seriously in our marriages.

7. What is your joint vision for your marriage? What are your goals as a couple for five years' time? What things would you need to do or prioritise in the short-term, medium-term, or long-term in order to meet your goals and fulfil your vision? If you want to adjust the time frame so it's shorter, e.g. one year, or longer, then feel free to select what suits you as a couple.

Spiritual Reflection Points

1. Pray to God and ask Him to forgive you both for the times when you
    have not been as faithful as you could have been in your marriage – for
    the times when you may have been 'lukewarm'. Ask God to help you to
    manage any feelings of dissatisfaction/disillusionment and to discover
    the resources that you need within your marriage, to be a creative and
    fruitful couple.

2. Ask God to show you how – on a spiritual, sexual, emotional, and
    physical level – you can bring an intoxicating, sparkling element to your
    relationship. Spend some time in silent meditation, perhaps with some
    worship music on in the background, and focus on the metaphor of
    turning the ordinary water into the sparkling wine in your marriage.
    Beforehand, you could read together about Jesus' first miracle where he
    turned water into wine if you would like to, see John 2:1–11. At the end
    of this time share with each other any thoughts, images or Bible verses
    that came to mind.

3. Pray together: *'Dear God, show us how to live life full of erotic morality in our
    marriage, trusting, celebrating and embracing the healthy sexual desires that you have
    given us. Amen.'*

Closing Reflections

Adam and Eve:
the beginning and the end

Relationship is not a project, it is a grace.

Thomas Moore, Soul Mates

Take a look at Adam and Eve as the ultimate template that God has given us for a couple relationship, and what do we see? Two individuals who are together, initially enjoying life; however, they disagree and try to negotiate the right way forward, but they make a mistake. The consequence is that they have to start over again, not in the Garden of Eden, but in the context of the new and painful reality of Earth. 'Blame' is a central theme for Adam and Eve, it crops up again and again in modern-day couple relationships and can lead to bitterness and resentment. After the mistake has been made, feelings of shame come into the marriage for the first time. This is perhaps another common theme in the modern couple relationship. However, God gives them a second chance to work things out, with the ultimate long-term goal of reconciliation through Jesus. The reality that we face probably hasn't changed much: the joy of togetherness; the disputes; the failed negotiations; and the having to start over again.

When I initially thought about Adam and Eve as the original template for the modern-day couple relationship, I experienced an inward sigh of relief. As a model, it helps to underline that we don't have to try to fit into the mould of a 'Stepford' wife or husband – always smiling and constantly happy, turning up to church with our hair done, nice outfit, and feeling an almost heavenly degree of marital bliss. This of course, may happen, but I realise now, after being married for a number of years, that it's okay if it is not always the case.

Right from the start, perhaps God has wanted to tell us that it's good not to be alone, but being together can be an interesting challenge. The reality seems to be that there is pleasure and pain involved in being in a relationship with one another. The perfect relationship, the perfect marriage, the perfect husband or wife, is nowhere to be found in the Bible. Even King David, who was 'a man after God's own heart', committed adultery. However, our hope perhaps rests on the consistent opportunities we have to start over again, to work things out together, and to try to move forward. In this way we become closer to one another through the sharing of life experiences, including the bad times as well as the good. Viewing our relationship as a grace can be helpful because it orients us towards the opportunities for personal and spiritual growth that can arise from living our lives together as a couple.

Thank you, Adam and Eve, for a glimpse of the reality, and a glimpse of the hope.

References

References

Bloch, A. & Bloch, C. (2006). *The Song of Songs*. New York: Modern Library Inc.

Bly, R. (2001). *Iron John: A book about men*. London: Rider.

Crittenden, P. M. (2006). A Dynamic Maturational Model of Attachment. *Australian & New Zealand Journal of Family Therapy, 27* (2), 105–115.

Grant, T. (1988). *Being A Woman: Fulfilling Your Femininity and Finding Love*. New York: Random House.

Grier, F. (2006). Ideals, Betrayal, Guilt and Forgiveness in Couple Psychotherapy. *British Journal of Psychotherapy, 23* (1), 37–48.

Haag, H., Chungel-Straumann, H., Wetzel, C., Elliger, K., Grohmann, M., Soelle, D. (2006). *Great Couples of the Bible*. Minneapolis: Fortress Press.

Hasseldine, R. (2017). *The Mother-Daughter Puzzle: A New Generational Understanding of the Mother-Daughter Relationship*. Durham: Women's Bookshelf Publishing.

Johnson, S. (2011). *Hold Me Tight: Your Guide to the Most Successful Approach to Building Loving Relationships*. London: Piatkus.

Jung, C. G.(1977). *Two Essays on Analytical Psychology, Volume 7*. London: Routledge.

Jung, C. G. (1978). *The Collected Works of C. G. Jung, Volume 9, Part II*. London: Routledge.

Kabat-Zinn, J. (1994). *Wherever You Go, There You Are: Mindfulness Meditation for Everyday Life*. London: Piatkus.

Kutz, I. (1989). Samson's complex: The compulsion to re-enact betrayal and rage. *Psychology and Psychotherapy: Theory, Research and Practice, 62* (2), 113–204.

LaCelle-Peterson, K. (2008). *Liberating Tradition: Women's Identity and Vocation in Christian Perspective*. Michigan: Baker Academic.

Miles, J. (1991). 'Two Trees' in Grana, J. (Ed.) *Images of Women in Transition* (p.58). Winona: Saint Mary's Press.

Moore, D. (2004). *Good Christians, Good Husbands? Leaving a Legacy in Marriage and Ministry*. Fearn: Christian Focus Publications.

Moore, R. & Gillette, D. (1990). *King, Warrior, Magician, Lover: Rediscovering the Archetypes of the Mature Masculine*. New York: Harper Collins.

Moore, T. (1992). *Care of the Soul: How to add depth and meaning to your everyday life*. London: Piatkus.

Moore, T. (1994). *Soul Mates: Honoring the Mysteries of Love and Relationship*. New York: HarperCollins.

Moore, T. (1998). *The Soul of Sex: Cultivating Life as an Act of Love*. New York: HarperCollins.

Orbach, S. (2009). Separated attachments and sexual aliveness in Clulow, C. (Ed.) *Sex, Attachment and Couple Psychotherapy: Psychodynamic Perspectives* (pp.63–74). London: Karnac.

Pembroke, N. (2007). *Moving Toward Spiritual Maturity: Psychological, Contemplative, and Moral Challenges in Christian Living*. New York: The Haworth Press.

Perry, P. (2019). *The Book You Wish Your Parents Had Read: (and Your Children Will Be Glad That You Did)* [Kindle DX version]. Retrieved from Amazon.co.uk

Rholes, W. S. & Simpson, J. A. (Eds) (2004). *Adult Attachment: Theory, Research and Clinical Implications.* Guilford Press: New York.

Ruszczynski, S. (2004). Reflective space in the intimate couple relationship: the "marital triangle". In Grier, F. (Ed.) *Oedipus and the Couple* (pp.31–48). London: Karnac.

Sampson, V. (2002). *Tantra: The Art of Mind Blowing Sex.* London: Vermilion.

Samuels, A. (1995). *Jung and the Post Jungians.* London: Routledge.

Schnarch, D. (2009). *Passionate Marriage: Love, Sex, and Intimacy in Emotionally Committed Relationships.* London: W.W. Norton & Company.

Shaddock, D. (1998). *From Impasse to Intimacy: How Understanding Unconscious Needs Can Transform Relationships.* London: Jason Aronson Inc.

Shinoda Bolen, J. (1999). *The Ring of Power: Symbols and Themes of Love vs Power in Wagner's Ring Cycle and in Us.* York Beach: Nicolas-Hays.

Steiner, J. (1993). *Psychic Retreats: Pathological Organizations in Psychotic, Neurotic and Borderline Patients.* London: Routledge.

Tverberg, L. (2006). *To Be the Image of God.* Retrieved from http://www.egrc.net/articles/director/articles_director_0806.html

Williams, M. & Penman, D. (2011). *Mindfulness: A practical guide to finding peace in a frantic world.* London: Piatkus.

Young, J. E. & Klosko, J. S (1994). *Reinventing Your Life: The Breakthrough Program to End Negative Behaviour and Feel Great Again.* London: Penguin Group.

Young-Eisendrath, P. (1984). *Hags and Heroes: A Feminist Approach to Jungian Psychotherapy with Couples.* Toronto: Inner City Books.